Manual of Regulation-Focused Psychotherapy for Children (RFP-C) with Externalizing Behaviors

Manual of Regulation-Focused Psychotherapy for Children (RFP-C) with Externalizing Behaviors: A psychodynamic approach offers a new, short-term psychotherapeutic approach to working dynamically with children who suffer from irritability, oppositional defiance, and disruptiveness. RFP-C enables clinicians to help by addressing and detailing how the child's externalizing behaviors have meaning that they can convey to the child. Using clinical examples throughout, Hoffman, Rice, and Prout demonstrate that in many dysregulated children, RFP-C can:

- Achieve symptomatic improvement and developmental maturation as a result of gains in the ability to tolerate and metabolize painful emotions by addressing the crucial underlying emotional component.
- Diminish the child's use of aggression as the main coping device by allowing painful emotions to be mastered more effectively.
- Help to systematically address avoidance mechanisms, talking to the child about how their disruptive behavior helps them avoid painful emotions.
- Facilitate development of an awareness that painful emotions do not have to be so vigorously warded off, allowing the child to reach this implicit awareness within the relationship with the clinician, which can then be expanded to life situations at home and at school.

This handbook is the first to provide a manualized, short-term dynamic approach to the externalizing behaviors of childhood, offering organizing framework and detailed descriptions of the processes involved in RFP-C. Supplying clinicians with a systematic, individual psychotherapy as an alternative or complement to PMT, CBT, and psychotropic medication, it also shifts focus away from simply helping parents manage their children's misbehaviors. Significantly, the approach shows that clinical work with these children is compatible with understanding the children's brain functioning, and posits that contemporary affect-oriented conceptualizations of defense mechanisms are theoretically similar to the neuroscience construct of implicit emotion regulation, promoting an interface between psychodynamics and contemporary academic psychiatry and psychology.

Manual of Regulation-Focused Psychotherapy for Children (RFP-C) with Externalizing Behaviors: A psychodynamic approach is a comprehensive tool capable of application at all levels of professional training, offering a new approach for psychoanalysts, child and adolescent counselors, psychotherapists, and mental health clinicians in fields including social work, psychology, and psychiatry.

Leon Hoffman, MD, is a child and adolescent psychiatrist and psychoanalyst, and is currently the director of the Pacella Parent Child Center at the New York Psychoanalytic Society and Institute, and Chief Psychiatrist at West End Day School.

Timothy Rice, MD, is assistant professor of psychiatry at the Icahn School of Medicine at Mount Sinai, New York City.

Tracy Prout, PhD, is assistant professor of psychology in the combined school-child clinical doctoral program at the Ferkauf Graduate School of Psychology at Yeshiva University. She is also in private practice working with children, adolescents, adults, and families.

"This book gives readers a bird's eye view into the organized and focused thought processes of the experienced psychodynamic clinician in handling children with disruptive behavior disorders. As such, this is a novel book and a must-read for clinicians who work with children, as it provides a systematic, operationalized, comprehensive treatment approach that is radically different from the ubiquitous cognitive behavioral approach. It is essential that these core treatment techniques, articulated so well in this manual, not get lost amid ever-narrowing treatments that are regularly imparted to clinicians who work with children."

– Barbara Milrod, MD, Professor of Psychiatry, Weill Cornell Medical College, expert in clinical trials in anxiety disorders in adults and children.

"This book addresses one of the most important issues of our modern times – how do children and adolescents learn to regulate their emotions and behaviors.

The intervention presented in this book has its basis in psychodynamic principles, especially defense mechanisms. It focuses on the emotional underpinnings of behavioral disruptions especially the avoidance of and reaction to painful emotions.

There is meaning in the child's behaviors, emotions, and communications. The clinician learns to understand this and communicates that understanding to the child and parents. This is done in a systematic, manualized manner which enables the child to better tolerate and deal with the unpleasant emotions.

This wedding of psychodynamic principles into a systematized, clear, and manualized approach is what makes this book so imaginative and modern in its approach to a very serious problem facing children, parents, mental health clinicians, and society."

– John D. O'Brien, MD, Clinical Professor, Training Director, Child/Adolescent Psychiatry Residency Program, Icahn School of Medicine at Mount Sinai.

"This book is of such scope it must be considered a magnum opus for the field of child clinical psychology and psychiatry. It is a unique blend of review of the most recent research on externalizing behavior in children, of the underlying neuroscientific features of the disorder and the most concise summary of psychoanalytic concepts related to the treatment of the disorder. There is no book quite like this one available. As a resource for teaching it is unique in its direct and clear writing style which make so accessible the psychotherapeutic techniques necessary for treating these often challenging cases. The book is more than a manual on delivering Regulation-Focused Psychotherapy for Children with Externalizing Behaviors, it is a manual on treating children with difficulties in regulating their affect in general and therefore is a 'must have' for every child clinician."

– Miriam Steele, PhD, Professor of Psychology, Director of Clinical Training, New School for Social Research, author of *Clinical Applications of the Adult Attachment Interview*, Routledge, 2008.

"This is a timely, masterful, comprehensive contribution to the sparse literature on Externalizing Disorders (ODD or DD). The authors provide rich examples from their clinical experience which will be of great value to all who treat children with aggressive behavior disorders. A must for child psychotherapists who wish to treat externalizing behavior disorders effectively. The authors provide an incredibly creative procedure that incorporates basic principles of psychodynamic treatments with findings from the affective neurosciences, developmental, and cognitive psychology and yet goes beyond. RFT goes beyond CBT because it gets at the underlying emotional component, promotes maturation of emotional regulation, and removes roadblocks to normal development. The authors get to the heart of the problem by highlighting the centrality of addressing painful emotions and maladaptive ways which children and adolescents have of avoiding and protecting themselves. Careful attention to how to approach such problems in an experience-near way as well as how to work with parents makes this a most comprehensive treatment approach, including a termination and evaluative process that lead to the development of protective measures that are adaptive and life changing."

– **Wendy Olesker, PhD, Training and Supervising Analyst at NYPSI and on the Faculty at the NYU Postdoctoral Program in Psychoanalysis and Psychotherapy.**

PSYCHOLOGICAL ISSUES BOOK SERIES

DAVID WOLITZKY
Series Editor

The basic mission of *Psychological Issues* is to contribute to the further development of psychoanalysis as a science, as a respected scholarly enterprise, as a theory of human behavior, and as a therapeutic method.

Over the past 50 years, the series has focused on fundamental aspects and foundations of psychoanalytic theory and clinical practice as well as on work in related disciplines relevant to psychoanalysis. *Psychological Issues* does not aim to represent or promote a particular point of view. The contributions cover broad and integrative topics of vital interest to all psychoanalysts as well as to colleagues in related disciplines. They cut across particular schools of thought and tackle key issues such as the philosophical underpinnings of psychoanalysis, psychoanalytic theories of motivation, conceptions of therapeutic action, the nature of unconscious mental functioning, psychoanalysis and social issues, and reports of original empirical research relevant to psychoanalysis. The authors often take a critical stance toward theories and offer a careful theoretical analysis and conceptual clarification of the complexities of theories and their clinical implications, drawing upon relevant empirical findings from psychoanalytic research as well as from research in related fields.

The Editorial Board continues to invite contributions from social/behavioral sciences such as anthropology and sociology, from biological sciences such as physiology and the various brain sciences, and from scholarly humanistic disciplines such as philosophy, law, and esthetics.

PSYCHOLOGICAL ISSUES BOOK SERIES

DAVID WOLITZKY
Series Editor

Members of the board

Sidney J. Blatt
Yale University School of Medicine
Wilma Bucci
Derner Institute, Adelphi University
Morris Eagle
Derner Institute, Adelphi University
Peter Fonagy
University College London
Robert Holt
New York University
Anton Kris
Beth Israel Hospital
Fred Pine
Albert Einstein College of Medicine
Herbert Schlesinger
Columbia University College of Physicians and Surgeons
Robert S. Wallerstein
University of California School of Medicine

PSYCHOLOGICAL ISSUES BOOK SERIES

DAVID WOLITZKY
Series Editor

Published by Routledge

74. *Manual of Regulation-Focused Psychotherapy for Children (RFP-C) with Externalizing Behaviors: A psychodynamic approach*, Leon Hoffman, Timothy Rice and Tracy Prout
73. *Myths of Termination: What patients can teach psychoanalysts about endings,* Judy Leopold Kantrowitz
72. *Identity and the New Psychoanalytic Explorations of Self-organization,* Mardi Horowitz
71. *Memory, Myth, and Seduction: Unconscious Fantasy and the Interpretive Process,* Jean-Georges Schimek & Deborah L. Browning
70. *From Classical to Contemporary Psychoanalysis: A Critique and Integration,* Morris N. Eagle

Published by Jason Aronson

69. *Primary Process Thinking: Theory, Measurement, and Research,* Robert R. Holt
68. *The Embodied Subject: Minding the Body in Psychoanalysis,* John P. Muller & Jane G. Tillman
67. *Self-Organizing Complexity in Psychological Systems, Craig Piers*, John P. Muller, & Joseph Brent
66. *Help Him Make You Smile: The Development of Intersubjectivity in the Atypical Child,* Rita S. Eagle
65. *Erik Erikson and the American Psyche: Ego, Ethics, and Evolution,* Daniel Burston

Published by International Universities Press

64. *Subliminal Explorations of Perception, Dreams, and Fantasies: The Pioneering Contributions of Charles Fisher,* Howard Shevrin
62/63. *Psychoanalysis and the Philosophy of Science: Collected Papers of Benjamin B. Rubinstein, MD,* Robert R. Holt
61. *Validation in the Clinical Theory of Psychoanalysis: A Study in the Philosophy of Psychoanalysis,* Adolf Grunbaum
60. *Freud's Concept of Passivity,* Russell H. Davis
59. *Between Hermeneutics and Science: An Essay on the Epistemology of Psychoanalysis,* Carlo Strenger
58. *Conscious and Unconscious: Freud's Dynamic Distinction Reconsidered,* Patricia S. Herzog
57. *The Creative Process: A Functional Model Based on Empirical Studies from Early Childhood to Middle Age,* Gudmund J. W. Smith & Ingegerd M. Carlsson

PSYCHOLOGICAL ISSUES BOOK SERIES

DAVID WOLITZKY
Series Editor

56. *Motivation and Explanation*, Nigel Mackay
55. *Freud and Anthropology*, Edwin R. Wallace IV
54. *Analysis of Transference, Vol. II: Studies of Nine Audio-Recorded Psychoanalytic Sessions*, Merton M. Gill
53. *Analysis of Transference, Vol. I: Theory and Technique*, Merton M. Gill & Irwin Z. Hoffman
52. *Anxiety and Defense Strategies in Childhood and Adolescence*, Gudmund J. W. Smith & Anna Danielsson Smith
51. *Cognitive Styles, Essays and Origins: Field Dependence and Field Independence*, Herman A. Witkin & Donald R. Goodenough
50. *Internalization in Psychoanalysis*, W. W. Meissner
49. *The Power of Form: A Psychoanalytic Approach to Aesthetic Form*, Gilbert J. Rose

47/48. *Intelligence and Adaptation: An Integration of Psychoanalytic and Piagetian Developmental Psychology*, Stanley I. Greenspan

45/46. *Hysteria: The Elusive Neurosis*, Alan Krohn

44. *Symbol and Neurosis: Selected Papers of Lawrence S. Kubie*, Herbert Schlesinger

42/43. *Modern Psychoanalytic Concepts in a General Psychology: General Concepts and Principles/Motivation*, Allan D. Rosenblatt & James T. Thickstun

41. *Freud in Germany: Revolution and Reaction in Science, 1893–1907*, Hannah S. Decker
40. *A Structural Theory of the Emotions*, Joseph De Rivera
39. *A History of Aggression in Freud*, Paul E. Stepansky
38. *Schizophrenia: Selected Papers*, David Shakow
37. *Emotional Expression in Infancy: A Biobehavioral Study*, Robert N. Emde, Theodore J. Gaensbauer, & Robert J. Harmon
36. *Psychology versus Metapsychology: Psychoanalytic Essays in Memory of George S. Klein*, Merton M. Gill & Philip S. Holzman

34/35. *Freud: The Fusion of Science and Humanism: The Intellectual History of Psychoanalysis*, John E. Gedo & George H. Pollock

33. *A Consideration of Some Learning Variables in the Context of Psychoanalytic Theory: Toward a Psychoanalytic Learning Perspective*, Stanley I. Greenspan
32. *Scientific Thought and Social Reality: Essays*, Fred Schwartz
31. *Else Frenkel-Brunswik: Selected Papers*, Nanette Heiman & Joan Grant
30. *Psychoanalytic Research: Three Approaches to the Experimental Study of Subliminal Processes*, Martin Mayman

PSYCHOLOGICAL ISSUES BOOK SERIES

DAVID WOLITZKY
Series Editor

29. *Similarity in Visually Perceived Forms*, Erich Goldmeier
28. *Immediate Effects on Patients of Psychoanalytic Interpretations*, Edith L. Garduk
27. *The Effect of Stress on Dreams*, Louis Breger, Ian Hunter, & Ron W. Lane
25/26. *Information, Systems, and Psychoanalysis: An Evolutionary Biological Approach to Psychoanalytic Theory*, Emanuel Peterfreund
24. *Ego Boundaries*, Bernard Landis
23. *A Psychoanalytic Model of Attention and Learning*, Fred Schwartz & Peter Schiller
22. *Toward a Unity of Knowledge*, Marjorie Grene
21. *Prediction in Psychotherapy Research: A Method of the Transformation of Clinical Judgments into Testable Hypotheses*, Helen D. Sargent, Leonard Horwitz, Robert S. Wallerstein, & Ann Appelbaum
20. *Psychoanalysis and American Medicine, 1894–1918: Medicine, Science, and Culture*, John Chynoweth Burnham
18/19. *Motives and Thought: Psychoanalytic Essays in Honor of David Rapaport*, Robert R. Holt
17. *The Causes, Controls, and Organization of Behavior in the Neonate*, Peter H. Wolff
16. *Freud's Neurological Education and Its Influence on Psychoanalytic Theory*, Peter Armacher
15. *Dragons, Delinquents, and Destiny: An Essay on Positive Superego Functions*, Wolfgang Lederer
14. *Papers on Psychoanalytic Psychology*, Heinz Hartmann, Ernst Kris, & Rudolph M. Loewenstein
13. *The Influence of Freud on American Psychology*, David Shakow & David Rapaport
12. *The Formation and Transformation of the Perceptual World*, Ivo Kohler
11. *Ego and Reality in Psychoanalytic Theory: A Proposal Regarding the Independent Ego Energies*, Robert W. White
10. *Topography and Systems in Psychoanalytic Theory*, Merton M. Gill
9. *Activation and Recovery of Associations*, Fred Rouse & Richard O. Schwartz
8. *Personality Organization in Cognitive Controls and Intellectual Abilities*, Riley W. Gardner, Douglas N. Jackson, & Samuel J. Messick
7. *Preconscious Stimulation in Dreams, Associations, and Images*, Otto Potzl, Rudolf Allers, & Jakob Teler
6. *The Structure of Psychoanalytic Theory: A Systematizing Attempt*, David Rapaport

PSYCHOLOGICAL ISSUES BOOK SERIES
DAVID WOLITZKY
Series Editor

5. *The Developmental Psychologies of Jean Piaget and Psychoanalysis*, Peter H. Wolff
4. *Cognitive Control: A Study of Individual Consistencies in Cognitive Behavior*, Riley W. Gardner, Philip. S. Holzman, George S. Klein, & Harriet Linton
3. *On Perception and Event Structure, and the Psychological Environment*, Fritz Heider
2. *Studies in Remembering: The Reproduction of Connected and Extended Verbal Material*, Irving H. Paul
1. *Identity and the Life Cycle: Selected Papers*, Erik H. Erikson

Manual of Regulation-Focused Psychotherapy for Children (RFP-C) with Externalizing Behaviors

A psychodynamic approach

Leon Hoffman, Timothy Rice, and Tracy Prout

LONDON AND NEW YORK

First published 2016
by Routledge
2 Park Square, Milton Park, Abingdon, Oxon, OX14 4RN

and by Routledge
711 Third Avenue, New York, NY 10017

*Routledge is an imprint of the Taylor & Francis Group,
an informa business*

© 2016 Pacella Parent Child Center

The right of Leon Hoffman, Timothy Rice and Tracy Prout to be identified as authors of this work has been asserted by them in accordance with sections 77 and 78 of the Copyright, Designs and Patents Act 1988.

All rights reserved. No part of this book may be reprinted or reproduced or utilised in any form or by any electronic, mechanical, or other means, now known or hereafter invented, including photocopying and recording, or in any information storage or retrieval system, without permission in writing from the publishers.

Trademark notice: Product or corporate names may be trademarks or registered trademarks, and are used only for identification and explanation without intent to infringe.

British Library Cataloguing in Publication Data
A catalogue record for this book is available from the British Library

Library of Congress Cataloging-in-Publication Data
Hoffman, Leon.
  Manual of regulation-focused psychotherapy for children (RFP-C) with externalizing behaviors : a psychodynamic approach / Leon Hoffman, Timothy Rice and Tracy A. Prout.
     pages cm. — (Psychological issues)
  Includes bibliographical references and index.
  1. Child psychotherapy. 2. Psychodynamic psychotherapy.
3. Psychotherapist and patient. I. Rice, Tim. II. Prout, Tracy A.
III. Title.
  RJ504.H64 2016
  618.92'8914—dc23
  2015014782

ISBN: 978-1-138-82373-0 (hbk)
ISBN: 978-1-138-82374-7 (pbk)
ISBN: 978-1-315-73664-8 (ebk)

Typeset in Times New Roman
by Apex CoVantage, LLC

The man who first flung a word of abuse at his enemy instead of a spear was the founder of civilization. Thus words are substitutes for deeds.

Sigmund Freud, 1897

We gratefully acknowledge the help and support from Barbara Milrod, MD.

Contents

Foreword by Nick Midgley   xvii

SECTION 1
Introduction and theoretical background   1

1 Introduction: rationale for regulation-focused psychotherapy for children with externalizing behaviors (RFP-C)   3

2 Basic psychoanalytic and psychodynamic perspectives   34

3 Defenses, defense mechanisms, and coping devices: an experience-near-observable construct   58

4 Affect, emotion regulation, and the research domain criteria   79

SECTION 2
Practice manual   91

5 Foreword to practice manual   93

6 Step 1: introductory meeting with the parents   103

7 Step 1: sessions 1 and 2: initial sessions with the child   120

8 Step 1: second meeting with the parents: feedback   145

9 Step 2: sessions 3–11: addressing child's avoidance of disturbing thoughts and feelings   158

10 Step 2: sessions 3–11: examination of the clinician/patient relationship in the treatment of children   179

11 Step 2: ongoing parent contact: check-ins and meetings   194

12	Step 3: sessions 12–16: termination	206
13	Conclusion	218
	Appendix A	221
	Appendix B	223
	Appendix C	229
	Index	232

Foreword

Anyone who works in mental health services for young people will know how common it is for children to be referred because parents and teachers are concerned by their overactivity, noncompliance, defiance, aggression, and poor regulation of impulses. These children may have a diagnosis of Attention Deficit/Hyperactivity Disorder (ADHD), Oppositional Defiant Disorder (ODD), or Conduct Disorder – all of which can be seen as part of the spectrum of "externalizing" or "disruptive behavior" disorders. Although there is considerable heterogeneity in the way these children present, there is a growing consensus about two points. First, that without appropriate help, these children are highly vulnerable to develop more serious forms of antisocial behavior in adolescence, and to having poor, long-term outcomes in terms of health, emotional well-being, and relationships. Second, that although there is good evidence that Parent Training Programs can be helpful for a substantial proportion of these children, there are many for whom these interventions appear to be less helpful, including children with more severe symptoms and those whose parents are less motivated to engage with services (Fonagy et al. 2014). Yet despite the need for interventions that can address the complex needs of this group of children and families, there is a lack of research into the efficacy of other forms of treatment, especially those that draw on a psychodynamic model of the mind.

This is where this new work by Leon Hoffman, Timothy Rice, and Tracy Prout comes in, and why it is such an important addition to the literature in this field. The contribution that this work makes is, I would suggest, three-fold.

First, Hoffman and his colleagues offer a way of thinking about the nature of externalizing problems that goes beyond a simple checklist of symptoms. In their masterful review of the diagnostic literature on ADHD, ODD, and Conduct Disorder, they draw upon contemporary research – especially from the field of affective neuroscience – to argue that the children who come to our services with these difficulties may share an underlying problem: A deficit in the capacity for implicit emotional regulation. The authors review the latest findings from developmental and neuroscience research to demonstrate why implicit affect regulation is so key to the many behaviors that disruptive children display; and they offer a way of understanding how these difficulties may have come about, drawing on both genetic and environmental factors. Most importantly, they argue that when a child presents to mental health services with oppositional or aggressive conduct, this is *not simply a behavior that needs to be managed; it is also a communication that needs to be understood.*

On the basis of this fundamental insight, the second major contribution that Hoffman and his colleagues make in this book is to set out a model of time-limited therapy that can address a child's deficits in implicit affect regulation, and offer support to their parents, who are so often struggling to cope with the impact of their child's difficulties. Because the intervention is manualized, it allows for the possibility that other clinicians can be trained to replicate the therapy; researchers can evaluate this approach to find out if it is effective and whether it can help in areas where Parent Training Programs have struggled. Moreover, the intervention that is set out here is linked directly to the conceptual model of disruptive disorders that the authors have described in the first part of the book. In other words, there is a conceptual coherence to the model: If externalizing problems can best be understood as resulting from deficits in implicit emotional regulation, then a therapy that attempts to promote this capacity, rather than simply trying to "manage" the disruptive behaviors, should be more effective. This is a change mechanism that can be clearly set out as a key hypothesis in future research, to be either supported or disproved. Rather than simply adding one more brand name treatment to the list of "empirically supported treatments," research into Regulation-Focused Psychotherapy for Children (RFP-C) offers a real possibility of reaching a greater understanding of *what makes treatment effective for this particular group of children*, by linking the underlying psychopathology with the treatment focus and methods of intervention.

As if this were not enough, there is a third area in which I believe this book makes a major contribution, although this area might be of more relevance to a specific professional community, and may matter less to the children and families who come to our services seeking help. The community I am referring to is that of psychodynamic therapists, whose role in child mental health services sometimes appears to be uncertain. For although there is broad recognition that psychodynamic thinking was a forerunner in child mental health research and practice, introducing many of the key ideas that are central to the way we think and work today, there is also a widely held view that psychodynamic models are "out-dated," and that they have not kept up with contemporary thinking or contemporary research. The lack of manualized treatments has prevented research from taking place, and although "lack of evidence" is not the same as "evidence for the lack of effectiveness," there is a widely held skepticism about whether psychodynamic approaches are compatible with contemporary scientific thinking, or have something specific to offer to the children and families who come to our services.

This book demonstrates magnificently how wrong that view is. Regulation-Focused Psychotherapy for Children is a model that clearly draws on the very latest developmental and neuroscientific research, and describes the approach using a language that is largely theory neutral and descriptive. This should ensure that the ideas are as accessible as possible to the whole community of child mental health practitioners, who have sometimes felt put off by the language of classical psychoanalysis. But for those who are interested, this book also spells out very clearly the way in which psychodynamic ideas – including the work of Freud and Anna Freud, Berta Bornstein, Paulina Kernberg, and others – should be absolutely central to the way in which "externalizing problems" are understood, and that therapy is provided.

In these pages you will find a fascinating discussion of the link between the concept of "defense mechanisms" and "implicit emotional regulation," and the way in which violent and hostile behavior of children with disruptive disorders can be understood in terms of defenses such as "projection" and "denial." There are many wonderful clinical vignettes that help to demonstrate the way in which a child's play or behavior in the consulting room can have a meaning that is closely linked to the difficulties that led the families to seek help. There are also clear illustrations of the value of paying attention to our own emotional reactions to these children, especially when the challenging and violent behavior comes into the consulting room, leaving us feeling punitive, controlling, or overwhelmed. Hoffman and his colleagues illustrate carefully how concepts such as "transference" and "countertransference" don't have to be seen as specialist terms belonging only to the field of psychodynamic therapy; they are instead *aids to thinking*, ones that can be of enormous value to almost all professionals working in child mental health.

Therapists working with children who present with "externalizing disorders" (and with the parents of those children) will find much clinical wisdom in the pages of this book. It is a clinical wisdom that has been "manualized," in a form that the model can be replicated and evaluated. Evaluation measures are proposed and measures of treatment adherence provided. Thanks to this, future research will be able to test the value of this approach and find out whether it offers something to children and families that complements (or supplements) what is already being offered. For the time being, we can be extremely grateful that these experienced clinicians have shared with us their thinking and added to the repertoire of what is possible when working with these very challenging young people. In the long term, this book is likely to contribute to a sea-change in the way that psychodynamic therapies are viewed, as their contemporary relevance and value to children and families comes to be gradually reestablished.

Nick Midgley, PhD, is a Child and Adolescent Psychotherapist at the Anna Freud Centre, and a lecturer at University College London. He is coauthor of a forthcoming manual of short-term psychodynamic psychotherapy for adolescents with depression.

Reference

Fonagy, P., Cottrell, D., Phillips, J., Bevington, D., Glaser, D., & Allison, E. 2014. *What works for whom? a critical review of treatments for children and adolescents,* New York, NY: Guildford Press.

Section 1

Introduction and theoretical background

Chapter 1

Introduction
Rationale for regulation-focused psychotherapy for children with externalizing behaviors (RFP-C)

The man who first flung a word of abuse at his enemy instead of a spear was the founder of civilization. Thus words are substitutes for deeds.
Sigmund Freud, 1893

This manual is the first attempt to systematize how clinicians can address a child's defenses (implicit affect regulation mechanisms) when addressing a child's disruptive behavior.

SUBJECTS COVERED IN THIS CHAPTER

The nature of externalizing behaviors
Lessons from a moment of therapeutic failure
Countertransference
Varieties of externalizing behaviors
Why the lack of effective psychological treatments for children with externalizing behaviors?
Historical context towards an affect-sensitive nosology
Emotional components in ODD
The work of Paulina Kernberg
Mentalization-informed child psychoanalytic psychotherapy
Regulation-focused psychotherapy for children with externalizing behaviors (RFP-C): towards an empirical study of its effectiveness

The nature of externalizing behaviors

Clinical vignette

One session with Stephanie, a seven-year-old girl who was a tomboy, demonstrates the problem we have to address when we consider children with externalizing behaviors. This active, athletic little girl was disruptive in school and needing disciplinary actions; she had one parent who was anxious, overindulgent, and inconsistent and another who was rigid, punitive, and emotionally unavailable. Her play in psychotherapy sessions consisted of a variety of ball games, often kickball. As is typical with young children, winning was of central importance for her. However, unlike with most children, the clinician's occasional point or win led to dramatic hysterics and accusations that the clinician was cheating (in other words, she utilized the defense mechanism of projection of her own wishes and actions onto the other person). "I am not cheating, you are cheating," was the implicit message to the clinician playing with her. This defense mechanism of projection was also utilized by the parents.

Stephanie is a typical example of children with externalizing behaviors, and in particular those who can be categorized as oppositional defiant disorder (ODD). These children demonstrate the defense mechanisms (DM) of denial and projection. It is the premise of RFP-C that the construct of unconscious DM (developed within the psychodynamic tradition) is similar to the construct of implicit emotion regulation (ER) (developed within the empirical findings of contemporary affective neuroscience) (Rice & Hoffman 2014). We discuss in more detail the similarity between DM and implicit ER in Chapter 4.

Therefore, we have chosen the term "Regulation-Focused Psychotherapy" instead of "defense-focused" for our therapeutic intervention because the term "regulation" is more descriptive and theory neutral than the term "defense." And, in fact, in the Research Domain Criteria (RDoC) of the NIMH (Insel 2014), a key feature in children with externalizing behaviors is an inability to regulate their affective responses to negative stimuli. It is important to note that the RDoC project of the NIMH is "intended to serve as a framework for neuroscience research." RDoC takes an approach different from that of DSM. It assumes (1) that mental disorders can be explained in terms of brain circuits and (2) that abnormalities of these circuits are identifiable and will lead to the discovery of "biosignatures," ultimately to be integrated with clinical data" (Colibazzi 2014, page 709).

Definition of emotion regulation

"Implicit emotion regulation may be defined as any process that operates without the need for conscious supervision or explicit intentions, and which is aimed at modifying the quality, intensity, or duration of an emotional response. Implicit emotion regulation can thus be instigated even when people do not realize that they are engaging in any form of emotion regulation and when people have no conscious intention of regulating their emotions" (Koole & Rothermund 2011, page 390).

Definition of defense mechanism

The definition of defense mechanisms (DM) is virtually identical. DM are "automatic psychological processes that protect the individual against anxiety and from the awareness of internal or external dangers or stressors. Individuals are often unaware of these processes as they operate. DM mediate the individual's reaction to emotional conflicts and to internal and external stressors" in the language of the DSM-IV (American Psychiatric Association 2000, page 751).

Children with externalizing behaviors utilize major reality-distorting defenses (such as projection and denial), which can be viewed as similar to developmental delays in their implicit emotion regulation (ER) capacities. An underdeveloped implicit ER system results in heightened prolonged limbic, hormonal, and autonomic nervous system arousal when these children are challenged with strong and painful emotions (Etkin et al. 2010). We hypothesize that these biochemical changes contribute to a tendency towards impulsive action and, when coupled by the cognitive distortions and errors in judgment afforded by their denials and projection, cause major and multiple problems in these children's lives.

RFP-C hypothetically removes roadblocks to normative development and promotes the maturation of ER processes. The procedures described herein have been conceptualized originally as specific to children with ODD, yet can be applied to other children with a variety of externalizing behaviors. Emotion regulation deficits may be the core deficit in not only ODD (Cavanagh et al. 2014), but it may also account for many of the behavioral disturbances and social deficits of attention deficit/hyperactivity disorder (ADHD; Shaw et al. 2014), disruptive mood dysregulation disorder (DMDD; Dougherty et al. 2014), and perhaps even some children with conduct disorder (CD; Deborde et al. 2014). These children's deficits render them unable to integrate or usefully consider *direct verbal interventions* by the clinician about their *actions*. In this manual, we illustrate how *premature direct verbal interventions about children's disruptive actions* are at best not useful and at worst may hamper the treatment. We describe an approach to children with externalizing behaviors in which the clinician carefully addresses the child's *unpleasant emotions* and the *defenses, such as denial and projection against these unpleasant emotions*. Iterative application of these procedures promotes maturation of ER capacities in these children, enabling successes, improved self-esteem, and self-mastery.

Regulation-focused approach to children with externalizing behaviors

The clinician carefully addresses the child's *unpleasant emotions*, particularly the *defenses, such as denial and projection against these unpleasant emotions.*

Lessons from a moment of therapeutic failure

Stephanie, the seven-year-old, often suffered a great deal of tension at home. At school, she was often threatened with suspension. The parents were dissatisfied with her treatment. In the psychotherapy sessions, cheating during games was rampant, and often the clinician felt provoked by the notorious cheating. Only retrospectively did the clinician become aware that her countertransference reactions to this little girl prevented her from addressing the cheating in a therapeutic manner.

> **The clinician has to be sensitive to his/her own countertransference reactions when working with children who exhibit externalizing behaviors.**
>
> **Is the universality of countertransference responses to disruptive children one of the sources for the lack of effective psychological treatments for children with externalizing behaviors?**

When the clinician discussed this session with colleagues, she became aware that her response to Stephanie was a result of countertransference feelings of which she was unaware at the time of the session. The clinician had said to Stephanie: "You know I really don't understand why it's so difficult for you to ever lose a point, even though you win every game." You certainly can hear in the clinician's words her own frustration and disguised aggression and wish that Stephanie would "shape up" so the treatment could continue.

The clinician addressed Stephanie's actions and not her emotions that were masked by her unsocialized actions.

Undoubtedly, the clinician's tone and affect towards Stephanie were similar to what Stephanie experienced from her teachers and parents. Everyone was, in essence, saying:

"If you just stopped it and shape up and act like other kids, all will be OK."

> **A clinician's job is not to tell a child to "shape up" and "act right."**
> **The clinician's task is to help a child with the emotions that trigger the disruptive maladaptive behavior.**

Stephanie ran out of the playroom to her mother and screamed inconsolably that the clinician was cheating. "She wants to cheat all the time and stops me from winning!" The extent of the projection was clear. What was unanticipated by the clinician, as a result of her countertransference, no doubt, was Stephanie's development of a sustained refusal to come into the office alone, precipitating the interruption of the treatment.

This brief vignette highlights a common clinical moment when a clinician may not be aware of his/her personal affective response and affective communication to the patient, and cannot appropriately address the child's emotional state. In this particular instance, the clinician was engaged in a communication in the cognitive sphere without being aware of the child's emotional state, affecting her cognitions.

As a result, the clinician did not address the patient's emotional sphere, the girl's feelings, or the protective role against painful emotions played by the externalizing behavior.

This moment of therapeutic failure provides us with a valuable lesson in how to address children with externalizing behaviors.

Disruptive symptoms result from impaired emotion regulation (ER) and are the only protection against painful emotions that a child with ODD can utilize.

The challenge:
 How to address the emotional sphere of the child with externalizing behaviors.

Countertransference

The lesson of the therapeutic failure with Stephanie is an example of the difficulty in the psychotherapeutic treatment of aggressive children. Aggressive children at times may exhibit a potential real threat to the clinician and his/her possessions. Counterreactions are inevitably evoked in the clinician. As with any other person, the clinician's experience of the patient is colored by residues from his/her own past (countertransference). That is why a clinician has to understand him/herself as much as possible. This is crucial since the clinician needs to discern clearly the degree to which his/her reactions to the child are derived from his/her own past and how much is provoked by the patient.

Children with regulation problems, such as children with ODD or DMDD, can become aware of their effects on their clinicians. In order to protect themselves from the painful emotions of powerlessness, shame, and distress that emerge in their relationship to the clinician (what is called activation of the attachment system and a reemergence of the distorted attachment patterns that are often present in these children), aggressive children may attempt to cope with those feelings by exhibiting an attitude of superiority or attempting to control the clinician. They attack the clinician; they follow the motto, "A good offense is the best defense." The provocations of the clinician and the attacks on the clinician are often a repetition of the behaviors that occur at home and/or at school. In the sessions, the child may respond with disruptive, attacking behavior to the clinician's absences, to the presence of other children in the waiting room, or to the clinician's attempts to discuss uncomfortable subjects. In order not to feel the shame of missing the clinician, the child will attack instead. These situations are often reenactments of significant precipitants of the disruptive symptoms in the child's life.

It may be that providing the therapist with a theoretical frame of reference and an active technique such as RFP-C enables the clinician to become aware sooner and more effectively of his/her countertransference and enables the clinician to respond therapeutically rather than in a countertransferential way, which can lead to an escalation of the externalizing behavior, such as occurred with Stephanie.

It is reasonable to conjecture that countertransference responses to disruptive children are universal. Such children learn the clinician's buttons very quickly and intuitively and learn how to push them. Can it be that this phenomenon is one of the sources for the lack of effective psychological treatments for children with externalizing behaviors?

It is interesting to note that the concept of countertransference has been neglected by the child psychiatry community. Rasic (2010) notes that this neglect may be due to several factors:

1 "An increasing emphasis on evidence-based psychiatry; at present, countertransference and countertransference reactions" – defined by the author as unconsciously-influenced clinician behaviors in response to the countertransference which can lead to enactments – "cannot be precisely measured, nor can their precise clinical effect;
2 "The natural discomfort resulting from the serious and honest self-examination that is required to identify and understand countertransference; child psychiatry may create particularly heightened anxiety and avoidance because admitting to having strong feelings (particularly negative ones) conflicts with our cultural values to protect and help children; and
3 "Countertransference was originally a psychoanalytic concept, and the psychoanalytic notion of analyzing children separate from their family and social context was abandoned by child psychiatry as a whole, perhaps explaining why the application of the concept of countertransference in relation to children, adolescents and families was largely forgotten" (page 251).

In Chapter 10, we will discuss in detail examples of the clinician's approaches to his/her countertransference.

Varieties of externalizing behaviors

Externalizing behaviors are one of the most significant mental health problems, if not the most significant, from which children and their families suffer. They are the most common reason for referral to specialty clinics (Loeber et al. 2000). The healthcare costs of children with disruptive behaviors outweigh those of chronic health conditions, such as asthma or diabetes (Guevara et al. 2003). Parents, teachers, caretakers, and other professionals are often at a loss with these children and, thus, seek mental health care. The adults believe that the child who is very disruptive needs an intervention even though the child believes that his/her problems would easily be solved if the environment changed. In fact, because of the difficulties these children pose for themselves and their caretakers and teachers, a significant number of them are treated with antipsychotic medications (Olfson et al. 2012). Stephanie, for example, felt that the clinician's cheating was the cause of her problem in the session.

> **Children with externalizing behaviors feel that the environment is the cause of their problems.**
> "If only the teacher would change."

Children with externalizing behaviors include those who can be diagnosed with ADHD, CD, DMDD, and ODD. Many of these children have a variety of symptoms so that they easily can be classified to be in more than one of these categories (comorbidities). In addition, some of these children have anxiety and/or depressive symptoms, either as subsyndromal states or which can be actually categorized to have comorbid disorders. Children with a primary ODD diagnosis, particularly very young children in preschool or early school years, form a group that is easily recognizable and easily contrasted with those children who are more adaptable and compliant and/or inhibited anxious/depressed. Some children with ODD also can be diagnosed with ADHD.

ODD is one of the most prevalent disorders of childhood (Lavigne et al. 2009). It is among the most frequent reasons for referral of young children to specialist care (Wilens et al. 2002). Between 4 and 8% of children and adolescents meet criteria for ODD (American Psychiatric Association 2013). This prevalence is consistent among different cultures and countries (Canino et al. 2010). Though ODD is traditionally considered more prevalent in boys (Maughan et al. 2004), some consider this to be an artifact of girls' less overt and less impairing symptom manifestations (Waschbusch & King 2006). A significant population of girls with impairment due to behavior problems may exist that fail to meet the current diagnostic criteria. The transformative applications of this manual may apply to many children not traditionally considered affected by ODD.

Children with ODD make themselves quite apparent to their environment. They may have frequent temper tantrums, argue excessively with adults, be actively defiant and refuse to comply with adult requests and rules, make deliberate attempts to annoy or upset people, blame others for their mistakes or misbehavior, be touchy or easily annoyed by others, have frequent anger and resentment, talk in a mean and hateful way when upset, and seek revenge for wrongs done to them (American Psychiatric Association 1994). In addition, many of these children have histories, dating especially back to their toddlerhood, of increased expressions of negative affect, particularly anger secondary to frustrations consistent with temperamental difficulties (Gartstein et al. 2012).

Aggression affects between 10 and 25% of youth (Scotto Rosato et al. 2012), and ODD is often a precursor to more serious psychopathology. Children with ODD do not, by definition, *yet,* have the essential features of CD (recurring and enduring pattern of behavior that violates the basic rights of others and deviates from important age-appropriate societal norms; Rowe et al. 2010). As such, they are treated as separate disorders in DSM-5.

Children with maladaptive aggression have emotion regulation deficits (Mullin & Hinshaw 2009). The association is even more pronounced when the heterogeneous concept of aggression is differentiated into independently valid constructs. Reactive aggression, or affectively driven aggressive outbursts that are "reactive" to frustration, is a major subtype of childhood aggression that appears integral to both oppositional defiant disorder and disrupted emotional regulation (Hubbard et al. 2010).

Despite the pervasiveness of the problem with aggressive children, it is striking that there are very few empirically validated approaches for children with severe oppositional symptoms. Helping parents *manage* the behavioral disturbance seems to be the major focus of the treatment of these children. For example, the Practice Parameters of the American Academy of Child Psychiatry for ODD (Steiner & Remsing 2007) state that:

> Parent management training (PMT) in the use of contingency management methods to help them better handle disruptive behavior is one of the most substantiated treatment approaches in child mental health (Brestan & Eyberg 1998; Kazdin 2005). The principles of these approaches can be summarized as follows:
>
> 1 Reduce positive reinforcement of disruptive behavior.
> 2 Increase reinforcement of prosocial and compliant behavior. Positive reinforcement varies widely, but parental attention is predominant. Punishment usually consists of a form of time out, loss of tokens, and/or loss of privileges.
> 3 Apply consequences and/or punishment for disruptive behavior.
> 4 Make parental response predictable, contingent, and immediate.
>
> (page 136)

Despite the fact that PMT (e.g., Kazdin 2005) is the main, validated, behavioral treatment, the Practice Parameters of the American Academy of Child and Adolescent Psychiatry stress that there is clinical evidence pointing to the value of dynamic therapies in the treatment of children with ODD.

A note of caution must be given considering there are few controlled clinical trials specific to ODD comparing modalities such as parent training versus individual approaches. Consequently, except for parent training and some pharmacological approaches, current recommendations regarding the use of modalities such as individual therapy are based on clinical wisdom and consensus rather than extensive empirical evidence. There is also some indication, from a retrospective analysis of a large case series, that dynamically oriented approaches may be useful (Fonagy & Target 1994a).

(Steiner & Remsing 2007, page 136)

Several evidence-based behavioral treatments that work directly with children with ODD, such as the expansive child group component of the Coping Power program (Lochman et al. 2008), have emerged since the drafting of the above-noted practice parameter. However, the vast majority of programs continue to be employed in parallel with a parent-training component, perhaps reflecting the difficulty of working directly with children with ODD. What is most important about the statement of the practice parameter is that this observation of the seeming value of dynamic therapies encourages the development of systematic methods to directly work with these children, in particular through a regulation-focused intervention, given the data of the last decade, which emphasizes a significant deficit in emotion regulation in these children. If, in fact, it could be systematically demonstrated that such an approach does consistently help children with externalizing behaviors, mental health clinicians, who have too few tools to help these children, would then have a valuable tool for the treatment of oppositional and disruptive behaviors.

There are also significant shortcomings of PMT. PMT may be suboptimally designed to help lower socioeconomic families where resources available to parents to ensure adherence and commitment to the intersession programming may be lacking (Kazdin 1990; Kazdin 1993; Kazdin & Mazurick 1994; Fernandez & Eyberg 2009). Younger mothers and those with lower intelligence scores are at greater risk for attrition in PMT (Hood & Eyberg 2003). Many parents of children with ODD have internal difficulties that prevent their full engagement in a structured behavioral treatment, and indeed maternal stress and maternal negative self-talk were also predictive of drop-out (Werba et al. 2006). Maternal stress may also lead to treatment interruption and drop-outs (Capage et al. 2008), and outcomes are likely to be significantly poorer for patients who fail to complete treatment (Boggs et al. 2008). Greater symptom severity predicts attrition (Kazdin 1990) in PMT. Individual work with children, rather than only focusing on parent interventions, may be especially helpful in families with these characteristics.

Why the lack of effective psychological treatments for children with externalizing behaviors?

It is crucial to reiterate that ODD is a significant public health problem. For example, "earlier age at onset of ODD symptoms conveys a poorer prognosis in terms of progression to CD and ultimately APD [antisocial personality disorder]" (Steiner & Remsing 2007, page 129). Even though ODD is milder compared to CD, about 30% of children with ODD do develop CD, a more serious and more difficult disorder to treat; and about 10% of children with ODD eventually develop APD, a severe and extremely difficult-to-treat adult personality disorder.

Despite the pervasiveness of the problem and the long-term problematic prognosis for a significant number of these children, the lack of effective psychological treatments prompts several considerations.

Stimulants and other medications

Certainly the responsiveness of ADHD to stimulant and other medications leads many practitioners to immediately utilize these medications to treat children with externalizing behaviors because many such children, such as those who can be categorized as suffering from ODD, do meet criteria consistent with a comorbid ADHD. However, stimulants may not address the problematic emotionality that is part of ADHD. Stimulants have been alternatingly reported to either improve (Ahmann et al. 1993) or to worsen (Gillberg et al. 1997; Short et al. 2004) symptoms of emotional labile states. The most methodologically sound study to date suggests that any symptomatic improvement, though statistically significant, is likely of a modest effect size (Katic et al. 2012). Additionally, stimulants may not work well for preschoolers (Greenhill et al. 2006), a critical time for the development of ODD (Comer et al. 2013).

> **Stimulants may not address the problematic emotionality that is part of ADHD.**

It is unclear whether the problematic emotionality observed in ADHD is actually part of the ADHD syndrome or a manifestation of the underlying temperamental difficulty in many children with ODD (Barkley 2010). Regardless, problematic emotionality sensitizes children who may be vulnerable to the development of ODD, unlike other children, to stresses and frustrations in their lives, leading to externalizing behaviors.

> **Problematic emotionality sensitizes children, who may be vulnerable to the development of ODD, to stresses and frustrations in their lives, leading to externalizing behaviors.**

Introduction: rationale for RFP-C   13

The utilization of antipsychotic medications is both a difficult and controversial approach (Olfson et al. 2012; Loy et al. 2012). Nevertheless, it is a common one: Disruptive disorders account for the majority of antipsychotic medication use in both children (63%) and adolescents (33.7%) (Olfson et al. 2012). Their use is expanding most rapidly among children of families with low income and of Hispanic ethnicity and African American race (Zito et al. 2013). The difficulty in accepting this practice lies in the well-established adverse effects of antipsychotic medications (Hampton et al. 2015). These effects may be particularly harmful to children. Evidence suggests vulnerability to antipsychotic medication induced weight gain and metabolic derangements (Maayan & Correll 2011). Youth may also be at greater risk for extrapyramidal symptoms and prolactin elevation (Correll 2011).

In addition to these side effects that are most easily recognizable as "biological" by merit of their manifestation within easily measurable parameters (body weight, lipid level, elevated prolactin), neuroleptics may even more profoundly adversely alter the child's experience of him/herself. Psychoanalyst and psychiatrist Donald Cohen writes:

> What does it mean for a child to lose control suddenly over his appetites, to be ravenous, insatiable and locked into battles with his parents because of his overeating? To feel sleepy and intoxicated? To feel, from still another cause, that his actions are not fully under his control, that his states of arousal and fatigue are related to what he takes in rather than to who he is? We know far too little about the long-term meaning of being medicated for several years or longer – both on the systems involved with autonomy and motivation as well as on brain receptors and structures. From a psychoanalytic perspective, we can see in such behavior the seeds of long-term alterations in the sense of self as the locus of integration of desires, initiatives, and affects.
>
> (Cohen 1991, page 205)

In children with ODD, DMDD, and other disorders of disruptive behavior and irritability, perhaps of all these consequences we are most concerned with the alterations supplied by medications to the child's experience of affect. As the act of accepting medication may be symbolized by the model of an external taking-in of an agent with the anticipated effect of calming or controlling negative affect, the child on medication disavows him/herself of the responsibility to process and self-regulate without the assistance of an agent that is outside him/herself. This creates a split within the child – between the "good" child and the "bad" child – which is to be controlled by medication. This is a similar split to that which is maintained in the PMT model and other behavioral approaches to childhood pathology. Often, these children develop fantasies concerning these "bad" selves. In prior times, they may have considered themselves bewitched or evil. Currently, many children, through the influence of our mental health field, employ a medical model and identify vague descriptors of "bad pathways in the brain" or "abnormal neurotransmitter levels" as the source of their distress. These binary simplifications impair the child's ability to see the process towards integration as within one's own control, and it ignores the ample evidence that psychotherapeutic work changes the underlying biological determinants of its targets (e.g., Buchheim et al. 2012; de Greck et al. 2011) even when psychotherapy is short-term (e.g. Woltering et al. 2011) and of a psychodynamic modality (e.g. Beutel 2010).

Most crucially to our model, this jettisoning of responsibility onto medicine short-circuits the opportunity for the child to develop internal implicit emotion regulation capacities. Some children may be immensely helped by the use of the medication, when anxiety or alternate negative effects are so consuming for the child, but the RFP-C clinician must consider whether the use of long-term medications – the conversion of the child into a chronic patient – may be useful or detrimental to his/her development. Thus, the use of medication in RFP-C is understood from a developmental rather than a biological perspective: Medication may be useful only when the child's development and emotion regulative capacities are seriously impaired; when they are at a level that impairs his/her ability to engage in the work of RFP-C.

The controversy of neuroleptics in children with ODD especially arises owing to the small base of empirical evidence upon which this practice stands. Practices have also been generalized from a select sample of children with intellectual deficits, leaving questions whether the results of these trials with these children are applicable to the greater population. As of 2012, only eight randomized controlled trials had investigated the use of antipsychotic medications in the management of aggression within the disruptive behavior disorders (Pringsheim & Gorman 2012). Seven of these trials investigated a single antipsychotic medication, Risperidone, and five of the trials investigated youth with subaverage-borderline intelligence quotients, yet children and adolescents with normal or high intelligence are also treated with a variety of antipsychotic medications (Pringsheim & Gorman 2012).

There is currently no Federal Drug Administration approval for the use of any psychotropic in the treatment of the externalizing behavior disorders in children. Nevertheless, off-label prescription with these described agents occurs routinely.

Nature of externalizing behaviors and response of the mental health clinician

A second conjecture that is stimulated by the lack of development of useful psychological treatments for children with externalizing behaviors, such as ODD, may be related to the nature of the problem and the responses from the mental health clinician (see the case of Stephanie at the beginning of this chapter).

Problems in children and adults may be broadly categorized as *externalizing* or *internalizing* (PDM Task Force 2006; Achenbach & Edelbrock 1978). *Internalizing* problems include behaviors that the child experiences as problematic, that is, problematic emotions that come from within. In contrast, *externalizing* behaviors refer to those situations in which the child expresses or reacts behaviorally to his/her conflicts or feelings instead of describing problematic feelings as emanating from within. Among externalizing disorders are those that can be globally categorized as Disruptive Disorders (DD). The rationale for this broad categorization is that in empirical studies, there is a great deal of comorbidity within both internalizing problems (anxiety and depression) and externalizing problems (ODD, CD, and ADHD). More recently, children who can be categorized with the new category of DMDD also exhibit many externalizing behaviors. At the internalizing end of the spectrum, we include children with the large variety of emotional disorders that have dysphoric affects and a great deal of overt self-recriminations, guilt, and/or shame (PDM Task Force 2006; Achenbach & Edelbrock 1978).

At the externalizing end of the spectrum, one tends to observe a seeming "lack of insight" into personal responsibility. If we think back to seven-year-old Stephanie, she could not think about the nature of her cheating, she did not have a sense of personal responsibility. Instead, she blamed the teachers for her problems in school and the clinician for her problems in the sessions.

It is crucial for us to consider that this apparent "lack of insight" may be a result of a maladaptive coping mechanism (a problem in her capacities to regulate her emotions [ER] effectively) and not just a cognitive defect. As a result of the clinician's countertransference, at the time, she did not conceptualize the child's behavior disturbance and lack of insight as manifestations of maladaptive coping or ER mechanisms.

There are, of course, various mixtures of internalizing and externalizing expressions.

Internalizing: Child feels problems are coming from within.
Externalizing: Child feels problems are caused by the environment.

Externalizing behaviors are problematic for other people in the child's life because, as a result of the manifest lack of insight and personal responsibility, the child, like Stephanie, blames the environment for his/her problems. Parents, caretakers, teachers, and others (often including clinicians) are blamed by the children for the problems. Sooner or later and with increasing intensity, these adults in the lives of children with disruptive behaviors have difficulty maintaining an empathic stance towards such children with severe behavioral disruptions. Mental health professionals, like the clinician with Stephanie, may also quickly lose their empathic connections with these children because of the children's negativistic responses and their lack of overt acceptance of responsibility.

It is no wonder that the major, effective psychotherapeutic techniques that have been developed, in essence, involve training the parents to train themselves and train the child to be more socialized. In a contemporary survey of 46 experts in the treatment of pediatric aggression, play therapy was rated the least appropriate and least essential of 18 therapeutic approaches (Pappadopulos et al. 2011). As such, contemporary guidelines, such as the Treatment of Maladaptive Aggression in Youth (T-MAY) guidelines (Knapp et al. 2012; Scotto Rosato et al. 2012), developed from this expert survey, stress behavior therapy and parent/family education.

These considerations prompt a central question that needs empirical exploration:

Are children with externalizing behaviors inherently so much more difficult to treat with psychological methods than children with internalizing problems? Or does the difficulty with psychological treatment ensue as a result of the inevitable problematic interactions between the child who externalizes and clinician (like between Stephanie and her clinician), with the clinician lacking the proper therapeutic tools to help the child with externalizing behaviors and, thus, allowing his/her countertransference to overwhelm the child?

Are children with externalizing behaviors inherently more difficult to treat with psychological methods than children with internalizing problems?

Disruptive children do not directly express their inner distress, nor do they directly manifest an inner sense of responsibility. Whether these difficulties are a result of a cognitive deficit or a result of emotional conflict, these children's difficulties may promote a prejudice against them by mental health professionals, whose mode of treatment with children always includes interactions, such as those that occur in psychotherapy. As a result, many clinicians come to believe that individual psychotherapies ("talking therapies" and "play therapies") are mainly, or actually, only, useful for children with internalizing problems, that is, children who openly acknowledge their distress and do not usually blame others for their problems. Can it be that there is a nihilism among mental health clinicians that leads them not to utilize psychological treatments with disruptive children, other than management-type treatments, such as PMT?

Mechanisms of action of psychological treatments

Contributing to the difficulty in the development of effective psychological treatments is the challenge of ascertaining the mechanism of action as well as the efficacy and effectiveness of psychological treatments, not just for externalizing behaviors but for most psychological disorders. Most importantly, in contrast to the large CBT-outcome literature, only in recent years have dynamic psychological treatments begun to be systematically evaluated. This is exemplified by the recent position statement by the American Psychological Association outlining the studies demonstrating the effectiveness of psychotherapy (American Psychological Association 2012[1]; Fonagy & Target 1994a, 1994b; Milrod et al. 2007; Busch et al. 2012).

Historical context towards an affect-sensitive nosology

ODD has been a controversial diagnosis since its inception in the DSM-III (American Psychiatric Association 1980). There was no clear precedent for ODD in the DSM-II (American Psychiatric Association 1968). Whereas the DSM-II diagnoses of unsocialized aggressive reaction of childhood, runaway reaction of childhood, and group delinquent reaction of childhood mapped to socialized and undersocialized CD, and hyperkinetic reaction of childhood mapped to attention deficit disorder, there was no equivalent diagnosis for ODD. Concern was expressed that ODD, or oppositional disorder as it was known in the DSM-III, was simply renaming normal developmental behavior as childhood pathology (Rutter 1980). In response, DSM-III-R (American Psychiatric Association 1987) eliminated less specific and more prevalent symptoms and increased the minimum required number of symptoms to the then-renamed ODD (Lahey et al. 1990). Prevalence of ODD fell in response to the changes (Lahey et al. 1992), and controversy moved to the demarcation between ODD and CD. Many argued that ODD and conduct were the same disorder (Werry et al. 1987). Most empirical studies published at that time lumped ODD and CD into a single diagnostic category (Werry et al. 1987). The majority of children who met criteria for CD before puberty also met criteria for ODD (Spitzer et al. 1990), and risk factors such as lower socioeconomic status, inadequate parenting, and parental antisocial behavior were identical for both diagnoses (Lahey & Loeber 1994).

However, other evidence favored retaining the distinction. This included the fact that a significant number of youth with adolescent-onset CD previously met criteria for ODD; however, not all children who meet criteria for ODD go on to meet criteria for CD (Loeber et al. 1991). Differences between the two disorders in age of symptom onset (Lahey et al. 1992), functional severity, and criterion covariations also supported this distinction.

The distinction was ultimately retained for the DSM-IV (American Psychiatric Association 2000), but the disorders, along with antisocial personality disorder (ASPD), became conceptualized hierarchically and developmentally as age-dependent manifestations of the same underlying disorder (Moffitt et al. 2008). Concurrent comorbidity was disallowed between the three disorders (ODD, CD, and ASPD), and ASPD required evidence of CD prior to age 15 (American Psychiatric Association 2000).

Though some recent evidence continues to support this developmental hierarchy (Bezdjian et al. 2011), a large number of studies since the publication of the DSM-IV have questioned this unidirectional organization of ODD. The high degree of ODD to CD progression seen in clinical settings (e.g., Campbell 1994; Lavigne et al. 1998) and prospective studies (Cantwell & Baker 1988; Lahey & Loeber 1994) were not replicated in the community. Only 40% of boys with ODD progressed to CD in The Great Smoky Mountain Study (Rowe et al. 2002). Eventually, as few as 9.2% of youth with CD were found to have been diagnosed with ODD at earlier study waves (Rowe et al. 2010). The findings from another large community study were in agreement; there was a low progression from ODD to CD (Loeber et al. 2009).

Concurrently, early, small-sized studies suggested a possible affective basis to ODD (Fischer et al. 1984; Hooks et al. 1988). A two-year prospective study of 79 boys found that up to a quarter developed mood or anxiety disorders in the follow-up period, and ODD was suggested to serve as a gateway to eventual affective/anxiety disorders, with risk increasing with age (Speltz et al. 1999). These studies, combined with a decreasing faith in an ODD to CD progression, set the stage for the reconceptualization of ODD to a disorder, in part, of disrupted affect.

Emotional components in ODD

There is theoretical validity to address the emotional component of ODD. The past decade has witnessed a radical reconceptualization of ODD. No longer is ODD considered strictly a behavioral disorder; the importance of affect has become pronounced. This has developed alongside gradual increased interest in the affective neurosciences (for example, Etkin et al. 2010).

There is recent evidence to suggest the centrality of the emotional component in children with ODD. A factor analysis suggests that the core deficit of ODD may be one of emotion dysregulation (Cavanagh et al. 2014); Stringaris and Goodman (2009b) have identified distinct dimensions within ODD that divergently correlate with emotional (i.e., irritable, touchy, angry) and behavioral (i.e., defying adults, annoying, blaming) dimensions of this disorder. The addition of DMDD to the Diagnostic and Statistical Manual of Mental Disorders (American Psychiatric Association 2013; Leibenluft et al. 2003) and the recent discussion of difficulties in emotional regulation in individuals with ADHD (Shaw et al. 2014) are further examples of the potential theoretical shift in the field, which highlights the emotional underpinnings of behavioral disruptions (Ambrosini et al. 2013; Reimherr et al. 2005).

ODD closely linked to emotional dysfunction: towards DSM-5

The interest in an affective component in children with ODD originated in the context of other nosologic controversies. Disappointment with the overdiagnosis of childhood bipolar disorder in both inpatients (Blader & Carlson 2007) and outpatients (Moreno et al. 2007) led to increased scrutiny of whether nonepisodic, chronic irritability exists as a true developmental presentation of mania, as some had proposed (Wozniak et al. 1995). As increasing evidence showed that it did not (Mikita & Stringaris 2013), new diagnostic concepts were proposed, including severe mood dysregulation (SMD) (Leibenluft 2011), deficient emotional self-regulation (DESR) (Barkley 2010), temper dysregulation disorder with dysphoria (TDD) (DSM-5 Work Group, 2010), and DMDD (DSM-5 Work Group, 2010). Simultaneously, as irritability may be defined as easy annoyance and touchiness that can manifest in anger and outbursts (Stringaris 2011), interest developed in whether the cluster of ODD criteria that include "is often touchy or easily annoyed," "is often angry or resentful," and "often loses temper" (American Psychiatric Association 2000) may be related to these constructs.

Stringaris and Goodman (2009a) published the first major study to draw attention to the differential symptom clusters within the current ODD construct. They divided ODD into three dimensions based on an ODD criteria profile. This profile resulted in an irritable dimension (touchy, angry, temper), a headstrong dimension (argues, annoys, blames, and defies), and a hurtful dimension (vindictive). They found that the irritable dimension predicted emotional symptoms and disorders to a greater extent than the others, whereas the headstrong dimension predicted ADHD and the nonaggressive symptoms of CD. In contrast, the hurtful dimension predicted the aggressive symptoms of CD. In a three-year follow-up study (Stringaris & Goodman 2009a), the authors hypothesize that children with ODD who scored high on the irritable dimension may benefit from interventions that addressed their emotional dysregulation. As a result, the DSM-5 reorganized ODD item criteria by these dimensions.

Dimensions in ODD from Stringaris and Goodman (2009a)

Irritable: temper outbursts, touchy or easily annoyed, and angry and resentful.

Headstrong: Argues with grownups, takes no notice of rules, or refuses to do as she/he is told, seems to do things to annoy other people on purpose, and blames others for his/her own mistakes or bad behavior.

Hurtful: spiteful and vindictive.

Children with ODD who score high on the irritable dimension may benefit from interventions that address their emotional dysregulation.

Rowe and colleagues (Rowe et al. 2010) used factor analysis of data from a large prospective trial of child and adolescent psychopathology, focusing on the irritable dimension delineated by Stringaris and Goodman. Rather than demarcate between the Stringaris and Goodman headstrong and hurtful dimensions, Rowe

20 Introduction and theoretical background

and colleagues chose to combine these two dimensions and retain the headstrong name for all five component symptoms of this combined dimension. Their result indicated that the irritable factor was a significant predictor of conduct, depressive, and anxiety disorders; whereas, the headstrong dimension predicted only conduct and depressive disorders.

Burke and colleagues (2010) also used factor analysis but with differing symptom cluster dimensions. They named the two dimensions negative affect (touchy, angry, and spiteful symptoms) and behavioral (argues, defies, loses temper). A clinical sample of boys and a community of sample of girls were both separately analyzed. The results showed that in both samples, the negative affect dimension predicted major depressive disorder and the behavioral dimension predicted CD. In the community sample of girls, the negative affect group also predicted CD. Leibenluft and colleagues (2006) also used differing symptom clusters and included the "argues" symptom within their respective irritable group. They found this group to prospectively predict major depressive disorder (MDD) in late adolescence.

Drabick and Gadow (2012) recategorized the irritable group as anger/irritability symptoms (AIS) and the broad headstrong group as noncompliant symptoms (NS) to reflect the differing uses of symptom clusters by the above studies. In a case-control study, they found that children with AIS had higher levels of mood and anxiety symptoms than their NS peers. In another publication, the NS children were found to be closer to controls than those with AIS (Gadow & Drabick 2012).

The diminished anger control in the irritable type, and even possibly the empathic failure of the hurtful type, may be manifestations of emotional dysregulation (Scott & O'Conner 2012), though there is debate whether the hurtful type may be more akin to the headstrong type of ODD (Rowe et al. 2010). The data of Scott and O'Conner now shows that these subtypes may be more responsive to treatment than their characteristically headstrong peers. In a randomized controlled trial of PMT (The Incredible Years), children of the hurtful and irritable types showed a greater reduction in conduct symptoms at a level of statistical significance than the headstrong type (Scott & O'Connor 2012).

Might this differential hold for individual, child-focused psychological treatment of ODD, such as RFP-C? The basis of RFP-C on the emotion regulation system suggests that it may be targeted to dysregulated emotionality to an even greater extent than the PMT. Thus, PMT may offer a more targeted approach to helping these children who are clearly responsive to treatment. Further research will be required to clarify the current confusion whether the hurtful subtype is more akin to the headstrong versus the irritable subtypes. For now, RFP-C has been designed to address the irritable subtype of ODD as well as all children with ODD by merit of the high association between subgroups within the disorder.

The work of Paulina Kernberg

Kernberg and Chazan (1991) created an affect-oriented approach to the disruptive behavior disorders before this empiric evidence had been discovered. Their work, *Children with Conduct Disorders: A Psychotherapy Manual*, presents a manualized approach to treating children with aggressive-socialized CD. In their overview, they state their conceptualization of aggressive behavior in children with disruptive disorders as "often an unconscious effort to ward off the awareness of feelings of being disregarded and devalued (p. 29)." They characterize the disruptive child as having developmental impairments that are understood under the dual theoretical perspectives of object relations and ego psychology. Interventions drawn from the schools of learning (Patterson 1976), attachment (Bowlby 1969), and temperament (Thomas et al. 1968) are also used.

Like its theoretical orientation, the intervention approach is multifaceted and flexible. Individual, play group, and parent training modalities are all used. In the manual, the recommended treatment for the individual child is driven by the underlying personality structure, whether the recommended treatment is individual, group, or parent training. Play groups are indicated if the child presents with peer difficulties as the main presenting problem. Individual therapy is indicated if low self-esteem, depression, or impulsivity is primary. Mild disorders and those clearly related to difficulties in parental management are treated through parent-training. Kernberg and Chazan saw problems as frequently presenting in different combinations and intensities of the above, and so often all modes were utilized.

Kernberg and Chazan believed that the goal is to increase the child's ability to tolerate affect through words in place of action; that is, to contain affective experience within the psychological realm. Interventions were made patient-near, and are similar to defense interpretations. As a means of organizing and defining their interventional system, Kernberg and Chazan devised The Hierarchy of Verbal Interventions (Liebowitz et al. 1988; Kernberg, Cohen et al. 1986). As children progress through stages of treatment within each therapeutic modality, Kernberg and Chazan comment on the intended relative increase and decreases of various verbal interventions. In RFP-C, a variety of supportive and expressive interventions are offered to the child. However, from the beginning to the end of treatment, the key intervention involves addressing the child's defenses against unpleasant emotions.

Mentalization-informed child psychoanalytic psychotherapy (MBT-C)

There is increasing empirical validation for the effectiveness of psychodynamic psychotherapy for children and adolescence (Midgley & Kennedy 2011). Contemporary research of psychological treatments of children has been spearheaded by Peter Fonagy and Mary Target, whose work builds on that of Anna Freud, Hansi Kennedy, Joseph Sandler, Phyllis and Robert Tyson, George Moran, and others at the Anna Freud Centre. Arguably, they have had the broadest impact in the field, trying to empirically sort out the efficacy and effectiveness of various psychoanalytic techniques with children. They state that the "classical model" is a technique "by which the patient is helped to recover threatening ideas and feelings that have been repudiated or distorted as a result of conflict and defense" (Fonagy & Target 1997, page 66). In contrast, they have stressed that a "mental process model" of treatment is one in which the clinician engages the patient directly by "focusing on the thoughts and feelings of each person and how the child understands these" (page 67).

This conceptualization implies that the "mental process model" is a more experience-near model; whereas the "classical" model is more experience-distant because they consider the "classical" model to be a more cognitive model. Fonagy and Target (1998) say that the classic model can be utilized with children who suffer from what has been classified as "neurotic disorders," whereas the mental process model is utilized with children who suffer from what can be classified as "developmental disorders."

Fonagy and Target (1998) state that "[c]hildren with limited mentalization or reflective abilities are unable to take a step back and respond flexibly and adaptively to the symbolic, meaningful qualities of other people's behavior. Instead, these children find themselves caught in fixed patterns of attribution; rigid stereotypes of response; non-symbolic, instrumental uses of affect – mental patterns that are not amenable to either reflection or modulation" (page 93).

They maintain that:

> Such patients need to learn to observe their own emotions and understand and label their emotional states, including their physiological and affective cues. They need help to understand both the conscious and the unconscious relationships between their behavior and internal states, for instance of frustration or anxiety. As part of that process, the analyst focuses children's attention on the circumstances that lead them, for example, to be aggressive in particular situations in which they feel misunderstood or made anxious by those around them. The analyst introduces a mentalizing perspective that focuses on children's minds as well as the mental states of people who are important to them.
>
> (page 105)

In a recent discussion of "Mentalization-Informed Child Psychoanalytic Psychotherapy" (MBT-C), Zevalkink et al. (2012) state that the overarching aims of MBT-C are "to facilitate the emergence of a coherent sense of self, to foster the capacity to handle emotional reactions, and to enhance that the child is the owner of his or her behavior" (page 131). They further state that "the process is more important than the content" and that the clinician has to have a "willingness to learn the child's perspective," "an attitude of curiosity, active questioning, active reference to possible feelings and thoughts, raise the possibility of thinking about wishes and longings of another person, ability to talk about his or her own 'mistakes,' and an ability to hold the child in mind" (page 139). The authors identify three groups of interventions: (1) attention regulation, (2) affect regulation, and (3) mentalization (page 142). The authors, which include Fonagy, conclude that "the clinical evidence needs to be substantiated with an empirical study of the effectiveness of MBT-C for children and their parents" (page 157).

The aim of this volume is to delineate a systematic therapeutic approach stressing one aspect of dynamic therapy: Addressing a child's difficulties with his/her implicit emotion regulation (defenses) when confronted with unbearable emotions. A key similarity between MBT-C and the approach described in this volume is that **process is stressed over content.**

Regulation-focused psychotherapy for children with externalizing behaviors (RFP-C): towards an empirical study of its effectiveness

The major proposition of this volume is to develop an approach to Regulation-Focused Psychotherapy for Children with Externalizing Behaviors (RFP-C) that can be systematically applied and evaluated.

The dynamic approach described in this manual considers externalizing behaviors as expressions of maladaptive emotion regulation or coping mechanisms (defenses) by the child to protect him/herself from painful emotions. The aggressive symptoms protect the child by masking and removing the painful emotions from the child's consciousness. The unbearable painful feelings may include guilt, shame, hurt, and/or worry. In this treatment approach, the clinician systematically addresses the avoidance mechanisms with the child and talks with the child about how the disruptive behavior helps the child avoid painful emotions. And, eventually the clinician helps the child find better ways to cope with painful feelings.

In one way or other, from the very beginning of the treatment, throughout the treatment, and until termination, the clinician is always (implicitly and explicitly) thinking about this question and, when appropriate, addressing the question with the child.

With this approach, from the first meeting with the child, the clinician carefully tries to understand, explore, and describe the child's current mental state – in terms of emotional pain – and then addresses with the child the avoidant mechanism he/she utilizes against allowing a full awareness of this emotional pain. This allows the child to expand his/her control, leading to greater mastery of emotions and more adaptive interactions with the environment. In some children, over time, there may be greater verbal elaboration of his/her feelings and fantasies while in others not. It is important to stress that, just like in MBT–C, the focus is on the process of the therapy (of what is occurring between clinician and patient at the moment) and not mainly on the content.

The central points in this volume are these:

1   There seems to be a general lack of appreciation of the centrality of the clinical dynamic concept of *regulation-focused interventions against painful emotions*. This intervention is particularly useful when utilizing

psychotherapeutic modalities in trying to help children with severe externalizing behaviors and who do not spontaneously express insight and *deny* their role into their problems.
2   The *regulation-focused intervention* is an experience-near technical intervention.
3   Even a cursory review of the clinical literature indicates that *regulation-focused interventions* are often utilized without appreciation of its significance and without attribution of its origins. These interventions are labeled "defense interpretation" in the clinical literature.
4   Demonstrating the therapeutic effectiveness of *regulation-focused interventions against painful emotions* for children with externalizing behaviors can help integrate this basic technical maneuver within the general psychotherapy research community, with the eventual goal of trying to understand the basic therapeutic ingredients, that is, the treatment mediators, in psychotherapy. The compatibility of RFP-C with affective neuroscience will enable efficacy demonstration through biomarkers of the emotion regulation system in addition to standardized rating scales, questionnaires, and clinical interview.
5   The scientific underpinnings of psychodynamic thinking will be increased as a result of these understandings.

Thus, in working with children, the clinician needs to:

1   Understand the nature of the child's affective communication in the session,
2   Understand the nature of the mechanisms the child uses to avoid experiencing unpleasant affects/emotions,
3   Communicate to the child how the clinician understands the nature of the child's avoidance mechanisms against such unpleasant emotions, and/or
4   Identify for the child the child's emotion in a manner that is consistent with, respectful of, and does not bypass the child's avoidance mechanisms against unpleasant emotions (Compare Yanof 1996, starting on page 108, the section entitled: "The analysis of defense in children").

Rationale for a regulation-focused approach

There is one major proposition that is assumed in the dynamic approach to mental health function and dysfunction: *All of a person's emotions, behaviors, verbal productions, activities, life choices, and other experiences and products have meaning.* This assumption is based on two observations that have been systematically verified: *Childhood events affect behavior, emotions, and personality later in life* and *a great deal of mental activity occurs outside of the individual's awareness.* A corollary to these two observations is that when a person is communicating, particularly in a therapy session, one can infer that there is a connection between two thoughts or two actions even though the connection may not be manifestly transparent.

Introduction: rationale for RFP-C 25

For example, a patient will be telling the clinician an episode about a problem he/she had while completing one of his/her projects and the mean, non-empathic behavior of his/her superior at work. After the story's natural ending, the patient, seemingly "out of the blue," tells a story about his childhood: When his/her father acted in a very mean way when the patient struck out in an important Little League game. The patient was not consciously aware that there was a common thread in the two stories and only later realized that he/she was so sensitive to his/her superior's behavior because of the continued power of the memory traces of his/her father's insensitivity. In other words, his/her past emotional experience with his/her father influenced his/her present emotional response to his/her superior.

A variety of mechanisms to *avoid painful emotions* are an important category of mental activities that often occur outside a person's awareness. For example, that same patient while talking about his/her father's behavior during the patient's Little League career suddenly said: "I don't want to talk about that anymore. I want to tell you about the Yankee game I attended last night." In this sequence, the patient may very well be communicating that he/she wants to avoid experiencing in the present the painful feelings that were reawakened as he/she remembered the events from his/her childhood, although he/she was not aware of this avoidance consciously.

This mechanism of *avoidance of painful feelings* is often observed in the treatment of children, and often consciously. For example, an eight-year-old boy was discussing how upset he was when his divorced parents had a big argument in front of him the previous weekend. While telling the clinician the story, the boy told the clinician: "Let's not talk about that anymore, let's go back to our chess game."

In contrast to the adult man, this boy was very conscious of his wish to avoid the painful emotions provoked by the fight between the parents. There were other situations, however, when this little boy would deny that the fights between the parents bothered him, or he would stress all of the good things the parents did. In those situations, one could see that the boy was not aware of the elements of avoidance of painful emotions involved in some of these discussions. In other words, in both adults and children, avoidance of painful emotions may be conscious or unconscious.

Can a dynamic approach be utilized with children with externalizing behaviors?

One can readily imagine utilizing a dynamic approach with children who manifest internalizing symptoms. One can easily imagine a little, four-year-old girl talking and playing with her clinician about her fears of dogs and her nightmares that a dog came and bit her and her parents were not there to protect her. In such a situation, one can envision the clinician trying to understand why the girl is afraid of dogs, the meaning of the fear, and how to help her address the fear. One can also imagine speaking with a depressed eight-year-old boy who responds to every problematic event as if he was the cause. One can talk about the genesis of this worry and its continued impact in his present life.

> ### The quandaries when working with children who demonstrate externalizing behaviors
>
> What do you do and say when a child wants to fight?
> When the child wants to mess up your toys?
> Wants to leave the session early?
> How does one approach a child with externalizing behaviors when one needs to fend off attacks from the child? Is there more than behavioral management in the treatment of children with externalizing behaviors?
>
> THERE IS MEANING TO THE EXTERNALIZING BEHAVIOR

It is more difficult to imagine trying to understand the *meaning* of the disruptive behaviors of children with externalizing behaviors. What do you do and say when a child wants to fight? When the child wants to mess up your toys? Wants to leave the session early? How does one approach a child with externalizing behaviors when one needs to fend off attacks from the child? Is there more than behavioral management in the treatment of children with disruptive symptoms?

The key element that can help the clinician approach disruptive children with a sense of equanimity is the conviction that *regardless of how disruptive, how seemingly un-empathic, how much the child denies self-responsibility, and only blames others, there is meaning in the child's behaviors, emotions, and communication.* In this frame of mind, the clinician approaches the child's externalizing behavior trying to understand its meaning while acknowledging that he/she may have to set limits and prevent harm to everyone in the room. An important aspect of trying to understand the meaning includes trying to understand how the aggression may be serving protective purposes for the child, following the football maxim of

> *"A good offense is the best defense."*

The clinician should always think to him/herself:

> *"The child came into my office wanting to fight with me. What is he afraid of? Why does he need to protect himself in that way? Why does he have to show that he is strong and not afraid?"*

Note

1 The statement includes the comment that "[i]n controlled trials and in clinical practice, psychotherapy results in benefits that markedly exceed those experienced by individuals who need mental health services but do not receive psychotherapy."

Bibliography

Achenbach, T.M. & Edelbrock, C.S., 1978. The classification of child psychopathology: a review and analysis of empirical efforts. *Psychological Bulletin*, 85(6), pp. 1275–1301.

Ahmann, P.A. et al., 1993. Placebo-controlled evaluation of Ritalin side effects. *Pediatrics*, 91, pp. 1101–6.

Ambrosini, P.J., Bennett, D.S., & Elia, J., 2013. Attention deficit hyperactivity disorder characteristics: II. Clinical correlates of irritable mood. *Journal of Affective Disorders*, 145(1), pp. 70–6.

American Psychiatric Association, 1968. *Diagnostic and statistical manual of mental disorders*, 2nd edition, Washington, DC: Author.

American Psychiatric Association, 1980. *Diagnostic and statistical manual of mental disorders*, 3rd edition, Washington, DC: Author.

American Psychiatric Association, 1987. *Diagnostic and statistical manual of mental disorders*, 3rd edition revised, Washington, DC: Author.

American Psychiatric Association, 1994. *Diagnostic and statistical manual of mental disorders*, 4th edition text revision, Washington, DC: Author.

American Psychiatric Association, 2000. *Diagnostic and statistical manual of mental disorders*, 4th edition, Washington, DC: Author.

American Psychiatric Association, 2013. *Diagnostic and statistical manual of mental disorders*, 5th edition, Washington, DC: Author.

American Psychological Association, 2012. *Resolution on the Recognition of Psychotherapy Effectiveness* [Press release].

Barkley, R.A., 2010. Deficient emotional self-regulation is a core component of ADHD. *Journal of ADHD and Related Disorders*, 1(2), pp. 5–37.

Beutel, M.E., Stark, R., Pan, H., Silbersweig, D., & Dietrich, S., 2010. Changes of brain activation pre-post short-term psychodynamic inpatient psychotherapy: an fMRI study of panic disorder patients. *Psychiatry Research*, 184(2), pp. 96–104.

Bezdjian, S. et al., 2011. The structure of DSM-IV ADHD, ODD, and CD criteria in adolescent boys: a hierarchical approach. *Psychiatry Research*, 188(3), pp. 411–21.

Blader, J.C. & Carlson, G.A., 2007. Increased rates of bipolar disorder diagnoses among U.S. child, adolescent, and adult inpatients, 1996–2004. *Biological psychiatry*, 62(2), pp. 107–14.

Boggs, S.R. et al., 2008. Child & family behavior therapy outcomes of parent-child interaction therapy: a comparison of treatment completers and study dropouts one to three years later. *Child and Family Behavior Therapy*, 26(4), pp. 1–22.

Bowlby, J., 1969. *Attachment and loss*, Harmondsworth, England: Penguin.

Brestan, E. & Eyberg, S., 1998. Effective psychosocial treatments of conduct-disordered children and adolescents: 29 years, 82 studies, and 5,272 kids. *Journal of Clinical Child Psychology*, 27(2), pp. 180–9.

Buchheim, A., Viviani, R., Kessler, H., Kächele, H., Cierpka, M., Roth, G., George, C., Kernberg, O.F., Bruns, G., & Taubner, S., 2012. Changes in prefrontal-limbic function in major depression after 15 months of long-term psychotherapy. *PLoS*, 7(3), pp. 1–8. doi: 10.1371/journal.pone.0033745.

Burke, J.D., Hipwell, A.E., & Loeber, R., 2010. Dimensions of oppositional defiant disorder as predictors of depression and conduct disorder in preadolescent girls. *Journal of the American Academy of Child and Adolescent Psychiatry*, 49(5), pp. 484–92.

Busch, F. N. et al., 2012. *Manual of panic focused psychodynamic psychotherapy-extended range*, New York, NY: Routledge/Taylor & Francis Group.
Campbell, S. B., 1994. Hard-to-manage preschool boys: externalizing behavior, social competence, and family context at two-year followup. *Journal of Abnormal Child Psychology*, 22(2), pp. 147–66.
Canino, G. et al., 2010. Does the prevalence of CD and ODD vary across cultures? *Social Psychiatry and Psychiatric Epidemiology*, 45(7), pp. 695–704.
Cantwell, D. P. & Baker, L., 1988. Issues in the classification of child and adolescent psychopathology. *Journal of the American Academy of Child and Adolescent Psychiatry*, 27(5), pp. 521–33.
Capage, L. C. et al., 2008. A comparison between African American and Caucasian children referred for treatment of disruptive behavior disorders. *Child & Family Behavior Therapy*, 23(1), pp. 1–14.
Cavanagh, M. et al., 2014. Oppositional defiant disorder is better conceptualized as a disorder of emotional regulation. *Journal of attention disorders*, pp. 1–9.
Cohen, D. J. 1991. Tourette's syndrome: a model disorder for integrating psychoanalysis and biological perspectives. *International Review of Psychoanalysis*, 18, pp. 195–208
Colibazzi, T., 2014. Journal watch review of research domain criteria (RDoC): toward a new classification framework for research on mental disorders. *Journal of the American Psychoanalytic Association,* 62, pp. 709–10.
Comer, J. S. et al., 2013. Psychosocial treatment efficacy for disruptive behavior problems in very young children: a meta-analytic examination. *Journal of the American Academy of Child and Adolescent Psychiatry*, 52(1), pp. 26–36.
Correll, C. U., 2011. Safety and tolerability of antipsychotic treatment in young patients with schizophrenia. *The Journal of Clinical Psychiatry*, 72(8), pp. e26. doi: 10.4088/JCP.9101tx5c.
Deborde, A.-S., Vanwalleghem Maury, S., & Aitel, S., 2014. [Emotion regulation in adolescents with conduct disorder and controls.]. *L'Encephale* [Epub ahead of print].
de Greck, M., Scheidt, L., Bölter, A. F., Frommer, J., Ulrich, C., Stockum, E., Enzi, B., Tempelmann, C., Hoffmann, T., & Northoff, G., 2011. Multimodal psychodynamic psychotherapy induces normalization of reward related activity in somatoform disorder. *World Journal of Biological Psychiatry*, 12(4), 296–308. doi: 10.3109/15622975.2010.539269.
Dougherty, L. R. et al., 2014. DSM-5 disruptive mood dysregulation disorder: correlates and predictors in young children. *Psychological Medicine*, pp. 1–12.
Drabick, D.A.G. & Gadow, K. D., 2012. Deconstructing oppositional defiant disorder: clinic-based evidence for an anger/irritability phenotype. *Journal of the American Academy of Child and Adolescent Psychiatry*, 51(4), pp. 384–93.
DSM-5 Work Group, 2010. *DSM-5 childhood and adolescent disorders work group: justification for temper dysregulation disorder with dysphoria*, Washington, DC: American Psychiatric Association.
Etkin, A. et al., 2010. Failure of anterior cingulate activation and connectivity with the amygdala during implicit regulation of emotional processing in generalized anxiety disorder. *The American Journal of Psychiatry*, 167(5), pp. 545–54.
Fernandez, M. A. & Eyberg, S. M., 2009. Predicting treatment and follow-up attrition in parent-child interaction therapy. *Journal of Abnormal Child Psychology*, 37(3), pp. 431–41.

Fischer, M. et al., 1984. Follow-up of a preschool epidemiological sample: cross-age continuities and predictions of later adjustment with internalizing and externalizing dimensions of behavior. *Child Development*, 55(1), pp. 137–50.
Fonagy, P. & Target, M., 1994a. The efficacy of psychoanalysis for children with disruptive disorders. *Journal of the American Academy of Child & Adolescent Psychiatry*, 33(1), pp. 45–55.
Fonagy, P. & Target, M., 1994b. Who is helped by child psychoanalysis? A sample study of disruptive children, from the Anna Freud Centre retrospective investigation. *Bulletin of the Anna Freud Center*, 17, pp. 291–315.
Fonagy, P. & Target, M., 1997. The problem of outcome in child psychoanalysis: contributions from the Anna Freud centre. *Psychoanalytic Inquiry*, 17(sup001), pp. 58–73.
Fonagy, P. & Target, M., 1998. Mentalization and the changing aims of child psychoanalysis. *Psychoanalytic Dialogues*, 8, pp. 87–114.
Freud, S. 1893. On the psychical mechanism of hysterical phenomena1. *The standard edition of the complete psychological works of Sigmund Freud, Volume III (1893–1899): early psycho-analytic publications.* London, England: The Hogarth Press and the Institute of Psychoanalysis, pp. 25–39.
Gadow, K. D. & Drabick, D.A.G., 2012. Anger and irritability symptoms among youth with ODD: cross-informant versus source-exclusive syndromes. *Journal of Abnormal Child Psychology*, 40(7), pp. 1073–85.
Gartstein, M.A., Putnam, S.P., & Rothbart, M.K., 2012. Etiology of preschool behavior problems: contributions of temperament attributes in early childhood. *Infant Mental Health Journal*, 33(2), pp. 197–211.
Gillberg, C. et al., 1997. Long-term stimulant treatment of children with attention-deficit hyperactivity disorder symptoms. A randomized, double-blind, placebo-controlled trial. *Archives of General Psychiatry*, 54(9), pp. 857–64.
Greenhill, L. et al., 2006. Efficacy and safety of immediate-release methylphenidate treatment for preschoolers with ADHD. *Journal of the American Academy of Child and Adolescent Psychiatry*, 45(11), pp. 1284–93.
Guevara, J.P. et al., 2003. National estimates of health services expenditures for children with behavioral disorders: an analysis of the medical expenditure. *Pediatrics*, 112, pp. 440–446.
Hampton, L.M. et al. (2015). Emergency department visits by children and adolescents for antipsychotic drug adverse events. *JAMA Psychiatry*. Published online January 14, 2015. doi:10.1001/jamapsychiatry.2014.2412
Hood, K.K. & Eyberg, S.S.M., 2003. Outcomes of parent-child interaction therapy: mothers' reports of maintenance three to six years after treatment. *Journal of Clinical Child and Adolescent Psychology*, 32(3), pp. 419–29.
Hooks, M.Y., Mayes, L.C., & Volkmar, F.R., 1988. Psychiatric disorders among preschool children. *Journal of the American Academy of Child and Adolescent Psychiatry*, 27(5), pp. 623–7.
Hubbard, J.A. et al., 2010. Reactive and proactive aggression in childhood and adolescence: precursors, outcomes, processes, experiences, and measurement. *Journal of Personality*, 78(1), pp. 95–118.
Insel, T.R., 2014. The NIMH research domain criteria (RDoC) project: precision medicine for psychiatry. *The American Journal of Psychiatry*, 171(4), pp. 395–7.

Katic, A. et al., 2012. Clinically relevant changes in emotional expression in children with ADHD treated with lisdexamfetamine dimesylate. *Journal of Attention Disorders*, 16(5), pp. 384–97.

Kazdin, A. E., 1990. Premature termination from treatment among children referred for antisocial behavior. *Journal of Child Psychology and Psychiatry, and Allied Disciplines*, 31(3), pp. 415–25.

Kazdin, A. E., 1993. Treatment of conduct disorder: progress and directions in psychotherapy research. *Development and Psychopathology*, 5, pp. 277–310.

Kazdin, A. E., 2005. *Parent management training: treatment for oppositional, aggressive, and antisocial behavior in children and adolescents*, New York, NY: Oxford University Press.

Kazdin, A. E. & Mazurick, J. L., 1994. Dropping out of child psychotherapy: distinguishing early and late dropouts over the course of treatment. *Journal of Consulting and Clinical Psychology*, 62(5), pp. 1069–74.

Kernberg, P. F. & Chazan, S. E., 1991. *Children with conduct disorders: a psychotherapy manual*, New York, NY: Basic Books.

Kernberg, P. F., Cohen, J., et al., 1986. *The global verbal interventions scale. A workshop on the differences and similarities between child psychoanalysis and child psychotherapy.* Conducted at the annual meeting of the American Psychoanalytic Association, New York, December 18, 1986.

Knapp, P. et al., 2012. Treatment of maladaptive aggression in youth: CERT guidelines I. Engagement, assessment, and management. *Pediatrics*, 129(6), pp. e1562–76.

Koole, S. L. & Rothermund, K., 2011. "I feel better but I don't know why": the psychology of implicit emotion regulation. *Cognition & Emotion*, 25(3), pp. 389–99.

Lahey, B. B. et al., 1990. Comparison of DSM-III and DSM-III-R diagnoses for prepubertal children: changes in prevalence and validity. *Journal of the American Academy of Child and Adolescent Psychiatry*, 29(4), pp. 620–6.

Lahey, B. B. et al., 1992. Oppositional defiant and conduct disorders: issues to be resolved for DSM-IV. *Journal of the American Academy of Child and Adolescent Psychiatry*, 31(3), pp. 539–46.

Lahey, B. B. & Loeber, R., 1994. A framework for a developmental model of oppositional defiant disorder and conduct disorder. In D. Routh, ed. *Disruptive behavior disorders in childhood*. New York, NY: Plenum, pp. 139–80.

Lavigne, J. V et al., 1998. Psychiatric disorders with onset in the preschool years: I. Stability of diagnoses. *Journal of the American Academy of Child and Adolescent Psychiatry*, 37(12), pp. 1246–54.

Lavigne, J. V et al., 2009. The prevalence of ADHD, ODD, depression, and anxiety in a community sample of 4-year-olds. *Journal of Clinical Child and Adolescent Psychology : The Official Journal for the Society of Clinical Child and Adolescent Psychology, American Psychological Association, Division 53*, 38(3), pp. 315–28.

Leibenluft, E., 2011. Severe mood dysregulation, irritability, and the diagnostic boundaries of bipolar disorder in youths. *The American Journal of Psychiatry*, 168(2), pp. 129–42.

Leibenluft, E. et al., 2003. Irritability in pediatric mania and other childhood psychopathology. *Annals of the New York Academy of Sciences*, 1008, pp. 201–18.

Leibenluft, E. et al., 2006. Chronic versus episodic irritability in youth: a community-based, longitudinal study of clinical and diagnostic associations. *Journal of Child and Adolescent Psychopharmacology*, 16(4), pp. 456–66.

Liebowitz, J. H., Kembar, J. C., Kernberg, P. F., Frankel, A. K., & Kruger, R. S., 1988. Judging mental health-sickness in children: development of a rating scale. *Journal of the American Academy of Child and Adolescent Psychiatry*, 27(2/March), pp. 193–9.

Lochman, J., Wells, K., & Lenhart, L., 2008. *Coping power child group program: facilitator guide*, New York, NY: Oxford.

Loeber, R. et al., 2000. Oppositional defiant and conduct disorder: a review of the past 10 years, part I. *Journal of the American Academy of Child and Adolescent Psychiatry*, 39(12), pp. 1468–84.

Loeber, R., Burke, J., & Pardini, D. A., 2009. Perspectives on oppositional defiant disorder, conduct disorder, and psychopathic features. *Journal of Child Psychology and Psychiatry, and Allied Disciplines*, 50(1–2), pp. 133–42.

Loeber, R., Lahey, B. B., & Thomas, C., 1991. Diagnostic conundrum of oppositional defiant disorder and conduct disorder. *Journal of Abnormal Psychology*, 100(3), pp. 379–90.

Loy J. H., Merry, S. N., Hetrick, S. E., & Stasiak, K. 2012. Atypical antipsychotics for disruptive behaviour disorders in children and youths. Cochrane Database of Systematic Reviews Issue 9. Art. No.: CD008559. doi: 10.1002/14651858.CD008559.pub2.

Maayan, L. & Correll, C. U., 2011. Weight gain and metabolic risks associated with antipsychotic medications in children and adolescents. *Journal of Child and Adolescent Psychopharmacology*, 21(6), pp. 517–35.

Maughan, B. et al., 2004. Conduct disorder and oppositional defiant disorder in a national sample: developmental epidemiology. *Journal of Child Psychology and Psychiatry, and Allied Disciplines*, 45(3), pp. 609–21.

Midgley, N. & Kennedy, E., 2011. Psychodynamic psychotherapy for children and adolescents: a critical review of the evidence base. *Journal of Child Psychotherapy* (September 2011), pp. 232–260.

Mikita, N. & Stringaris, A., 2013. Mood dysregulation. *European Child & Adolescent Psychiatry*, 22 Suppl 1, pp. S11–16.

Milrod, B. et al., 2007. A randomized controlled clinical trial of psychoanalytic psychotherapy for panic disorder. *The American Journal of Psychiatry*, 164(2), pp. 265–72.

Moffitt, T. E. et al., 2008. Research review: DSM-V conduct disorder: research needs for an evidence base. *Journal of Child Psychology and Psychiatry, and Allied Disciplines*, 49(1), pp. 3–33.

Moreno, C. et al., 2007. National trends in the outpatient diagnosis and treatment of bipolar disorder in youth. *Archives of General Psychiatry*, 64(9), pp. 1032–9.

Mullin, B. C. & Hinshaw, S. P., 2009. Emotion regulation and externalizing disorders in children and adolescents. In *Handbook of Emotion Regulation*. New York, NY: Guilford Press, pp. 523–41.

Olfson, M. et al., 2012. National trends in the office-based treatment of children, adolescents, and adults with antipsychotics. *Archives of General Psychiatry*, 71(1), pp. 81–90.

Pappadopulos, E. et al., 2011. Experts' recommendations for treating maladaptive aggression in youth. *Journal of Child and Adolescent Psychopharmacology*, 21(6), pp. 505–15.

Patterson, G. R., 1976. The aggressive child: victim and architect of a coercive system. In L. Hamerlynck, L. Handy, & E. Mash, eds. *Behavior modification and families: theory and research*. New York, NY: Brunner/Mazel., pp. 267–316

PDM Task Force, 2006. *Psychodynamic Diagnostic Manual*, Silver Spring, MD: Alliance of Psychoanalytic Organizations.

Pringsheim, T. & Gorman, D., 2012. Second-generation antipsychotics for the treatment of disruptive behaviour disorders in children: a systematic review. *Canadian Journal of Psychiatry/Revue Canadienne de Psychiatrie*, 57(12), pp. 722–7.

Rasic, D., 2010. Countertransference in child and adolescent psychiatry—a forgotten concept? *Journal of the Canadian Academy of Child and Adolescent Psychiatry/Journal de l'Académie Canadienne de Psychiatrie de l'Enfant et de l'Adolescent*, 19(4), pp. 249–54.

Reimherr, F.W. et al., 2005. Emotional dysregulation in adult ADHD and response to atomoxetine. *Biological Psychiatry*, 58(2), pp. 125–31.

Rice, T.R. & Hoffman, L., 2014. Defense mechanisms and implicit emotion regulation: a comparison of a psychodynamic construct with one from contemporary neuroscience. *Journal of the American Psychoanalytic Association*, 62(4), pp. 693–708.

Rowe, R. et al., 2010. Developmental pathways in oppositional defiant disorder and conduct disorder. *Journal of Abnormal Psychology*, 119(4), pp. 726–38.

Rowe, R., Maughan, B., Pickles, A., Costello, E.J., & Angold, A. 2002. The relationship between DSM-IV oppositional defiant disorder and conduct disorder: findings from the Great Smoky Mountains Study. *Journal of Child Psychology and Psychiatry, and Allied Disciplines*, 43(3), pp. 365–73.

Rutter, M., 1980. *Changing youth in a changing society*, Cambridge, MA: Harvard University Press.

Scott, S. & O'Connor, T.G., 2012. An experimental test of differential susceptibility to parenting among emotionally-dysregulated children in a randomized controlled trial for oppositional behavior. *Journal of Child Psychology and Psychiatry, and Allied Disciplines*, 53(11), pp. 1184–93.

Scotto Rosato, N. et al., 2012. Treatment of maladaptive aggression in youth: CERT guidelines II. Treatments and ongoing management. *Pediatrics*, 129(6), pp. e1577–86.

Shaw, P. et al., 2014. Emotion dysregulation in attention deficit hyperactivity disorder. *The American Journal of Psychiatry*, 171(3), pp. 276–93.

Short, E.J. et al., 2004. A prospective study of stimulant response in preschool children: insights from ROC analyses. *Journal of the American Academy of Child and Adolescent Psychiatry*, 43(3), pp. 251–9.

Speltz, M.L. et al., 1999. Preschool boys with oppositional defiant disorder: clinical presentation and diagnostic change. *Journal of the American Academy of Child and Adolescent Psychiatry*, 38(7), pp. 838–45.

Spitzer, R.L., Davies, M., & Barkley, R.A., 1990. The DSM-III-R field trial of disruptive behavior disorders. *Journal of the American Academy of Child and Adolescent Psychiatry*, 29(5), pp. 690–7.

Steiner, H. & Remsing, L., 2007. Practice parameter for the assessment and treatment of children and adolescents with oppositional defiant disorder. *Journal of the American Academy of Child and Adolescent Psychiatry*, 46(1), pp. 894–921.

Stringaris, A., 2011. Irritability in children and adolescents: a challenge for DSM-5. *European Child & Adolescent Psychiatry*, 20(2), pp. 61–6.

Stringaris, A. & Goodman, R., 2009a. Longitudinal outcome of youth oppositionality: irritable, headstrong, and hurtful behaviors have distinctive predictions. *Journal of the American Academy of Child and Adolescent Psychiatry*, 48(4), pp. 404–12.

Stringaris, A. & Goodman, R., 2009b. Three dimensions of oppositionality in youth. *Journal of Child Psychology and Psychiatry, and Allied Disciplines*, 50(3), pp. 216–23.

Thomas, A., Chess, S., & Birch, H.G., 1968. *Temperament and behavior disorders in children*, New York, NY: New York University Press.

Waschbusch, D.A. & King, S., 2006. Should sex-specific norms be used to assess attention-deficit/hyperactivity disorder or oppositional defiant disorder? *Journal of Consulting and Clinical Psychology*, 74(1), pp. 179–85.

Werba, B.E. et al., 2006. Predicting outcome in parent-child interaction therapy: success and attrition. *Behavior Modification*, 30(5), pp. 618–46.

Werry, J.S., Reeves, J.C., & Elkind, G.S., 1987. Attention deficit, conduct, oppositional, and anxiety disorders in children: I. A review of research on differentiating characteristics. *Journal of the American Academy of Child and Adolescent Psychiatry*, 26(2), pp. 133–43.

Wilens, T.E. et al., 2002. Psychiatric comorbidity and functioning in clinically referred preschool children and school-age youths with ADHD. *Journal of the American Academy of Child and Adolescent Psychiatry*, 41(3), pp. 262–8.

Woltering, S., Granic, I., Lamm, C., & Lewis, M.D., 2011. Neural changes associated with treatment outcome in children with externalizing problems. *Biological Psychiatry*, 70(9), 873–9.

Wozniak, J. et al., 1995. Mania-like symptoms suggestive of childhood-onset bipolar disorder in clinically referred children. *Journal of the American Academy of Child and Adolescent Psychiatry*, 34(7), pp. 867–76.

Yanof, J., 1996. Language, communication, and transference in child analysis. II. Is child analysis really analysis? *Journal of the American Psychoanalytic Association*, 44(1), pp. 100–16.

Zevalkink, J., Verheugt-Pleiter, A., & Fonagy, P., 2012. Mentalization-informed child psychoanalytic psychotherapy. In A. Bateman & P. Fonagy, eds. *Handbook of mentalizing in mental health practice*. Arlington, VA: American Psychiatric Publishing, pp. 129–158.

Zito, J.M. et al., 2013. Antipsychotic use by medicaid-insured youths: impact of eligibility and psychiatric diagnosis across a decade. *Psychiatric Services (Washington, DC)*, 64(3), pp. 223–9.

Chapter 2

Basic psychoanalytic and psychodynamic perspectives

Psychoanalytic perspectives

There are a variety of perspectives and constructs that are important in the psychoanalytic theory of the mind:

1. Developmental perspective.
2. Unconscious mental activity.
3. Influence of past on present.
4. Ubiquity of psychological conflict.
5. Defenses and defense mechanisms to cope with and attempt to master conflicted emotional states.
6. Transference and countertransference.

The *developmental perspective* needs to be mentioned first, since any theorizing or clinical application of techniques derived from any theory has to take into consideration the gradual development of the person from the antenatal and neonatal period through infancy, toddlerhood, childhood, adolescence, and adulthood. This developmental frame of reference includes considering the importance of other people in all of our lives, beginning from the first days of life. In other words, all development takes place within a relational context.

Attachment theory is one overarching rubric that emphasizes the significance of the nature of the attachments between baby and caretaker. Several psychoanalytic perspectives, or "schools," have defined themselves around attachment theory and the developmental perspective. In fact, infant research has validated many core concepts of this perspective (Stern 1985). Such studies continue to progress today (e.g., Seligman & Harrison 2012).

The ubiquity and importance of *unconscious mental activity*, of course, is the central discovery of psychoanalysis. Contemporary neuroscience has now empirically confirmed validity of the concept of unconscious mental activity. A 1987 article in the journal *Science* initiated a growth in interest in the empirical study of unconscious processes (Kihlstrom 1987). This study and the early studies that followed focused on cognitive procedures and processes that had nominal clinical relevance to psychoanalysis. Today, the empirically studied processes are highly relevant to clinical work. For example, Susan Andersen and colleagues have demonstrated the occurrence of the unconscious process resulting in the concept of transference in multiple experimental studies (Andersen & Przybylinski 2012). Elements of the dynamic unconscious have been delineated and expanded in a variety of studies, as described, for example in Berlin (2011) and Berlin and Koch (2009).

The influence of the past on the present is mediated via unconscious mental mechanisms, of which the person is not often aware. As a result of this continuity between the past and the present, as development unfolds, events, particularly interactions with primary caretakers, have a profound influence. The nature of relationships later in life, the vocational choices a person makes, the likes and dislikes, and various personality and symptom patterns are all influenced by unconscious factors, particularly early experiences. As noted above, the transference studies of Susan Andersen provide strong empirical support for the impact of past relations on the choice of relationships in the present.

Most central for the thesis of this volume is the ubiquity of conflict within our minds and the utilization of defenses and defense mechanisms as ways of coping with and attempting to master conflicted emotional states. This is the central idea of therapeutic work from a psychodynamic perspective and will be greatly expanded upon throughout this volume. Through a discussion of implicit emotion regulation (ER), we advance an empirical model addressing the connection between implicit ER and unconscious defense mechanisms (See Chapter 4 of this volume and Rice & Hoffman 2014).

Understanding and addressing defenses (how people cope with and attempt to master conflicted emotional states) is a central idea in therapeutic work utilizing a psychodynamic perspective.
Implicit emotion regulation mechanisms = Defense mechanisms.

Id, ego, superego

In order to present a sketch of the nature of defenses, defensiveness, defense mechanisms, and coping devices, as well as how defenses function (Chapter 3), we first present a schematic outline of development from the psychoanalytic perspective which stresses the presence and evolution of inner conflict.

Psychological conflict is a product of the constant interplay among various agencies of the mind, historically labeled as id, ego, and superego (Freud 1923; Freud 1926). These three constructs, developed by Freud and then extended over the last century by a myriad of theoreticians and clinicians, are abstractions that refer to three general functions of the mind common to all people.

The id

The id refers to the wishes and desires people have, many of which the person may not be consciously aware. Conceptualization of the id has changed dramatically since its introduction by Freud. Freud initially posited that the id was predominantly a sexual drive, which he termed *libido*. Aggression, central to the theories of Adler, was seen as secondary to libido within the id. Later, Freud posited that in addition to libido, there was also a "death drive," or Thanatos. Neither of these drives was empirically testable. The creation of a theory of psychology on the foundation of untestable and unobservable principles posed problems.

Over the last several decades, there have been a variety of debates among psychoanalysts concerning the primacy of drives versus the centrality of relationships in human development (Greenberg & Mitchell 1983; Hoffman 1999; Levenson 2010). To some extent this dichotomy (between the centrality of drives versus the centrality of relationships) is artificial because, from the earliest moments of life, all "drives" are always experienced in interaction with another person, that is, what has been called "drive derivatives" (Brenner 1982). To an extent, these debates within psychoanalytic theory mirror the debates in biology and psychology concerning the false split between nature and nurture: All behavior is a result of "innate" factors interacting with environmental factors (Goldhaber 2012).

From a psychoanalytic perspective, attachment between mother (or other maternal figure) and infant occurs within moments after birth. It begins with close contact between mother and baby. Within this context, the earliest desires that are observed in newborns are the desires to suck and to be held close to another body. As the child develops, his/her wishes evolve. The wish to not be left alone, the wish to be loved, the wish to marry mommy or daddy, and the wish to have an intact body are all wishes that little children express directly and indirectly at different times. The internalization of these wishes by the child continues to have an impact, often outside of consciousness, throughout life. They affect one's personality, behavior, and interactions with other people.

> **Id = Basic human desires.**

A model that stresses the primacy of interaction over drives has certain advantages (Cooper 2008). However, such a model that abandons a central, intrapsychic drive concept of unconscious thought results in a loss. By proposing *just* a two-person interactive perspective without consideration of internal motivators creates distance from the other fields of medicine and biology. While two-person modes of investigation are inarguably pervasive, the perspective we advance in this manual retains a focus on individual neurobiology, individual psychology, and the ongoing interaction between the brain/mind and the environment, particularly the important relationships in a child's life (Hoffman 2000). However, through our conversation with emotion regulation (Rice and Hoffman 2014) and the dyadic origins of emotion regulation in the parent-child dyad (Calkins & Hill 2009), we acknowledge the importance of both the intrapsychic (internal emotion regulation) and the interpersonal (external emotion regulation) in human life. This dual emphasis is in some way reminiscent of Brenner's conception of "drive derivative," where the innate is always interdependent with the people in one's life.

Affects or emotions

Auchincloss and Samberg (2012) define *affect* as a complex psychophysiologic state that consists of a subjective feeling, associated ideas and fantasies, observable biological phenomena, and a behavioral response or emotional expression as a result of the person's state of mind (page 8). Panksepp and Pincus (2004) state, "we should reserve the term *affect* for the subjective experiential components of emotions and the term *emotion* for the superordinate category that includes [a variety of] components" (page 198). Gross (2014) views *affect* as an umbrella term for emotions, stress responses, and moods (page 5). It is clear from this brief synopsis that there is no clear distinction between the two terms and it is more parsimonious to consider the terms *affect* and *emotion* as synonyms.

As do many contemporary theoreticians and neuroscientists, we believe in the centrality of affect as the primary motivator of behavior, or drive. Silvan Tomkins founded affect theory (Tomkins 1962) by inverting the drive–affect relationship. Tomkins argued that affects were the primary motivational system, or drive, of human experience. This position implicitly valued behavioral learning theory. For example, Tomkins showed that sexuality, rather than being the primary motivator of behavior, was easily overcome when associated with affects of shame or anxiety. Affects were demonstrated as sufficient motivators in the absence of drives. Greenson (1967), Basch (1976), Nathanson (1992, 1996), and Lichtenberg (1983) all incorporated the centrality of affect as proposed by Tomkins into their analytic models (Harrison 1986; Mccullough 1997). And, most recently, O. Kernberg (2012) has proposed that "affects are hardwired and organize the two superordinate drives, libido and aggression, which determine the overall motivational system involved in unconscious intrapsychic conflict" (Hoffman 2012). Kernberg's (2012) idea proposes that affects are the primary motivating system and that integration between psychoanalytic affect theory and neuroscience is possible.

Lotterman (2012), in his review of the analytic literature, found very few references to how and when to address affects in the clinical situation. He notes that, in contrast to ideas and fantasies, affect "is an especially good marker of the workable psychic surface. Affect is part of a very early signaling system that alerts the individual and others about the status of the self. It is a rapid response and a largely automatic reaction that is only partially controlled by the ego and its defenses. Affects by their very presence mark the fact that a certain mental element has become significant to the self; therefore, affect can be a particularly consistent and helpful barometer of what is currently on the patient's mind" (page 330).

These formulations help merge psychoanalytically informed treatments with contemporary affective neuroscience by focusing on affect, an observable construct with defined biomarkers (Rice and Hoffman 2014). Contemporary cognitive neuroscientists have described a variety of core emotional systems (Panksepp 2007). These include the two classic drives of psychoanalytic theory. Panksepp has operationalized and empirically validated those "drives" as the organized motivational systems of sex or LUST and aggression or RAGE. The construct of the id, in essence, refers to these basic subcortical expressions of primary emotions.

The ego

The ego is roughly equivalent to the cognitive sphere (Rizzolatti et al. 2014). It includes cognitive functions such as attention, memory, perception, and judgment. Ego functions also include what cognitive neuroscientists call executive functions, or prefrontal lobe functions, as these complex processes are dependent upon large-scale, intrinsic networks between hierarchical brain systems that include the evolutionarily-more-recent frontal lobe of the brain. Ego functions have been theorized to be synonymous with these brain systems (Carhart-Harris & Friston 2010). They allow for impulse control, behavior modulation, and reflection upon the consequences of our behavior. They help us to decide what to do and what not to do. With them we may anticipate and plan, assign relative values to our wants within a motivational system, and perform what we need to do to attain those wants effectively. They are affected by development (immaturity or maturity) and by emotional states, which may affect or cloud our judgment (e.g., Pessoa 2008).

A major, if not the prime, function of the ego as theorized by Freud is to mediate between the desires of the Id and the realities of the world. From the affect-oriented conception of the Id that we have described above, this theory may be restated as follows: The primary function of the ego is to mediate between internal affective states and world realities, particularly the vicissitudes of the interactions with the important people in the child's life. The Default Mode Network (DMN), or the brain's activity and connectivity during wakeful rest, which has been hypothesized to be identical with the ego, regulates the activity of limbic structures that receive input from subcortical/hypothalamic centers mediating drives and motivations while controlling and modulating information coming from the external world. It connects the brain regions associated with internal affect and perception of reality (Carhart-Harris and Friston, 2010). Emotion regulation is a recent and developing concept (Gross 1998, 2013) that signifies the emotion modulating functions of the brain and its underlying neural correlates.

Structurally, emotion regulation seems similar to Freud's construct of *defense mechanisms*. Freud theorized that defense mechanisms play an important role in the ongoing balance between a person's emotional desires (id) and the need to keep those desires within some reasonable control that would be socially appropriate (ego). There is an ongoing interactive balance between the person's emotional state and his/her self-regulation that, from the perspective of psychology, is manifested by a variety of defense mechanisms. Gradually, the child gains greater prefrontally mediated processing capacities that continue to develop upon maturation into adolescence and then into adulthood. In other words, the individual develops greater control of the impact of his/her emotions. In the words of Freud (1933): *"Where id was ego shall be"* (page 80).

We hypothesize that defense mechanisms are similar to emotion-regulative processes of brain neural networks (Rice and Hoffman, 2014). These processes mature through normative development (Stegge & Terwogt 2007; Cramer 2006). Highly related to the development of defenses is language.

The classic work of Anny Katan (1961) illustrates the importance of verbalization for the control of impulsive actions, and how, in the balance between ego and id, language plays a crucial mediating role. Katan describes how a child verbalizes his/her perceptions of the outer world before he/she can verbalize feelings. She stresses that verbalization of feelings by the child leads to greater control and mastery. Verbalization helps the child distinguish between what is fantasy and what is real. These functions promote a greater sense of integration in the child. Katan (1961) makes a crucial point:

> *Children whose acting upon their feelings predominates over verbalizing their feelings can in this way establish a pattern which predisposes them to become 'actors out' in later life.*
>
> (page 186)

In other words, in modern parlance, and directly related to the topic of this manual, we would say that children who have difficulties consciously experiencing their painful emotions and putting those emotions into words have a tendency to develop externalization behaviors. Emotion regulation and language acquisition are two related processes. Thus, we have a neural basis for a therapeutic approach that addresses defenses and affect.

Ego = cognitive control (language) of emotional states.

Superego and its development: aid towards socialization

The superego, or the expression of one's personal morality, is the third mental agency described by Freud. The superego develops gradually during the child's early years.

We have discussed how the id represents the person's innate drive for pleasure, which begins at the beginning of life. The child, however, cannot experience these pleasurable sensations endlessly. At some point, he/she is weaned; left by him/herself and not held continually; encouraged to begin toilet training, perhaps even compelled to do so; instructed overtly or covertly that genital stimulation is not permitted to occur in all situations; and instructed in the social rules of sharing and self-control and that there are limits to the child's emerging wish for autonomous function.

Child rearing always involves the parents promoting a balance between gratifying the child's wishes and frustrating them. Restrictions are a normal part of child rearing. If the child were to be allowed limitless gratification, his/her progressive development towards autonomy *within* the social environment would be greatly compromised. In all of our lives, when we share our space within a community, we always balance our autonomous desires with respect for the perspective of other people. Cognitive psychology has recognized this important function. Mentalization (Bateman & Fonagy 2011) is a theoretical construct describing a mental state whereby one understands that the other person has his/her own independent mind with wishes, desires, and aspirations, which may not be in concert with our own desires.

Therefore, very early in life, the child begins to learn that he/she needs to erect barriers to the immediate gratification of his/her desires. These barriers, which are called defenses or defense mechanisms, oppose immediate gratification of desires. Any action or thought, in fact, can be used to oppose the gratification of a desire. For example, a child may have a very strong desire to mess, whether this is to make a mess of feces in his/her pants or to mess up his/her food on the table. This child begins to learn that mommy or daddy would be very pleased if he/she were neat and clean. Thus, when a child messes, the child may consciously or unconsciously worry that mommy or daddy may not love him/her or may leave him/her if the child were messy. The child then develops traits of cleanliness and orderliness. Later on in life, as a result of a combination of factors both innate and experiential, such a person may persist with exaggerated unconscious worries that if he/she were messy, important people in life would leave. This person may become super polite, extremely orderly, and very clean without any conscious awareness that the function of these character traits is to prevent important people from leaving him/her or not loving him/her. From the perspective of defense mechanisms, as we will discuss in the next chapter, this person has erected powerful barriers against certain desires and does the opposite of gratifying those desires, that is, the person has developed strong *reaction formations.*

As can be seen from this example, what starts out as an external conflict (between a child's desires and the environment's prohibition of the gratification of the desire) becomes an internal conflict between the desire and an internal prohibition. The child wishes to gratify a desire, yet his/her parents oppose the gratification of this desire. In order to not lose the parents' love, or the parents themselves, the child curbs his/her desires. Gradually, the external prohibitions become part of the child's own psychic make-up. They become internalized. Not all internal conflict is a result of parental prohibition. Very often, the child can develop severe internal prohibitions that are more intense than actual external parental prohibitions.

Thus, in addition to the conceptualization of the two agencies of the mind, *id* and *ego*, or the impulse to gratify wishes and the defensive barriers against their direct gratification, one can conceive of a third mental agency, the *superego* – or that aspect of the mind that is defined by its moral content.

> **Superego = development of the sense of right and wrong (morality). Prohibitions by the parents become internal prohibitions.**

It is important to stress that the terms *id*, *ego*, and *superego* are theoretical constructs and not independent entities in themselves. They are not to be reified or anthropomorphized.

An important part of psychoanalytic theory includes the understanding of the inevitable evolution of the child's focus of desire. Between the ages of four to six years, the child, who usually has a good command of his/her language, of his/her body, and the body of others, becomes focused on his/her genitals. During this time, the child's passionate feelings may become very intense and are directed towards parents. This is the period traditionally called Oedipal. Usually these intense passions cannot be gratified genitally. We need not elaborate on the fact that we have all seen or read about the pathologic effects of situations where these passions have not been curbed and the young child has been sexually abused.

During this period, issues of right and wrong (morality) become very important. To a four year old, morality means: "Will mommy and daddy love me or punish me for the things I do, want to do, have not done yet, have done, or think I have done because I fantasized that I wanted to do?" We stress these various hypothetical situations in order to indicate the importance of the child's fantasy and not simply focus on what the child may or may not have actually done or the nature of objective external prohibitions.

In fact, the child's fantasies can be stimulated by the inevitable seductive aspects of parent–child interactions such as feeding, bathing, and for that matter any affectionate contact. For this reason, the child's imagined transgressions and anticipated parental prohibitions are, in general, more severe than would be warranted by actual parental reactions. The child worries that if he/she transgresses the almost-imagined parental prohibitions, then the parents might leave or won't love him/her anymore. (In analytic terms, the child feels threatened by the loss of the "object" or the "object's love.") During the Oedipal period, the child's most intense pleasure is focused on his/her genitals, which for that reason are considered precious. Therefore, the child not only worries that the parents may leave or that they may no longer love him/her: The child also becomes concerned that the parents may inflict damage to those very organs where he/she experiences pleasure as a retribution for forbidden desires. As a result of the intensity of the desire, the child develops unpleasant feelings and worries that he/she will be punished. These unpleasant feelings trigger defenses to curb intense desires. As a result of these complicated mental phenomena during the Oedipal period (intense desire and the accompanying intense unpleasure), superego formation takes place. This special psychological agency reflects attitudes of right and wrong. In addition, maturational cognitive (ego) changes during this time of life contribute to the formation of an independent psychic agency: the superego.

In this context of the complex interplay of mental forces, defense mechanisms or defenses play a very important role in development. The child, and later adolescent and adult, uses a variety of mechanisms to deal with conflicted emotions, particularly passionate feelings towards loved ones or angry and aggressive feelings towards rivals or those who frustrate the gratification of his/her desires.

Defenses mediate the interplay among the mental forces.

During middle childhood, or latency, the child learns to curb his/her passions and focuses on social and academic learning. In adolescence, in great part due to hormonal upsurges, there is a resurgence of desire. The adolescent begins to shift his/her attachment from the parents to people in the outside world. Adolescence is a phase of development where the young person has a great many emotions to master and often expresses intense feelings in nearly all situations. In early adulthood, as the person's personality patterns become established, each person develops his/her own individualized repertoire of defense mechanisms that intensify during times of stress in order to help the person cope.

Psychodynamic psychotherapy

Psychodynamic psychotherapy developed within the psychoanalytic tradition as a more general rubric to describe a psychotherapeutic treatment (less intensive than psychoanalysis) that takes into consideration the dynamic nature of the human mind's proclivity to balance a variety of forces. As described above, these forces include the wishes a person has, the dangers that may be provoked by the expression of those wishes, the coping mechanisms or defenses or the person's moral strictures with which the person tries to protect him/herself from the expression of some of these forbidden wishes. In any conflicted situation, the person develops compromises by balancing these various forces.

As can be seen from these thoughts, psychoanalysis or psychodynamic thinking denotes both a theory of the functioning of the mind as well as a method of treatment of mental dysfunction based on the two basic assumptions: (1) that a great deal of mental activity occurs outside a person's conscious awareness (which in fact has been corroborated by neuroscientists as noted above); and (2) that there is a continuity of thoughts, which operates both when an adult is "free associating" during an analytic or therapy session, when a child is playing spontaneously in free play (i.e., suspending conscious control over his/her trend of thought or play), or relating personal history, i.e., that there is a connection between what went on in the person's past and what goes on in the person's present. The person who is talking freely or the child who is playing freely may not be aware of the connection between one element and the next. Nor may the person be aware that there is a connection between what is happening in the present life with what went on earlier in life.

The impact of childhood experiences with parental figures on the adult's later relationships has been amply demonstrated outside the psychotherapeutic situation (Andersen & Przybylinski 2012). It is important to stress that a person may not have any conscious awareness of the connections between his/her past experiences and his/her present life feelings or behaviors.

> **Unconscious memories of a person's primary relationships with his/her caretakers impact his/her relationships with other people (including the therapist).**
> **This is the construct of transference.**

These two basic postulates enable the clinician to organize the conscious mental productions of a patient during an analysis or a dynamic therapy, whether with a child, adolescent, or adult. In a dynamic treatment, the clinician gradually helps the patient increase his/her conscious awareness of connections between disparate events in the present as well as connections between present life and the past.

Listening to children from the psychodynamic perspective

There is one key factor in a psychodynamic approach that aids in the understanding of how a person thinks, feels, and acts. This factor, an abstract construct, called the *psychodynamic factor*, indicates that there are a *variety of forces* based on the workings of the id (or emotions or affects), ego, and superego within a person's mind. Some work in conjunction with one another, while others work in an antagonistic fashion. The way a person contends with or balances these various forces consciously, as well as outside his/her awareness, contributes to the person's personality style, characteristics, and traits; choices of interpersonal relationships; vocational choices; and adaptive and maladaptive responses to everyday situations. These forces within a person's mind are derived from an amalgamation of his/her inborn genetic make-up, life experiences from infancy onward, interactions with caretakers and other people, and the specific, unique events in the person's life.

> **Psychodynamic factor = balancing of mental forces.**

Here is a very simplified example: A child may want to take a toy that does not belong to him/her. The parents say: "No, you cannot have it, because it belongs to your sister." There are two opposing forces which the child has to balance: Do I take the toy? Or, do I please my parents and not take it? Most children, even very young children, most of the time, come to eventually choose to please the parents, beginning their road toward a socialized existence, which requires a certain amount of curbing of the immediate gratification of one's desires. Such parental prohibitions are gradually taken on by the child as the child's own, and a set of prohibitions become part of a child's internal moral outlook. They come to believe, for example, that it is *not* right for a person to take something that belongs to someone else. The child feels like a "good boy" or a "good girl" when the parental rules are followed. This inner good feeling in essence is greater than the pleasure that he or she would have had if the sister's toy would have been taken against the parents' injunction. This balancing act becomes an internal one: Is it right for me to do this activity? Or, do I ignore prohibitions because my needs are too great?

> **Inner conflict:**
> **Do I take my sister's toy?**
> **Or, do I please my parents?**

In this simplified example, these two forces, or demands, evolve throughout the person's life and affect the nature of relationships between the person and other people. Sometimes, for either constitutional and/or experiential reasons (or actually the interaction of genetics and experience), the child's need to feel gratified or avoid feeling deprived are much more intense than the aim to please the parents. The child may imagine that when the parents say "no," they prefer the sister to him/her. Over time, such a child may develop unsocialized externalizing behaviors, such as taking possessions that belong to someone else. In other words, such a child can develop so that prohibitions are experienced as if the authority figures were unreasonably restricting his/her needs and wishes. *This constellation may be the genesis of a child who develops an externalizing behavior.*

> **Children who are prone to develop externalizing behaviors experience prohibitions by others as unreasonable.**

At other times, the child develops a moral sense so that the rule to follow the parents' prohibitions completely overrides his/her wishes to please him/herself independent of the parents' desires. Such a child may develop an extremely inhibited approach to life and becomes very afraid to take anything for him/herself; the child may develop the fantasy that taking for oneself is the equivalent of stealing from the other person. This is the opposite resolution than that of the child who may develop externalizing behaviors. In this simplified situation, the inhibited child may become an adult who deprives him/herself of earning sufficient income because he/she then would be stealing from someone else. In other words, such a child as he/she becomes an adult takes on the moral sense that prohibitions have to be followed to the ultimate degree. As an extreme example, gaining pleasure, such as earning a good living, is forbidden by his/her moral value. *This constellation may lead to anxiety or depression.*

> **Children prone to develop severe inhibitions may experience "normal" pleasure as prohibited.**

In a psychodynamic treatment, the clinician tries to disentangle how the various forces contribute to the development of symptoms (maladaptive reactions) and maladaptive personality traits. In a therapy session, for example, a child who exhibits externalizing behaviors may want to take the clinician's toys for him/herself and disregard clinician statements that the toys are for all of the children who come to the playroom. The goal in the treatment is to help the child understand *why* the child wants the toy so much. Does the child feel deprived? Does the child feel that the clinician prefers the other children because the clinician won't let him/her take the toys home? Is it easier for the child to provoke a fight with the clinician about the toy than to *reveal* his/her worry that the clinician does not like him/her? Acknowledging certain feelings would cause a great deal of shame. Helping the child *understand how* he/she copes with unpleasant emotions in a particular situation and *why* he/she has particular symptoms contributes to the child's relief of distress and leads to the development of more effective and adaptive coping responses in life.

> **In a psychodynamic treatment, the clinician helps the child develop more adaptive responses to conflict.**

In Chapter 1, we described the case of Stephanie, the seven-year-old girl who cheated in games in the session. The clinician's countertransference prevented her from trying to understand Stephanie's motivations for cheating. In essence the clinician tried to "coerce" the child to stop her "bad" behavior. This had a disastrous effect on the treatment.

> **How do you help the child understand his/her motives instead of attempting to coerce the child to "stop" his/her "bad" behavior?**

This manual of Regulation-Focused Psychotherapy for Children with Externalizing Behaviors (RFP-C) outlines a systematic psychotherapeutic method that can help clinicians follow an approach in which the clinician tries *to understand*

1 The *meaning* of a child's symptomatic externalizing behaviors.
2 How the externalizing behaviors are used to *defend against (cope with) unpleasant emotions.*

Helping the child gain an *understanding, for him or herself,* about the sources of the externalizing behaviors can lead to greater self-control by the child and the development of more adaptive responses and interactions with other people. As we discuss below, a key element in this psychotherapeutic technique involves the *clinician systematically addressing the child's defenses.* To our knowledge, there has only been one systematic study of the impact of clinicians addressing defenses (Winston et al. 1994), but no study of clinicians addressing defenses with children.

> **This manual is the first attempt to systematize how clinicians can address a child's defenses or implicit emotional regulatory mechanisms.**

Clinical example of an approach to a child's behavior and play understanding the maladaptive implicit emotional regulatory mechanisms (defenses)

A five-year-old boy, Jimmy, came for treatment because of severe temper tantrums for the two years following the birth of his sister. Although he had been an irritable baby and toddler, his behavior markedly worsened after the sister's birth, including attempts to hit her. In addition, he suffered from sleep problems because he felt there were monsters under his bed.

In one early session, he told the clinician to go away and that he was going to lock her in the closet with all of the toys and that the clinician would have to stay there by herself. The clinician reminded him that during the previous session he was angry at her because he did not want to stop the session. She said that she knew that leaving the session was hard for him. He tried to hit the clinician for saying that but continued to play, saying that the clinician died and went underground where snakes and wolves ate her.

Thinking process of a psychodynamic clinician:

1 Understanding why a child is angry at the clinician, including what painful feeling is being avoided.
2 Communicating that understanding to the child.
3 Clinician's comments are *experience-near*, what clinician and child observe at the moment.
4 Utilization of play as source of information about the child's inner life.

This simple example illustrates the nature of the thought process of a psychodynamic clinician and choice of intervention.

The clinician hypothesized that the child's desire to abandon her were expressed by his words: "Stay by yourself." This was connected to Jimmy's reactions to the prior session where the child was angry that he had to leave the clinician's office. Furthermore, the clinician also hypothesized that ultimately the child was repeating with the clinician the abandonment he felt from his mother when the sister was born. However, the clinician's thoughts about the mother and sister were not relevant at the moment since there was no evidence from the child that those thoughts were near consciousness. These thoughts could be considered to be *experience-distant thoughts.*

However, the child's reaction to the clinician at the end of the prior session and his actions in this session allowed the clinician to proffer an intervention that was *experience-near*. The clinician reminded the child of his reaction to the end of the prior session, adding a comment about what she surmised to be the child's *emotional state* at the end of the previous session: Leaving the clinician was hard for him.

With that comment, the clinician utilized the information the child provided (playing out that he wanted the clinician to stay by herself) without directly addressing the play. The aim at this point was to try to help the child *observe* the *trigger* for his feelings: *Anger at being abandoned* by the clinician. The child's defensiveness ("don't say that") and attempt to hit the clinician indicated that the child had to *ward off the painful feelings associated with being abandoned.*

In his play, the child continued to communicate his aggression towards the clinician in a metaphoric sense (the clinician dying and animals eating her) and softened his attempts to hit the clinician. Over time, the clinician could point out to the child that he was *doing to the clinician* (abandoning the clinician and fighting with her) what the *clinician did to him* (abandoning the child). This mechanism is called *turning passive into active*.

In this treatment, there were a variety of repetitive iterations of these themes, including direct expressions of his anger towards the clinician's other patients – "Why does she see them and not just him?" The safety of the relationship with the clinician allows the child to experience and express anxiety-provoking situations. Anxiety and other painful emotions are mastered through a process called *working through*, a repetitive process whereby emotionally disturbing triggers are repeatedly experienced with the clinician and their intensity gradually lessened (Brodsky 1967, page 490; see also, Kernberg et al., 2012). At appropriate moments, the clinician connected Jimmy's jealousy of her other patients with his jealousy of his sister's interaction with their mother; there was a gradual abatement of his symptoms and greater comfort with his sister.

Nature of psychodynamic interventions

Expressive interventions

Regardless of the label given to a dynamic treatment, we can conceptualize therapeutic encounters as falling within a broad spectrum. At one end are "expressive interventions," where the clinician facilitates the patient's elaboration of personal thoughts, memories, and feelings and fosters the patient's immersion in his/her emotional experience (regardless of whether one conceptualizes the treatment as focusing on intrapsychic issues and/or relational issues). Within such an in-depth experience, both patient and clinician are emotionally engaged, with the clinician, of course, modulating his/her emotional responses to the patient in order to maintain clinical boundaries. With these kinds of interventions, the clinician facilitates the patient's understanding of his/her motives, how the patient responds to and defends him/herself against unpleasant emotions, and how the relationship between the patient and clinician is experienced by the patient and by the clinician (transference/countertransference). Within certain theoretical orientations there is an attempt to understand the connection between the patient's transference feelings and their origins in important figures in the patient's life.

Therapeutic work with another five-year-old child illustrates the value of not automatically responding to a child's provocation but rather trying to understand the meaning of the child's behaviors. This child often did not want to leave the sessions and often messed up the office when he was told that the session was soon over. The clinician responded to the child's disruptive behavior in a particular way. The clinician *did not* reprimand the child, but instead would often say:

"I guess my telling you that we had to stop was hard to hear and maybe that is why you made a mess."

In the various iterations of this kind of interaction, the child at first refused to acknowledge the clinician's comment and continued messing, forcing the clinician to insist that the session was over. Subsequently, the child, without acknowledging the veracity of the comment, said: *"OK, I will stop."* Later on, the child could say, *"I don't like it when we have to stop, it makes me feel bad."* In other words, the clinician, from the outset, attempted to make connections between the child's misbehavior and emotions; that is, that the misbehavior masked the painful emotion that was difficult to put into words. Gradually, the child could verbally and directly express those emotions.

> **Making connections between a child's misbehavior and his/her emotions.**

Transference

Transference is a critical phenomenon in all psychodynamic treatments. The phenomenon of transference is one of discoveries of Sigmund Freud (Freud 1900, page 562) that has stood the test of time and has been demonstrated to exist in everyday interpersonal interactions (Andersen & Przybylinski 2012).

Transference is a universal psychological phenomenon in which a person's relation to another person has elements that are similar to and/or are based on his/her earlier attachments, especially to parents, siblings, and significant others. In a psychodynamic treatment, particularly the more intense the treatment, a relationship between patient and clinician is fostered in which intense feelings are accentuated. As in any other relationship, the patient sees the clinician not only objectively but imputes qualities to the clinician that are based on qualities of other important figures in his/her earlier life. In real relationships, the other person gratifies or rejects, demands gratification or provokes rejection, or both parties may mutually gratify or mutually reject. In a therapeutic relationship, one member of this dyad, the clinician, attempts to be relatively neutral by attempting to limit his/her automatic social responses by limiting his/her direct expressions of anger and/or love.

With the two five-year-old children described above, the clinician was able to retain her/his composure when the child was provocative and thus was able to connect the child's reactions to the clinician with reactions in the child's family life. Of course, since the clinician is human, there may be personal responses by the clinician to the child's attempts for limitless gratifications and the child's attempts to provoke the clinician. These emotional responses by the clinician are called countertransferences. Neither patient nor clinician is necessarily aware that some of the responses to one another reflect issues from their own pasts. The clinician's ability to understand him/herself is enormously helpful. A clinician's self-reflection or discussion with colleagues or own therapist can be helpful to sort out how issues from the clinician's present and past life affect the interactions with the patient. The clinician can then sort out for him/herself the degree to which the responses to the patient are a result of the patient's provocations and the degree to which they are a result of the reawakening of personal issues.

Children with externalizing behaviors can be very keen in learning which activities personally affect the clinician. In the session described in Chapter 1, the clinician responded to the child's cheating as a personal attack rather than as a problem to be understood. The clinician eventually understood that she, herself, had a strong sense of right and wrong and fairness. The clinician's countertransference feelings to the child's cheating was a result of her own personal angry responses to people who cheated and memories of particular events in her own past. This prevented her from approaching the child's behaviors as symptoms that needed to be addressed.

> **Transference and countertransference:**
>
> **When we relate to other people, all of us are influenced by factors from our own pasts.**
>
> **The more a clinician is aware of his/her own countertransference, the more effective he/she can be when working, particularly with a child who demonstrates externalizing behaviors and who learns very quickly the therapist's buttons to push.**

In the setting of a dynamic treatment, the clinician attempts to understand the meaning of the patient's verbal and nonverbal communications. The clinician communicates his/her understanding to the patient in order to broaden the patient's view of him/herself. During this process, rather than gratifying or rejecting the patient, the clinician examines the nature of the patient's conscious and unconscious desires, defenses, and moral demands as they may be reproduced in the relationship to the clinician/analyst. The clinician communicates this understanding, or interpretation, to the patient.

One child with oppositional symptoms spontaneously described a situation at home where his parents became furious with him because he threw a ball at a lamp when his father praised the sister for a picture she drew. *"I guess that made you feel terrible, when your dad praised your sister,"* the clinician said. The child agreed and the clinician added, *"Bad feelings are such a problem for you that it is easier to get into trouble with your mom and dad than to let yourself feel those bad feelings."* After further discussion, the clinician added, *"That reminds me, you were furious at me last time you were here, when you saw another child's picture lying on the floor."* Clinician and patient could then go on and compare the responses to the clinician and the similarity to the responses with the parents.

Supportive interventions

At the other end of the spectrum are *supportive interventions*, where, in contrast to expressive interventions, there is an attempt to keep the emotional engagement within certain bounds and to avoid greater emotional immersion. The clinician uses encouragement, reassurance, perhaps promotion of logical thoughts and reasoning, clarification and reframing of internal and external dangers, promotion of autonomy, and management (such as setting limits with explanations), education, and facilitation of understanding of cause and effect, thus helping with developing a more realistic appraisal of aspects of life.

All treatments, regardless of what they are labeled, use a variety of both interventions. At one end, psychoanalysis utilizes more expressive interventions. At the other end, supportive psychotherapy and other directive therapies utilize more supportive techniques. But all treatments have a mixture of both kinds of elements to varying degrees. We know this empirically from prospective studies of psychotherapeutic modalities (Wallerstein 1986). Rather than consider the value of and indications for "expressive" versus "supportive" treatments, it has been suggested that, in every therapy, one should evaluate the relative value of expressive and supportive interventions, particularly with regard to how and when to use them.

Often times, with children who exhibit externalizing behaviors, especially early in the treatment, a clinician will have to prevent a child from damaging materials in the play room. The clinician may have to gently accompany the child to the waiting room when the session is over. He/she may have to repeat the comment that in the sessions, the child can say whatever he/she wants, but cannot hurt him/herself, the clinician, or the materials in the playroom. When five-year-old Jimmy was angry at the clinician and tried to hit her, the clinician gently held his arms and stopped the attempted attack. In such a situation, the clinician communicated that she could not allow any damage to the patient, the clinician, or the property. At the same time, if the clinician is aware of a proximate cause to the aggression, he/she states that to the child while preventing damage. If the clinician is not aware of the proximate cause of the aggression, the clinician simply says that the child's wish to hit reflects some feelings that are hard to put into words.

In all treatments, the approach can be one that is open-ended or one that is time limited (as the treatment described in this manual). This may be explicitly stated or implicitly motivated by either patient or clinician. In all techniques, fostering expressive exploration by direct confrontation with unconscious mental activity (experience-distant comments) is contraindicated regardless of the treatment and particularly in the beginning of treatment because (1) there may be no evidence for the comment and (2) issues may emerge too quickly that could be emotionality difficult for the patient. Addressing the observable defenses that a patient demonstrates in the sessions with the clinician avoids those pitfalls.

The general process of psychodynamic psychotherapy with children is described by Kernberg, Ritvo, & Keable (2012):

> Most psychological change is slow. In psychodynamic psychotherapy this gradual change is facilitated through a process of repetition and elaboration called working through. The intensity of the one on one experience in the therapy gives momentum to the change process. The clinician responds to as many repetitions of the child's expressions of developmental difficulties, maladaptive relational patterns, internal conflicts, and the child's attempts at new solutions as necessary for the child to internalize the new solutions. These many repetitions allow for the elaboration of variations of the themes and for the child to actively master the past difficulties. As old patterns change the child may develop new psychological resources to begin to work on conflicts or difficulties that were deeper or pushed aside by the earlier difficulties. This potential for further issues to be uncovered means that one of the tasks of the middle phase [there are three phases to the treatment – an opening, middle, and ending – termination phase] of therapy is continual updating of the formulation of the case, continued assessment and adjustments in the clinician's and patient's thinking.
>
> (page 544)

In addition to verbal interactions between child and clinician, a child communicates via play and activities, jokes and puns, motoric actions, and a whole variety of nonverbal communications such as grimaces and a variety of facial and bodily expressions. Many children easily talk about dreams and fantasies and create imaginary stories.

There are several factors that the dynamic clinician must keep in mind when working with the child. These include the child's development, the internal conflicts the child is experiencing, the nature of the transference that the child develops towards the clinician (how does the relationship to the clinician mirror relationships in the child's real life – past and present), and most importantly, how the child copes with threatening thoughts and feelings in the sessions. In other words, in what situations does the child *resist* expressing feelings, elaborate thoughts, or continue play? As we shall soon see, trying to observe these coping devices or *defenses* is a very important part of the dynamic treatment of children with externalizing behaviors.

All dynamic treatments have expressive elements and supportive elements, which include limit setting.

All effective interventions have to be experience-near.

Internal conflict and the utilization of defenses

> **Internal mental conflict and utilization of defenses are ubiquitous in both health and disease.**

Internal conflict, conscious and unconscious, is inevitable. The fact that conflict is ubiquitous in the mind results in an ongoing need to develop compromises between how much gratification to allow and how much restriction to impose. This is an inevitable conundrum of development – to try to achieve a balance between gratification and control.

Freud's (1909) description of the inner battle of the five-year-old boy, Little Hans, who had developed a phobia, is a marvelous example of the complex nature of our internal conflicts as we struggle (often unconsciously) with our complex mixed feelings (ambivalence) towards the people we love. We can love and hate them simultaneously.

> But this father, whom he could not help hating as a rival, was the same father whom he had always loved and was bound to go on loving, who had been his model, had been his first playmate, and had looked after him from his earliest infancy: and this it was that gave rise to the first conflict. Nor could this conflict find an immediate solution. For Hans's nature had so developed that for the moment his love could not but keep the upper hand and suppress his hate – though it could not kill it, for his hate was perpetually kept alive by his love for his mother.
>
> (page 134)

Little Hans was in a quandary. He loved his father and loved his mother. He hated his father because he saw him as a rival for his mother's affection. He feared retaliation from the father for the hate he felt towards the father. As a result of this conflict, he developed a maladaptive solution, a phobia of horses. Eventually Freud (1926) understood that one of the important factors that led to Little Hans' resolution of his phobia was the use of one of the defense mechanisms, *repression*. By modifying his anger at his father, he could establish a balance between his love for his mother and his love for his father. Freud (1926) writes:

> The instinctual impulse which underwent repression in 'Little Hans' was a hostile one against his father.
>
> (page 102)

In a series of papers, Charles Brenner (1982, 1987, 1992, 1994, 2002) has explicated the idea that psychoanalysis is a theory of the mind that looks at mental functioning from the point of view of internal mental conflict. When the opposing mental forces, as described above, work in concert towards the achievement of a goal, they are not observed. When they are in conflict with one another, one can observe them. In the case of Little Hans, for example, during the time he was conscious of his aggression towards his father and feared retaliation, he developed his symptomatic behavior because the conflict was quite active. After the utilization of the defense mechanism of repression of his anger, the conflict was no longer active, and thus not observable.

It is also important to stress that mental conflict is ubiquitous both in health as well as in disease. All human activity when considered from this point of view can be seen to have elements of conflict. For example, there are many factors that contribute to life choices: Native endowment, intelligence, socioeconomic status, ethnic identifications, familial interactions, and the many accidental fortunes and misfortunes of life. However, one may be able to discern the role of inner mental conflict to a person's choice of vocation.

When someone who works in some aspect of the caring professions is in analysis, for example, one may discover that an important determinant in his/her choice of vocation was a severe illness in childhood. Or, in another clinical situation, one may discover that the patient's severe aversion of hospitals is derived from his/her severe childhood illness. In other words, two very similar traumas may lead to very different outcomes as a result of differing compromises among each individual's mental forces. In all of these cases, an individual person utilizes a variety of defense mechanisms to try to master difficult feelings. The person who suffered a severe illness and now takes care of the sick may be utilizing the defense mechanism of *turning passive into active* to master the passivity he/she felt as a child. The person who avoids hospitals may be utilizing the defense mechanisms of *avoidance* or *denial* because the hospital triggers too many painful memories that cannot be mastered in any other way.

Children with externalizing behaviors: utilization of defenses

As one can plainly see, children with externalizing behaviors have not developed sufficient controls and mastery over their impulses. Avoidance, denial and turning passive into active are the defense mechanisms typically used by these children. Understanding these defenses can help us gauge the difficulties these children have in achieving an adaptive balance between their desires for immediate gratification and mastery and control of these impulses, as required by the norms of the social group, whether it is with the family, or in school, or with other children and adults. Defenses and defense mechanisms will be explored in depth in Chapter 3 as well as throughout this manual. We will discuss the clinical development of the technique of *interpreting defenses against unpleasant emotions*, which we define as *Regulation-Focused Psychotherapy*, since defenses are, in essence, emotional regulation mechanisms. We will present the significant contemporary data that oppositional defiant disorder as well as other externalizing behaviors may be, in part, a result of difficulties of consciously dealing with disturbed affect, and will proceed to develop RFP-C as an evidence-based therapeutic model to address these deficits. We will explore and address the conjecture that deficient capacities for emotion regulation observed in these externalizing behaviors of childhood have recently defined neurobiological correlates. A focus upon children's ability to master painful affects and their utilization of higher-adaptive processes of implicit emotional regulation is the essence of RFP-C. In this chapter, the beginnings of a comprehensive theoretical groundwork has been laid.

Bibliography

Andersen, S.M. & Przybylinski, E., 2012. Experiments on transference in interpersonal relations: implications for treatment. *Psychotherapy*, 49(3), pp. 370–83.

Auchincloss, E. & Samberg, E., 2012. *Psychoanalytic Terms & Concepts*, New Haven, CT: Yale University Press.

Basch, M., 1976. Psychoanalysis and communication science. *The Annual of Psychoanalysis*, 4, pp. 385–421.

Bateman, A. & Fonagy, P., 2011. *Handbook of mentalizing in mental health practice*, Arlington, VA: American Psychiatric Publishing.

Berlin, H.A., 2011. The neural basis of the dynamic unconscious. *Neuropsychoanalysis*, 13(1), pp. 5–31.

Berlin, H.A. & Koch, C., 2009. Neuroscience meets psychoanalysis. *Scientific American Mind*, 20(2), pp. 16–19.

Brenner, C., 1982. The concept of the superego: a reformulation. *The Psychoanalytic Quarterly*, 51(4), pp. 501–25.

Brenner, C., 1987. A structural theory perspective. *Psychoanalytic Inquiry*, 7(2), pp. 167–171.

Brenner, C., 1992. The structural theory and clinical practice. *Journal of Clinical Psychoanalysis*, 1, pp. 369–80.

Brenner, C., 1994. The mind as conflict and compromise formation. *Journal of Clinical Psychoanalysis*, 3(4), pp. 473–88.

Brenner, C., 2002. Conflict, compromise formation, and structural theory. *The Psychoanalytic Quarterly*, 71(3), pp. 397–417.

Brodsky, B., 1967. Working through: its widening scope and some aspects of its metapsychology. *The Psychoanalytic Quarterly*, 36(4), pp. 485–96.

Calkins, S.D. & Hill, A., 2009. Caregiver influences on emerging emotional regulation: biological and environmental transactions in early development. In J.J. Gross, ed. *Handbook of emotion regulation*. New York, NY: Guilford Press, pp. 229–48.

Carhart-Harris, R.L. & Friston, K.J., 2010. The default-mode, ego-functions and free-energy: a neurobiological account of Freudian ideas. *Brain: A Journal of Neurology*, 133(Pt 4), pp. 1265–83.

Cooper, A.M., 2008. American psychoanalysis today: a plurality of orthodoxies. *The Journal of the American Academy of Psychoanalysis and Dynamic Psychiatry*, 36(2), pp. 235–53.

Cramer, P., 2006. *Protecting the self: defense mechanisms in action*, New York, NY: Guilford Press.

Freud, S., 1893. The psychotherapy of hysteria from studies on hysteria. In *The standard edition of the complete psychological works of Sigmund Freud, Volume II (1893–1895): studies on hysteria.* London, England: The Hogarth Press and the Institute of Psychoanalysis, pp. 253–305.

Freud, S., 1900. The interpretation of dreams. In *The standard edition of the complete psychological works of Sigmund Freud, Volume IV (1900): the interpretation of dreams (first part).* London, England: The Hogarth Press and the Institute of Psychoanalysis, pp. ix–627.

Freud, S., 1909. Analysis of a phobia in a five-year-old boy. In *The standard edition of the complete psychological works of Sigmund Freud, Volume X (1909): two case histories ("Little Hans" and the "Rat Man").* London, England: The Hogarth Press and the Institute of Psychoanalysis, pp. 1–150.

Freud, S., 1923. The ego and the id. In *The standard edition of the complete psychological works of Sigmund Freud, Volume XIX (1923–1925): the ego and the id and other works.* London, England: The Hogarth Press and the Institute of Psychoanalysis, pp. 1–66.

Freud, S., 1926. Inhibitions, symptoms and anxiety. In *The standard edition of the complete psychological works of Sigmund Freud, Volume XX (1925–1926): An autobiographical study, inhibitions, symptoms and anxiety, The question of lay analysis and other works.* London, England: The Hogarth Press and the Institute of Psychoanalysis, pp. 75–176.

Freud, S., 1933. New introductory lectures on psycho-analysis. In *The standard edition of the complete psychological works of Sigmund Freud, Volume XXII (1932–1936): new introductory lectures on psycho-analysis and other works.* London, England: The Hogarth Press and the Institute of Psychoanalysis, pp. 1–182.

Goldhaber, D., 2012. *The nature–nurture debates bridging the gap*, Cambridge, UK: Cambridge University Press.

Greenberg, S.A. & Mitchell, S.A., 1983. *Object relations in psychoanalytic theory*, Cambridge, MA: Harvard.

Greenson, R., 1967. *The technique and practice of psychoanalysis.* Vol.1. New York, NY: International Universities Press.

Gross, J.J., 1998. The emerging field of emotion regulation: an integrative review. *Review of General Psychology*, 2(3), pp. 271–99.

Gross, J.J., 2013. Emotion regulation: taking stock and moving forward. *Emotion (Washington, D.C.)*, 13(3), pp. 359–65.

Gross, J.J., 2014. Emotion regulation: conceptual and empirical foundations. In J.J. Gross, ed. *Handbook of emotion regulation, Second Edition.* New York, NY: Guilford Press, pp. 3–20.

Harrison, I., 1986. A note on the nature and the developmental origins of affect. In A.D. Richards & M.S. Willick, eds. *Psychoanalysis: the science of mental conflict (essays in honor of Charles Brenner).* Hillsdale, NJ: Analytic Press, Inc., pp. 191–208.

Hoffman, L., 1999. Passions in girls and women. *Journal of the American Psychoanalytic Association*, 47, pp. 1145–68

Hoffman, L., 2000. The exclusion of child psychoanalysis. *Journal of the American Psychoanalytic Association*, 48(4), pp. 1617–18.

Hoffman, L., 2012. Book review: the inseparable nature of love and aggression: clinical and theoretical perspectives. *Journal of the American Psychoanalytic Association*, 60(6), pp. 1334–9.

Katan, A., 1961. Some thoughts about the role of verbalization in early childhood. *The Psychoanalytic Study of the Child*, 16, pp. 184–8.

Kernberg, O.F., 2012. *The inseparable nature of love and aggression: clinical and theoretical perspectives*, Washington, DC: American Psychiatric Publishing.

Kernberg, P.F., Ritvo, R., & Keable, H., 2012. Practice parameter for psychodynamic psychotherapy with children. *Journal of the American Academy of Child and Adolescent Psychiatry*, 51(5), pp. 541–57.

Kihlstrom, J.F., 1987. The cognitive unconscious. *Science*, 237(4821), pp. 1–2.

Levenson, E.A., 2010. The schism between drive and relational analysis: a brief historical overview. *Contemporary Psychoanalysis*, 46(1), pp. 7–9.

Lichtenberg, J.D., 1983. *Psychoanalysis and infant research*, Hillsdale, NJ: Analytic Press, Inc.

Lotterman, A.C., 2012. Affect as a marker of the psychic surface. *The Psychoanalytic Quarterly*, 81(2), pp. 305–33.

Mccullough, L., 1997. *Changing character: short-term anxiety-regulating psychotherapy for restructuring defenses, affects, and attachment*, New York, NY: Basic Books.

Nathanson, D.L., 1992. *Shame and pride: affect, sex, and the birth of the self*, London, England: W.W. Norton and Co.

Nathanson, D.L., 1996. *Knowing feeling: affect, script, and psychotherapy*, London, England: W.W. Norton and Co.

Panksepp, J., 2007. Criteria for basic emotions: is DISGUST a primary "emotion"? *Cognition & Emotion*, 21(8), pp. 1819–28.

Panksepp, J. & Pincus, D., 2004. Commentary. *Neuropsychoanalysis*, 6, pp. 197–203.

Pessoa, L., 2008. On the relationship between emotion and cognition. *Nature Reviews. Neuroscience*, 9(2), pp. 148–58.

Rice, T.R. & Hoffman, L., 2014. Defense mechanisms and implicit emotion regulation: a comparison of a psychodynamic construct with one from contemporary neuroscience. *Journal of the American Psychoanalytic Association*, 62(4), pp. 693–708.

Rizzolatti, G., Semi, A.A., & Fabbri-Destro, M., 2014. Linking psychoanalysis with neuroscience: the concept of ego. *Neuropsychologia*, 55, pp. 143–8.

Seligman, S. & Harrison, A., 2012. Infancy research, infant mental health, and adult psychotherapy: mutual influences. *Infant Mental Health Journal*, 33(4), pp. 339–49.

Stegge, H. & Terwogt, M., 2007. Awareness and regulation of emotion in typical and atypical development. In J.J. Gross, ed. *Handbook of Emotion Regulation*. New York, NY: Guilford Press, pp. 269–86.

Stern, D., 1985. *The interpersonal world of the infant: a view from psychoanalysis and developmental psychology*, New York, NY: Basic Books.

Tomkins, S.S., 1962. *Affect imagery consciousness: volume I, the positive affects*, London, England: Tavistock.

Wallerstein, R., 1986. *Forty-two lives in treatment: a study of psychoanalysis and psychotherapy*, New York, NY: Guilford Press.

Winston, B. Samstag, L.W., Winston, A., & Muran, J.C., 1994. Patient defense/therapist interventions. *Psychotherapy: Theory, Research, Practice, Training*, 31(3), pp. 478–91.

Chapter 3

Defenses, defense mechanisms, and coping devices
An experience-near-observable construct

> **Defenses are automatic protective responses to:**
> 1 External stress.
> 2 Threats to the sense of self.
> 3 Internal anxiety and distress.

Addressing defenses in psychodynamic psychotherapy

As discussed in the last chapter, conflict among various mental agencies is ubiquitous in mental life. People utilize defenses and defense mechanisms, mainly unconsciously, to negotiate ongoing mental conflict and to cope with the unpleasant emotional states provoked by the conflict. Defenses are automatic protective responses to external stress, threats to the sense of self, or internal anxiety and distress. As George Vaillant (1977, page 77) notes, defenses are "[p]erhaps . . . Freud's most original contribution of man's understanding of man." Unlike other psychodynamic concepts, defenses are relatively easy to define operationally.

> **Defenses**
> "Freud's most original contribution of man's understanding of man."

A review of the literature reveals that though defenses may be defined with some ease, there is some overlap in its definition with the terms of alternate branches of psychology and psychiatry. Coping skills, for example, can be considered a more conscious process in contrast to defense mechanism, which are most often conceptualized as unconscious processes. Coping can be thought of as "a process of adaptation that permits the person to work to the attainment of his or her goal" (Hentschel et al. 2004, page 15), whereas "[w]e need defenses only when change in our lives happens faster than we can accommodate" (G. Vaillant 1993, page 108). In other words, defenses reduce the experience of distress; while coping describes a process with a desired outcome (which may or may not be successful). The emerging distinction between implicit and explicit processes of emotion regulation (Gross 2013) provides an organizing model for this distinction between conscious and unconscious processes as well as communication with the affective neurosciences.

All children and adults have a variety of coping skills and defense mechanisms; some result in adaptive states and some in maladaptive states. Some are conscious and some are unconscious. Some defense mechanisms are more adaptive while others are maladaptive. Similar defenses may be used in adaptive or maladaptive ways depending on the particular situation and the child's temperamental and other developmental issues. Utilizing a narrow range of defenses or employing them in a way that is inflexible may also be problematic.

In psychodynamic psychotherapy, clinicians utilize a variety of techniques, including discussing with the patient how he/she utilizes defense mechanisms in real life as well as in the treatment situation with the clinician. In fact, defense interpretations are utilized more frequently than transference interpretations in treatments, not only in psychodynamic psychotherapy, but also in CBT (Olson et al. 2011). Yet, although there have been descriptions about the utilization of defenses in nontreatment situations and clinical descriptions of the utilization of defense interpretations, there has been a paucity of systematic study of defense interpretations in contrast to the systematic study of transference interpretations (Olson et al. 2011). Studying defenses systematically, as Olson and colleagues suggest, can contribute a great deal to the enterprise of trying to understand how interventions are effective (or ineffective, for that matter).

This manual is an attempt to describe a procedure where defenses are systematically addressed in the treatment situation.

Sigmund Freud

From the beginning of his career, Sigmund Freud (1892) was aware of the centrality of defense in mental life. Yet, in his early formulations, defense and pathology were equivalent. At first, Freud maintained that in order to bring about therapeutic change, the analyst's job was to attempt to forcibly overcome the patient's defenses (or what has been called resistance to uncovering unconscious material) in order to allow for free awareness and expression of unconscious wishes. For example, Freud's (1893) early approach to addressing resistances seemed to be equivalent to a battle with a pathological force, where Freud described "the important part played by the figure of the physician in creating motives *to defeat* the psychical force of resistance" (page 301 [italics added]).

For our purposes, defenses and resistance in therapy are synonymous concepts because the term resistance is simply how a patient consciously or unconsciously prevents unpleasant associations to emerge in his/her discussions with the clinician because revealing them would be too threatening, too painful, too anxiety provoking, too shameful, or provoke other unpleasant emotion. It is important to underline that the patient (child or adult) should not be considered to be "uncooperative" when the patient has difficulty revealing painful emotions in therapy, even if the patient consciously avoids revealing important affectively loaded thoughts and memories.

In fact, all clinicians periodically ask a patient: "Can you tell me what's on your mind?" It would be much more valuable to say "I see that it's difficult to tell me what's on your mind." The second comment addresses the defense, while the first question tries to "overcome" or "overpower" the defense.

"Can you tell me what's on your mind?" versus "I see that it's difficult to tell me what's on your mind."

The second comment addresses the defense, while the first comment tries to "overcome" or "overpower" the defense.

Freud's (1923, 1926) central change in technique involved understanding the inevitable defensive responses that arise in treatment. Freud came to appreciate that these resistances to uncovering (that is, defensive reactions) were automatically expressed by the patient and were unconscious themselves. He came to see that these defenses had to be respected and addressed in analysis rather than forcibly overcome.

Defenses are to be respected and addressed in therapy and not simply overcome.

Anna Freud's ego and the mechanism of defense

Although Sigmund Freud was acutely aware by 1926 that to help a patient, one needed to address and discuss defenses with a patient and not attempt to overcome them forcibly, it was Anna Freud (1936) who began the first systematic study of defenses and defense mechanisms. In that volume, she discusses defense-mechanisms, such as repression (already discussed in depth by Sigmund Freud), regression, reaction-formation, isolation, undoing, projection, identification, sublimation, displacement, transformation into the opposite, and turning against one's self. In addition, there were three other defenses, which are most relevant to RFP-C: *Denial in fantasy, denial in word and act,* and *identification with the aggressor.*

Defense mechanisms relevant to children with externalizing behaviors:
- **Denial in fantasy.**
- **Denial in word and act.**
- **Identification with the aggressor.**

Revisiting ego and the mechanisms of defense

Over a period of a year in 1972–73, Anna Freud with Joseph Sandler and others at the Hampstead Clinic (later, the Anna Freud Center in honor of Anna Freud after her death in 1982; Sandler & Freud 1985) studied Anna Freud's original volume (1936). For the purposes of this manual, we highlight the group's discussion of three defense mechanisms that are relevant to understanding the nature of regulation-focused psychotherapy with children with externalizing behaviors. As mentioned above, these three defenses are the ones that A. Freud labels *denial in fantasy, denial in word and act,* and *identification with the aggressor*.

With *denial in fantasy*, the child creates a variety of fantasies to deny painful realities. Regardless of how the child expresses his/her worries and concerns, the trigger for disturbance feels objectively true. Anna Freud describes how Sigmund Freud's (1909) patient, Little Hans, who had a horse phobia, really worried that his father would retaliate against him, so he denied this "fact" by shifting his anxiety to a horse which he could then avoid by restricting his actions (page 123). He denied his aggression through the creation of a fantasy surrounding a horse. Restriction of their lives, like a child with a phobia, is a mechanism that is seen in children with what we are calling "internalizing behaviors." These children restrict their lives to try to cope with their anxieties and fears. For example, when children fear going to sleep because there are monsters in their rooms, they believe that the ghosts are *real* and that they need the protection of their parents. Like with Little Hans, such children *deny* their fears of their aggression connected to their parents, such as, for example, a reaction to the birth of a sibling.

Children with externalizing behaviors often have such symptoms as a result of *denial in fantasy*, but much more importantly and much more maladaptive are behaviors that result from the utilization of the defenses of *denial in word and act* and *identification with the aggressor* by children with externalizing behaviors.

These defensive maneuvers are observed in some of the children described in this manual. The child who was cheating was convinced that the clinician was the one who cheated. Children who are convinced that the clinician will throw them out of the office at the end of a session believe that their fantasy is an objective fact. Those who are convinced that the clinician prefers other patients to them also experience with certainty that their assessment is an objective fact. In all of these situations, the children respond to the clinician in a way to counteract their conviction of the "fact" of the clinician's *transgression against* them. The child who cheated *spoke and acted* in a convincing way, believing that the clinician was the one who cheated and therefore deserved to be punished by the patient, that is, by the patient abandoning the clinician. Children who repeatedly feel abandoned or displaced by the clinician *speak and act* in a way to retaliate against the clinician because, in fact, they are convinced that the clinician is harming them. These children deny the painful feelings generated in the transference through word and act.

Sometimes it may be that children have been mistreated in their real lives; these memories of the mistreatment are transferred to the figure of the clinician from whom they assume similar treatment. At other times, children with a variety of sensory and temperamental difficulties interpret the "normative" limitations of everyday life by parents and teachers as "real" maltreatment. They, then, expect the same maltreatment from the clinician.

Children with externalizing behaviors often believe that their fantasies of being maltreated are facts which need to be retaliated against.

Sandler and Anna Freud (Sandler & Freud 1985) discuss these issues (pages 342–43). They stress that defensive maneuvers occur when a reality is unpleasant for the child and the reality affects the child's self-esteem or causes him/her too much anxiety. On the one hand, the child may develop a more pleasant fantasy to cope with the unpleasant reality, or the child may pretend by way of action that the painful reality does not exist (page 345). Anna Freud notes that to pretend without action occurs developmentally later than to pretend with action.

Children with externalizing behaviors simply cannot utilize fantasies to cope with unbearable stress and must act to retaliate, for example, to the birth of a sibling or in the sessions with a clinician becoming convinced that the clinician prefers another patient and thus deserves to be attacked in retaliation. In addition, many children with externalizing behaviors utilize the defense of *identification with the aggressor*. The child who experienced the end of sessions as expulsions by the clinician played repetitively that he abandoned the clinician and that the clinician was alone without toys and the patient had all of the toys for himself. In other words, the patient took on the role of the aggressor, the one who abandons, because the conviction that he is abandoned is too painful too bear. By doing this, he converted the *passive experience of being abandoned into the active experience of being the one who does the abandoning*. It is more gratifying, with a more accepting sense of oneself, to be the active one inflicting harm than to be the passive one experiencing harm. A dramatic, clinical example of this mechanism is observed in abused children who become abusers themselves; children who are bullied by the adults in their lives in turn become bullies in school; or most commonly, children who feel betrayed and hurt by the birth of a sibling, can inflict hurt on their peers.

It is more gratifying, with a more accepting sense of oneself, to be the active one inflicting harm than to be the passive one experiencing harm.

Evaluation of defenses

In addition to Freud and Anna Freud, many theoreticians, clinicians, and researchers have stressed the importance of understanding and evaluating defenses and defense mechanisms and addressing them in psychotherapy. George Vaillant (Vaillant et al. 1986; Vaillant 1971) most prominently developed a hierarchy of maturity of defenses. His work has been furthered systematically by, among others, Bond, Perry, and colleagues (Bond 1986; Perry & Cooper 1989; Perry & Henry 2004) and eventually incorporated into the Diagnostic and Statistical Manual of Mental Disorders (DSM; American Psychiatric Association 1987).

DSM-IV-TR (American Psychiatric Association 2000, pages 807–8) provides the following definition:

> *Defense mechanisms* (or coping styles) are automatic psychological processes that protect the individual against anxiety and from the awareness of internal or external dangers or stressors. Individuals are often unaware of these processes as they operate. Defense mechanisms mediate the individual's reaction to emotional conflicts and to internal and external stressors. The individual defense mechanisms are divided conceptually and empirically into related groups that are referred to as *Defense Levels.*

High adaptive-level defenses include self-observation and sublimation. Mental inhibitions level includes reaction formation and undoing. Minor image-distorting level includes devaluation and omnipotence. Disavowal level includes denial and projection. Major image distorting levels include projective identification and splitting. Action level includes acting out and passive aggression. And level of defensive dysregulation includes psychotic distortion and delusional projection (American Psychiatric Association 2000, pages 807–9). Unfortunately, DSM-5 excludes this discussion of defense mechanisms.

Evaluation of defenses in children

There is much less work on the systematic evaluation of defenses in children, other than the work of Phebe Cramer (1991, 1997, 1998, 2007). She has studied defense mechanisms in children most extensively, collating a great deal of her work in 2006 (Cramer 2006). She distinguishes defense mechanisms, defensiveness, and coping. She identifies coping as a more conscious activity, defense mechanisms are more unconscious, and defensiveness as a more general term (page 8). Through factor analysis, Cramer identified three broad categories of defense mechanisms: Denial, projection, and identification. Denial is utilized by young children, projection by school-aged children, and identification becomes most prominent in adolescence. As development proceeds, the earlier defense mechanisms are given up and the next one/s becomes more prominent. In shorthand, Cramer considers denial a mechanism where the child utilizes avoidance of unpleasant perceptions; that is, not seeing something that is there, whereas with projection, the child sees something out there that is not there (page 69). There are some parallels between this hierarchy and with that of Anna Freud in her distinction between denial by fantasy and denial by word and act. Whereas both clinicians directly observed children in the formulation of their thoughts, one important difference and potential advantage of the system of Cramer is its correlation with what we currently know of brain development and maturation: Children begin to stop using the denial cluster defenses and begin to rely upon projective defenses in middle childhood just as pre-frontally-mediated brain networks of emotion regulation system begin to emerge (Lewis et al. 2006; Rothbart et al. 2011).

Cramer maintains that projection (seeing something that is not there) requires greater cognition; that is, projection requires putting ideas to the outside of one self. In contrast, identification requires even greater cognition in order to be able to take in a part of someone else to become part of oneself.

In terms of development, she very cogently states: "Once a person understands the connection between motive and the mental mechanism of defense, she gives up the defense because its adaptive purpose is no longer functional" (Cramer 2006, page 13). In other words, when there is greater understanding, the defense is no longer useful. Cramer and Blatt (1993) have noted that immature defenses change during therapy.

> **Phebe Cramer notes that denial is greater in children with conduct disorders.**

Most important for Regulation-Focused Psychotherapy, Cramer notes that denial is greater in children with conduct disorders (Cramer 2006, page 137). As we discuss in this manual, the primary focus of our understanding of children with externalizing behaviors involves the observation that they *deny unpleasant emotions.* The clinician has to recognize how the child does this and address this with the child from the beginning of the regulation-focused psychotherapy (RFP-C).

Others who have systematically looked at defenses in children include Laor and Wolmer (Wolmer et al. 2001; Laor et al. 2001) who developed the Comprehensive Assessment of Defense Style (CADS). They found three factors that were derived from responses by parents about their children. They found one mature defense factor, one immature defense factor expressed in relations with the environment (other-oriented), and one of defenses expressed in relations with the self (self-oriented). "The other-oriented factor included eight defenses that predominantly engage the other in an attempt to cope with stress (usually in an anger-provoking way): projection, acting out, devaluation, splitting, passive aggression, rationalization, regression, and displacement. Suppression, the mature capacity to temporarily put a stressful stimuli out of awareness, loaded negatively on this factor" Laor, et al. 2001, page 365). The self-oriented factor included the defense of denial. Again, parallels exist between this work and the work of Anna Freud and Phebe Cramer.

Daniel Benveniste (2005) has written about defenses in the drawings and play of children in therapy. He describes a variety of examples of defenses in children: (1) Play disruption (A. Freud 1936, page 38), (2) Play interruption (Erikson 1950, page 223), (3) Sublimation, (4) Displacement, (5) Turning passive into active, (6) Regression (Peller 1954), (7) Turning against the self – destroying like in depression, (8) Rationalization defense against regression, (9) Identification with the aggressor, and (10) Projection as in cops and robbers.

Tallandini and Caudek (2010) assessed defense mechanisms in children via dollhouse play; and our group (Nimroody et al. In Process) is attempting to systematize the use of defenses in children who were administered the MacArthur Story Stem Battery (MSSB). This project aims to develop a manual that will reliably rate defense mechanisms as evidenced in five- to seven-year-old children's doll play stories. We are analyzing videotaped play sessions attempting to achieve interrater reliability on our assessment of defense mechanisms in the play.

Defenses as observed by the clinician

A patient's defensive activity in a session can be observed directly by the clinician.

Since the defensive activities utilized by a patient in psychotherapy can be observed directly by the clinician, there are many opportune times to discuss those defensive activities that the clinician observes without needing to conjecture about the dynamics of the patient. Paul Gray (1973) states:

> Let us take a patient who refers to some clearly competitive situation and then expresses some passive form of response to it. It may be valid to point out to the patient that he characteristically deals this way with competition in his life. On the other hand, if he can be shown that the passive trend he adopted *while talking about the particular situation* represented a form of defense *at that moment*, he will be in a better position to work toward analytic changes of such character traits.
>
> (pages 477–8)

In other words, addressing the patient's activity in the session is a much more experience-near technique that promotes emotional resonance in the patient instead of the more experience-distant cognitive/intellectual discussion about the patient's patterns in his/her life.

> **An experience-near intervention is more much more emotionally effective than an experience-distant cognitive/intellectual discussion.**

J. Christopher Perry (Perry & Henry 2004, page 168) provides a useful table in which he delineates what he calls "Anomalies or signs that defensive activity may be occurring" (he discusses adults), and this is used to rate sessions utilizing both combination of written transcript and voice. This is the guide for the clinician to look for defenses:

- Showing an unexpected affect.
- A sudden change in tone of voice.
- Showing an affect that is not compatible with the ideas in the text.
- The absence of affect, when it is expected.
- Showing an affect but not being able to talk about it accurately or directly.
- Gross disturbance in the prosody of flow of speech, e.g., undue hesitation.
- Expressing an idea that is highly unlikely to be true.
- A clear contradiction between two or more ideas without resolution.
- Unexpected statements about the interviewer.
- Sudden, loud, or uncontrolled speech or behavior.
- An unexpected change in topic or the object of conversation.
- Talking that appears to avoid the immediate topic.
- Talking about a topic in an emotionally charged and excessive way.
- Taking offense, when there seems little reason to see any actual offense.
- Descriptions of the self and others that appear distorted, unrealistic, or excessively good or bad.
- The meaning is obscured.
- Reasons are given that appear to cover up or distort the truth.

What is interesting about these phenomenal observations is that they are very similar to the description of the phenomena discussed by Berta Bornstein (as we discuss below) and is a central tenet of Regulation-Focused Psychotherapy for Children with Externalizing Disorders.

Both Gray and Perry stress that it is important for the clinician to observe the changes, actions, verbalizations, etc. of the patient in the session and base interventions on what has been observed without needing to refer to conjectured, inferred dynamics, which although they may be absolutely correct, may not be usefully integrated by the patient.

Clinician addressing defenses

Unlike the wealth of material referring to the systematic evaluation of defenses, there has been a dearth of work systematically evaluating how defenses are addressed in treatment. As Olson et al. (2011) state: "How and when clinicians interpret defenses, however, has received little empirical examination" (page 142). To our knowledge, one study from two decades ago by Beverly Winston and colleagues (Winston et al. 1994) is the only published systematic evaluation of how clinicians address defenses in sessions.

Winston and colleagues studied patient defensive behavior and clinician addressing defense (TAD) in short-term dynamic psychotherapy and brief adaptive psychotherapy in 28 adult patients with personality disorders, coding three levels of defense (immature, intermediate, and mature). The authors note that the clinicians addressed defense more frequently (greater TAD) when the patients exhibited more immature and intermediate defensive behavior. Of note, however, the authors conclude that:

> Post-hoc analysis of the relationship between clinician addressing defense and outcome revealed that the more the clinician addressed defensive behavior the better the outcome on TC's (Target Complaint). In addition, there was a significant finding in quartile four for STDP on the Composite outcome score. While this finding is in good agreement with one of the major principles of short-term dynamic psychotherapy, namely, that the clinician needs to be active, and consistently to confront and interpret patient defensive behavior, it conflicts with that of Crits-Christoph, Cooper, & Luborsky (1988), who found that interpreting wishes and expectations from significant others predicts positive outcome, whereas interpreting defenses does not. However, in general, it does support the work of several researchers (Foreman & Marmar 1985) who found that confronting defensive behavior both in short-term group and individual treatment led to improvement on outcome measures, whereas patients who were confronted infrequently improved less on these measures. It is hypothesized that this type of approach will enable patients to recover hidden memories, fantasies, and dreams within a meaningful affective and cognitive framework which will be mutative.
>
> (pages 489–90)

Olson and colleagues (2011) conclude their review of the clinical literature on defense interpretation with the recommendation for the continued

> development of specific empirically supported guidelines for interpreting defenses. These guidelines would be particularly beneficial to novice clinicians, but also to seasoned clinicians who can run into difficult or novel situations in which directions on how to proceed are needed. Currently, this knowledge is limited to clinical wisdom, based on individual experience.

This report leads us to consider the role that interpretation of defenses should play in psychotherapy. Although transference interpretation has traditionally received more interest in the literature, in practice, defense interpretations are utilized more frequently by clinicians. Finally, the literature related to defense interpretations is broad and covers much of the breadth of psychotherapy in general. This may be indicative that defense interpretations have been undervalued in the theoretical literature thus far.

(page 162)

Bond (1986) reviewed the clinical and theoretical literature of 15 authors who have addressed defense interpretations (such as Fenichel, Greenson, Annie Reich, Sandler and Anna Freud, and Paul Gray). A number of themes clustered into several domains. The predominant domain was "Characteristics of the Patient and Defense Material," which encompassed most of the themes. One example of a theme in this domain was "[s]tart with interpreting material easily observable to the patient, then progressively move to more unconscious components, like motive and history" (page 147).

Two domains contained relatively few themes: "Characteristics of the Clinician," exemplified by the comment "[a]void making interpretations based on countertransference reactions" (Bond 1986, page 154) and "Characteristics of the Treatment," exemplified by the comment "[i]nterpretation is better at the beginning of the session" (page 155). The fourth broad domain, "General Characteristics Affecting Outcome of Defense Interpretations" contained more themes, such as "[p]oor timing of interpretation is ineffective" (page 156) and "[e]ffective interpretations result in a dynamic change in patients' behavior" (page 157).

Some of the themes uncovered by Bond (1986) relate to addressing affects and emotions, including Brenner's (1982) conceptualization that any activity can be used defensively to protect the individual from painful emotions. Two specific examples follow:

> The question, 'Why is the patient resisting?' can be reduced to: 'what painful affect is he trying to avoid.' The answer to this question is closer to consciousness usually than the answer to the question 'what instinctual impulses or traumatic memories make for the painful affect.
>
> (Greenson 1967, page 107)

> When affects are completely lacking the defensive function of this lack is relatively easy to demonstrate. One need then only guard against the mistake of analyzing contents which to the patient would be interesting conversation, while no work at all would be done at points decisive from the economic viewpoint.
>
> (Fenichel 1941, page 94)

Addressing defenses against affects in therapy have been described by Paul Kline (2004). Among a variety of defense mechanisms, he lists defenses against affects: Postponement of Affect (Freud 1918), Displacement of Affect (Freud 1909), and Identification with the Aggressor (Freud 1936).

Interestingly, in a recent communication, Lotterman (2012) noted that, in his review of the analytic literature, he found very few references regarding how and when to address affects in the clinical situation. Lotterman notes that, in contrast to ideas and fantasies, affect

> is an especially good marker of the workable psychic surface. Affect is part of a very early signaling system that alerts the individual and others about the status of the self. It is a rapid response and a largely automatic reaction that is only partially controlled by the ego and its defenses. . . . Affects by their very presence mark the fact that a certain mental element has become significant to the self; therefore, affect can be a particularly consistent and helpful barometer of what is currently on the patient's mind.
>
> (page 330)

Both Olson et al. (2011) and Lotterman (2012) address the analytic and psychotherapeutic work with adults, they do not discuss children. Perhaps that is why, although the work of Anna Freud is cited, both authors *omit reference to the work of Berta Bornstein* (1945) *and her role in the development of the technique of addressing defenses against painful affects*. A central tenet of RFP-C is that children with externalizing behaviors have an extraordinarily difficult time experiencing painful affects, resulting in the utilization of maladaptive coping and defensive activity.

Central challenges in the treatment of children with externalizing behaviors

1 They cannot cope with the stresses and strains in their lives.
2 Do not have inner resources to deal with the painful emotions of stressful events in a symbolic manner.
3 Aggression is clearly a coping mechanism, albeit a maladaptive one.
4 A regulation-focused approach promotes the child's symbolic capacity.
5 RFP-C promotes child's coping with stresses in a more adaptive way.

Berta Bornstein: interpreting defenses against unpleasant emotions[1]

In the literature on the nature of defense mechanisms (adaptive and maladaptive, immature and mature ones) there is both a lack of study of therapists addressing a patient's affects, defenses motivated by affects, and also an absence of the recognition of the work of Berta Bornstein, who was a critical force in the evolution of the technique of interpreting defenses against unpleasant emotions.

> Centrality of verbalization of emotions and automatic avoidance of painful emotions.

Historical development of the technique of interpretation of defenses against unwelcome affects

In the 1920s, Anna Freud (A. Freud 1926a) observed that children generally did not develop a transference neurosis. Melanie Klein (Klein 1927) maintained that this failure to demonstrate a transference neurosis was a result of the preparatory phase (where the analyst acted in an exaggeratedly benign and giving way). Anna Freud (Freud 1945) argued that "even if one part of the child's neurosis is transformed into a transference neurosis as it happens in adult analysis, another part of the child's neurotic behavior remains grouped around the parents who are the original objects of his pathogenic past" (page 130). In contrast, Klein (1927) espoused the idea that in analytic work with children, the analyst should not be concerned with the child's relationship to the outside world; and that reality issues and work with the parents were unnecessary and corrupting factors in a child's analysis because they interfered with the development of a transference neurosis.

Anna Freud (1926b) continued to stress that, as superego and auxiliary ego figures for the child, parents were crucial to the child's life and therefore were needed to maintain the treatment. She recommended that the analyst needed to form an alliance with the child, so the child could trust the analyst, and as well as with the parents, in order to help them support the analysis both emotionally and realistically.

One resolution to the conflicting approaches between the Kleinian view and the Anna Freudian view was accomplished with the development of defense analysis with children. This technique may be an unacknowledged forerunner of Paul Gray's (2005) conceptualizations about the lag in the utilization of defense analysis with adults (Hoffman 2000).

Anna Freud (1966) explained:

> So far as we were concerned, we explored above all the alterations in the classical technique as they seemed to us necessitated by the child's inability to

use free association, by the immaturity of his ego, the dependency of his superego, and by his resultant incapacity to deal unaided with pressures from the id. We were impressed by the strength of the child's defenses and resistances and by the difficulty of interpreting transference, the impurity of which we ascribed to the use of a nonanalytic introductory period. This latter difficulty was removed later by Berta Bornstein's ingenious use of defense interpretation for creating a treatment alliance with the child patient.

(page 9)

In her classic 1945 paper, Berta Bornstein (1945) clearly and succinctly introduced the technical approach to help children, particularly children who do not or cannot directly express their painful emotions. Bornstein described in great detail the technique of interpreting defenses against painful feelings in children. By clinical example, she demonstrated how this can be done without inflicting painful narcissistic injury on patients. By addressing the child's defenses against painful emotions instead of directly confronting the child's unwelcome thoughts and fantasies, the therapist can connect with the child in a much more sensitive and, thus, effective way. Bornstein's ideas form the basis of the contemporary approach to addressing a patient's defenses, including the utilization of Regulation-Focused Psychotherapy in children with Externalizing Behaviors.

> **Essence of a dynamic psychotherapy:**
> **Trying to understand how a patient protects him/herself from painful emotions.**

Interpretation of defenses against painful affects

The first step in any therapeutic endeavor, of course, is engaging the patient. Without such an engagement, treatment is not possible. In this manual, we are suggesting that there is a fundamental technical approach to a child's introduction to treatment (or, any patient's, for that matter): Understanding, addressing, and interpreting the patient's defenses against unwelcome affects.

> **A child's introduction to treatment by a clinician:**
> **Understanding, addressing, and interpreting the patient's defenses against unwelcome affects.**

With regard to terminology, Samuel Abrams has said, "I prefer protection instead of defense (it's a different implied metaphor) and I use explain rather than interpret – partly because it diminishes the authoritative position of the clinician and shifts the relationship toward one of co-operative partner" (personal communication, July 1, 2005). Although Abrams's language is certainly more descriptive, atheoretical, and closer to the language one uses with patients, the terms "defense" and "interpret" are ingrained in the lexicon not only of psychoanalysis and psychology, but also of the general intellectual community. Abrams is certainly correct that all interpretive communications to patients should not be made as if *ex cathedra*, but within the context of the relationship between analyst and patient.

As we note throughout this volume and in Rice and Hoffman (2014), we propose that the modern neurocognitive concept of implicit emotional regulation (ER) is equivalent to unconscious automatic defense mechanisms. Therefore we have chosen the term "regulation-focused" instead of "defense-focused" for our therapeutic intervention because the term "regulation" is more descriptive and theory neutral than the term "defense." And, in fact, an inability to regulate their affective responses to negative stimuli is a key feature in children with externalizing behaviors.

The psychoanalytic literature on the nature of interpretation – via verbal as well as nonverbal communication – is vast. Most clinically relevant is to consider an interpretation to be a communication from clinician to patient in which the clinician tries to explain something about the patient to the patient that the latter is not fully aware of (Brenner 1996, page 29). In that sense, the analyst's communication is a hypothesis or a conjecture about the meaning of some aspect of the patient's verbal or nonverbal activity (Bibring 1954, page 758; Spence 1984, page 594; Brenner 1996, page 29).

Historically, analysts have made a distinction between clarification and interpretation. Bibring (1954) states that in therapy, clarification (a term he cites as originating with Carl Rogers) addresses "those vague and obscure factors (frequently below the level of verbalization) which are relevant from the viewpoint of treatment; it refers to those techniques and therapeutic processes which assist the patient to reach a higher degree of self-awareness, clarity and differentiation of self-observation which makes adequate verbalization possible" (page 755).

> In contrast to clarification, interpretation by its very nature transgresses the clinical data, the phenomenological-descriptive level. On the basis of their derivatives, the analyst tries to "guess" and to communicate (to explain) to the patient in form of (hypothetical) constructions and reconstructions those unconscious processes which are assumed to determine his manifest behavior. In general, interpretation consists not in a single act but in a prolonged process. A period of "preparation" (e.g., in form of clarification) precedes it.
> (pages 757–58)

In other words, from Bibring's classical analytic perspective, clarifications refer to *experience-near interventions*, whereas interpretation refers to both an evolving process as well as to a more *experience-distant*. From the perspective of this manual, the phrase "*interpretation of the defenses against painful affects*" refers to an *experience-near intervention*, which is an amalgamation of the concepts clarification and interpretation. When addressing a child's defenses against awareness of unpleasant affects, the clinician must not stray very far from the surface and **should not** "transgress the clinical data" (Bibring's idea of an interpretation), but rather stay as experience-near as possible.

> **The phrase "*interpretation of the defenses against painful affects*" refers to an *experience-near intervention*, which is an amalgamation of the concepts clarification and interpretation.**

This preferential focus on the process of defense against disturbing affects includes the caution not to focus prematurely on a patient's unconscious libidinal or aggressive wishes or, in fact, defenses about which the patient has no awareness at all. The clinician should try to avoid "guessing" what's on the patient's mind, although inevitably a certain amount of guessing always takes place. The ideas in this manual are consistent with Sugarman's (1994, 2003) application with children of Paul Gray's technique. In Sugarman's (1994) words, the child is helped to expand "the control of the conscious ego over other structures of the psyche" (page 329).

> **The clinician should avoid guessing what is on the child's mind.**

With this approach, from the very beginning of the therapeutic work, the clinician first tries to understand, then judiciously explore, and eventually describe the child's current mental state in terms of the defenses against a conscious awareness of the emotional pain that the child seems to be experiencing. As the clinician understands how the child is hiding the emotional pain from him/herself (consciously or unconsciously keeping bad feelings out of awareness, avoiding direct verbalization, or disavowing the painful feeling states), the clinician needs to discern ways of addressing such defenses. When the clinician understands how the child is protecting him/herself from painful feelings, the clinician can try to communicate this understanding verbally or nonverbally to the child.

The child's defensive maneuvers are explored and eventually interpreted to the child in a careful, respectful, and developmentally appropriate way. Exploration of the defenses that the child utilizes to mask the emotional pain, ideally, leads to a situation where the child feels less threatened by the painful feeling states. This allows the child to share the feelings with the other person in a more direct or more elaborate, though disguised, way. The child then feels in greater control of him/herself, leading to greater mastery of affects and more adaptive interactions with the environment. In some children, over time, there may be greater verbal elaboration of his/her feelings and fantasies and exploration of the origins of the painful feelings. However, for many children, the clinician's interpretation of the child's defensive avoidance of painful affects allows the child ONLY to discuss the painful feelings more openly. In other words, there is evidence of greater mastery of feelings and diminishment of maladaptive defenses without direct verbal exploration of the origins of the overwhelming states.

Defenses and emotional regulation

There is an ever-expanding literature on the problems with emotional regulation in children with externalizing behaviors (Rice & Hoffman 2014). In fact, sad or hurtful feelings are difficult for these children to tolerate/regulate because they require higher order cognition, that is, the utilization of more mature defense mechanisms. The lack of these higher order functions results in a decreased capacity to self-regulate, resulting in less socially appropriate behavior.

> **Lack of higher order functions results in a decreased capacity to self-regulate, resulting in less socially appropriate behavior.**

Avoidance or denial of sad feelings is a less mature defense in contrast to defenses that allow a greater tolerance of the sad feelings, such as repression, humor, sublimation, and acceptance of reality. If these defenses are not operative, aggression is uncontrolled since children with externalizing behaviors cannot accept or suppress painful feelings.

Children with externalizing behaviors are overresponsive to negative affects. For example, the presence of a sibling promotes intense sadness at the displacement that cannot be mastered and, thus, reactively leads to impulsive aggression. In that sense, the aggression is a "defensive" response to avoid the unpleasant emotion and not just an attack against the imagined enemy. By addressing the aggressive action as a defensive maneuver on the child's part, the clinician avoids a direct labeling of the underlying sad affect, which would increase the defensiveness and increase the defensive aggression. By addressing the aggression as a defensive response to an unpleasant event ("You became very angry with me when I ended the session"), the clinician prepares the child for the next step where the unpleasant event is specified ("You became angry because you don't like it when you have to leave and another child gets to come in here"). At some later session, the clinician would add: "You felt sad when we ended last time." This slow iterative process is consistent with the concept of "cognitive reappraisal."

For example, Lyoo et al (2011) write:

> Emotion-regulating cognitive strategies, such as reappraisal of negative events and suppression of unpleasant memories, are associated with increased DLPFC and decreased limbic activities.
>
> (page 709)

It may very well be that addressing and interpreting defenses against painful emotions, that is, pointing out and working through the avoidance of the negative event, leads to a reappraisal of this strategy and to the utilization of higher defense mechanisms.

Note

1 Some of the ideas in this section are based on a talk by Leon Hoffman and Ruth Karush at the Classic Paper Series: On "Clinical Notes on Child Analysis" by Berta Bornstein (1945) at the New York Psychoanalytic Society and Institute, November 20, 2010, and included in Hoffman, L., 2015. Berta Bornstein's Frankie: the contemporary relevance of a classic to the treatment of children with disruptive symptoms. *The Psychoanalytic Study of the Child* 68, 152–76.

Bibliography

American Psychiatric Association, 1987. *Diagnostic and statistical manual of mental disorders,* 3rd edition revised, Washington, DC: Author.

American Psychiatric Association, 2000. *Diagnostic and statistical manual of mental disorders* 4th edition text revision, Washington, DC: Author.

Benveniste, D., 2005. Recognizing defenses in the drawings and play of children in therapy. *Psychoanalytic Psychology*, 22(3), pp. 395–410.

Bibring, E., 1954. Psychoanalysis and the dynamic psychotherapies. *Journal of the American Psychoanalytic Association*, 2, pp. 745–70.

Bond, M.P., 1986. Defense style questionnaire. In G.E. Vaillant, ed. *Empirical studies of ego mechanisms of defense*, Washington, DC: American Psychiatric Press.

Bornstein, B., 1945. Clinical notes on child analysis. *Psychoanalytic Study of the Child*, 1, pp. 151–66.

Brenner, C., 1982. The concept of the superego: a reformulation. *The Psychoanalytic Quarterly*, 51(4), pp. 501–25.

Brenner, C., 1996. The nature of knowledge and the limits of authority in psychoanalysis. *The Psychoanalytic Quarterly*, 65(1), pp. 21–31.

Cramer, P., 1991. *The development of defense mechanisms: theory, research and assessment*, New York, NY: Springer-Verlag.

Cramer, P., 1997. Evidence for change in children's use of defense mechanisms. *Journal of Personality*, 65(2), pp. 233–47.

Cramer, P., 1998. Freshman to senior year: a follow-up study of identity, narcissism, and defense mechanisms. *Journal of Research in Personality*, 32(2), pp. 156–72.

Cramer, P., 2006. *Protecting the self: defense mechanisms in action*, New York, NY: Guilford Press.

Cramer, P., 2007. Longitudinal study of defense mechanisms: late childhood to late adolescence. *Journal of Personality*, 75(1), pp. 1–24.

Cramer, P. & Blatt, S., 1993. Change in defense mechanisms following intensive treatment, as related to personality organization and gender. In U. Hentschel et al., eds. *The concept of defense mechanisms in contemporary psychology*. New York, NY: Springer-Verlag.

Crits-Christoph, P., Cooper, A., & Luborsky, L., 1988. The accuracy of therapists' interpretations and the outcome of dynamic psychotherapy. *Journal of Consulting and Clinical Psychology*, 56(4), pp. 490–5.

Erikson, E., 1950. *Childhood and Society*, New York, NY: Norton.

Fenichel, O., 1941. *Problems of psychoanalytic technique*, New York, NY: Psychoanalytic Quarterly Press.

Foreman, S.A. & Marmar, C.R., 1985. Therapist actions that address initially poor therapeutic alliances in psychotherapy. *The American Journal of Psychiatry*, 142(8), pp. 922–6.

Freud, A., 1926a. An hysterical symptom in a child of two years and three months old. *International Journal of Psychoanalysis*, pp. 227–9.

Freud, A., 1926b. Introduction to the technique of the analysis of children. In *Writings Volume 1*. New York, NY: International Universities Press, pp. 3–69.

Freud, A., 1936. *The ego and the mechanisms of defense*, New York, NY: International Universities Press.

Freud, A., 1945. Indications for child analysis. *The Psychoanalytic Study of the Child*, 1, pp. 127–49.

Freud, A., 1966. A short history of child analysis. *The Psychoanalytic Study of the Child*, 21, pp. 7–14.

Freud, S., 1892. Draft K. The neuroses of defense (A Christmas fairy tale), January 1, 1896. The complete letters of Sigmund Freud of Wilhelm Fliess, 1887–1904. In *The standard edition of the complete psychological works of Sigmund Freud, volume I (1886–1899): pre-psycho-analytic publications and unpublished drafts*. London, England: The Hogarth Press and the Institute of Psychoanalysis, pp. 162–9.

Freud, S., 1893. The psychotherapy of hysteria from studies on hysteria. In *The standard edition of the complete psychological works of Sigmund Freud, volume II (1893–1895): studies on hysteria*. London, England: The Hogarth Press and the Institute of Psychoanalysis, 253–305.

Freud, S., 1909. Analysis of a phobia in a five-year-old boy. In *The standard edition of the complete psychological works of Sigmund Freud, volume X (1909): Two case histories ("Little Hans" and the "Rat Man")*. London, England: The Hogarth Press and the Institute of Psychoanalysis, pp. 1–150.

Freud, S., 1918. From the history of an infantile neurosis. In *The standard edition of the complete psychological works of Sigmund Freud, volume XVII (1917–1919): an infantile neurosis and other works, 1–287*. London, England: The Hogarth Press and the Institute of Psychoanalysis, pp. 1–124.

Freud, S., 1923. The ego and the id. In *The standard edition of the complete psychological works of Sigmund Freud, volume XIX (1923–1925): the ego and the id and other works*. London, England: The Hogarth Press and the Institute of Psychoanalysis, pp. 1–66.

Freud, S., 1926. Inhibitions, symptoms and anxiety. In *The standard edition of the complete psychological works of Sigmund Freud, volume XX (1925–1926): an autobiographical study, inhibitions, symptoms and anxiety, the question of lay analysis and other works*. London, England: The Hogarth Press and the Institute of Psychoanalysis, pp. 75–176.

Gray, P., 1973. Psychoanalytic technique and the ego's capacity for viewing intrapsychic activity. *Journal of the American Psychoanalytic Association*, 21(3), pp. 474–94.

Gray, P., 2005. *The ego and the analysis of defense* 2nd ed., Northvale, NJ: Jason Aronson.

Greenson, R., 1967. *The techniques and practice of psychoanalysis*, New York, NY: International Universities Press.

Gross, J.J., 2013. Emotion regulation: taking stock and moving forward. *Emotion (Washington, D.C.)*, 13(3), pp. 359–65.

Hentschel, U. et al., 2004. Defense mechanisms: Current approaches to research and measurement. In U. Hentschel et al., eds. *Defense mechanisms: theoretical, research, and clinical perspectives*. Amsterdam: Elsevier, pp. 3–41.

Hoffman, L., 2000. The exclusion of child psychoanalysis. *Journal of the American Psychoanalytic Association*, 48(4), pp. 1617–18.

Klein, M., 1927. Symposium on child-analysis. *International Journal of Psychoanalysis*, 8, pp. 339–70.

Kline, P., 2004. A critical perspective on defense mechanisms. In *Defense mechanisms: theoretical, research, and clinical perspectives*. Amsterdam: Elsevier.

Laor, N., Wolmer, L., & Cicchetti, D. V, 2001. The comprehensive assessment of defense style: measuring defense mechanisms in children and adolescents. *The Journal of Nervous and Mental Disease*, 189(6), pp. 360–8.

Lewis, M.D., Granic, I., & Lamm, C., 2006. Neurophysiological correlates of emotion regulation in children and adolescents. *Journal of cognitive neuroscience*, 18(3), pp. 430–43.

Lotterman, A.C., 2012. Affect as a marker of the psychic surface. *The Psychoanalytic Quarterly*, 81(2), pp. 305–33.

Lyoo, I.K. et al., 2011. The neurobiological role of the dorsolateral prefrontal cortex in recovery from trauma. Longitudinal brain imaging study among survivors of the South Korean subway disaster. *Archives of General Psychiatry*, 68(7), pp. 701–13.

Nimroody, T. Principal Investigator (with Hoffman, L., & Christian, C.), In Process. Development of a defense mechanism ratings manual for children's play. Pacella research center, NY: Psychoanalytic Society and Institute. Retrieved from http://www.nypsi.org/#Continuing_Education_and_Research/Pacella_Research_Center

Olson, T.R. et al., 2011. Addressing and interpreting defense mechanisms in psychotherapy: general considerations. *Psychiatry*, 74(2), pp. 142–65.

Peller, L.E., 1954. Libidinal phases, ego development and play. *Psychoanalytic Study of the Child*, 9, pp. 178–98.

Perry, J.C. & Cooper, S.H., 1989. An empirical study of defense mechanisms. I. Clinical interview and life vignette ratings. *Archives of General Psychiatry*, 46(5), pp. 444–52.

Perry, J.C.J. & Henry, M., 2004. Studying defense mechanisms in psychotherapy using the defense mechanism rating scales. In U. Hentschel et al., eds. *Defense mechanisms: theoretical, research, and clinical perspectives*. Amsterdam: Elsevier, pp. 165–94.

Rice, T.R. & Hoffman, L., 2014. Defense mechanisms and implicit emotion regulation: a comparison of a psychodynamic construct with one from contemporary neuroscience. *Journal of the American Psychoanalytic Association*, 62(4), pp. 693–708.

Rothbart, M.K., Sheese, B.E., Rueda, M.R., & Posner, M.I., 2011. Developing mechanisms of self-regulation in early life: Emotion review. *Journal of the International Society for Research on Emotion*, 3(2), pp. 207–13.

Sandler, J. & Freud, A., 1985. *The analysis of defense: the ego & the mechanisms of defense revisited*, New York, NY: International University Press.

Spence, D.P., 1984. Discussion. *Contemporary Psychoanalysis*, 20, pp. 589–94.

Sugarman, A., 1994. Toward helping child analsys and observe mental functioning. *Psychoanalytic Psychology*, 11(3), pp. 329–39.

Sugarman, A., 2003. Dimensions of the child analyst's role as a developmental object. Affect regulation and limit setting. *The Psychoanalytic Study of the Child*, 58, pp. 189–213.

Tallandini, M.A. & Caudek, C., 2010. Defense mechanisms development in typical children. *Psychotherapy Research: Journal of the Society for Psychotherapy Research*, 20(5), pp. 535–45.

Vaillant, G., 1977. *Adaptation to life*, Boston, MA: Little, Brown.

Vaillant, G., 1993. *The wisdom of the ego*, Cambridge, MA: Harvard University Press.

Vaillant, G.E., 1971. Theoretical hierarchy of adaptive ego mechanisms: a 30-year follow-up of 30 men selected for psychological health. *Archives of General Psychiatry*, 24(2), pp. 107–18.

Vaillant, G.E., Bond, M., & Vaillant, C.O., 1986. An empirically validated hierarchy of defense mechanisms. *Archives of general psychiatry*, 43(8), pp. 786–94.

Winston, B. et al., 1994. Patient defense/therapist interventions. *Psychotherapy: Theory, Research, Practice, Training*, 31(3), pp. 478–91.

Wolmer, L., Laor, N., & Cicchetti, D.V, 2001. Validation of the comprehensive assessment of defense style (CADS): mothers' and children's responses to the stresses of missile attacks. *The Journal of Nervous and Mental Disease*, 189(6), pp. 369–76.

Chapter 4

Affect, emotion regulation, and the research domain criteria

Introduction

We have introduced Regulation-Focused Psychotherapy for Children (RFP-C; Chapter 1), described its psychodynamic theoretical orientation (Chapter 2), and discussed the pragmatics of working with children in this orientation (Chapter 3). In this chapter, our goal is to describe the hypothesized neural underpinnings of the RFP-C approach through a discussion of defense mechanisms and the implicit emotion regulation system.

The similarity of these two constructs permits the psychodynamic orientation of RFP-C to enter into a dialogue with the affective neurosciences. The focus in RFP-C upon affects and their defenses is understood in the RFP-C framework to be a specific intervention targeted to the implicit subdivision (Gyurak et al. 2011) of the emotion regulation system. This grounding enables RFP-C to be targeted to what emerging evidence suggests may be the core deficit of children with externalizing behaviors including those with oppositional defiant disorder (ODD; Cavanagh et al. 2014). More broadly, it additionally permits conversation with dimensional models of psychopathology that focus upon brain-based models, including that of the Research Domain Criteria project (RDoC; Insel et al. 2010 and Insel 2014). We believe that this theoretical foundation will permit opportunities for further studies, which may integrate RFP-C within an emerging recategorization of psychiatry and its links to biological medicine.

To recap the prior discussions of Chapters 1, 2, and 3, it may be summarized without great sacrifice that the essence of the difference between behavioral approaches to ODD and RFP-C lie in the proposition within RFP-C that disruptive behaviors have meaning. In RFP-C, disruptive behaviors are understood to be either a product or a consequence of underdeveloped defenses. Elsewhere, we have discussed the similarity in which the psychodynamic concept of defense mechanisms shares a great similarity with the contemporary concept of emotion regulation (Rice & Hoffman 2014). RFP-C is designed in theory to target the deficient implicit emotion regulation capacities of children with ODD. Whereas PMT for ODD originated within a categorical nosological framework based upon constellations of observable symptoms, RFP-C originates within a dimensional framework based on neural circuit processes.

The secondary aim of this chapter is to describe the means and the benefits of the transition from the earlier Diagnostic and Statistical Manual (DSM) system to the RDoC system. The structural and functional neuroanatomy of the emotion regulation system is reviewed. The relevance of this system to ODD and other categorical disorders of externalizing behaviors are discussed. Reorganization within the RDoC framework of domain constructs follows. The means by which RFP-C may be employed in hypothesis testing at various levels of units of analysis is demonstrated. Comparisons with existing psychotherapeutic projects among children and adolescents are discussed. A review of the benefits of this approach concludes the chapter.

The overall objective of this chapter is to demonstrate how RFP-C fits within the RDoC purview. Broadly, it affirms the strength of an affect-oriented approach to ODD and other externalizing behaviors of childhood through its focus on emotion regulation.

> This chapter demonstrates how RFP-C fits within the Research Domain Criteria of the NIMH (RDoC).

From categorical to the dimensional

The transition from the DSM system to the RDoC system has been appreciated as a challenge for research design by other authors of psychotherapeutic approaches to child and adolescent psychopathology. Many categorical diagnoses may be the manifestation of deficits in multiple and diverse neural pathways and therein be comprised of multiple RDoC domain constructs. Others have made the transition by creating hierarchies of priority of multiple functional domain constructs hypothesized to be implicated in categorical DSM diagnoses. Items on the hierarchy are then addressed through a typology of therapeutic triage (e.g., see Blom et al. 2014) in relation to adolescent Major Depressive Disorder (MDD). This approach arguably limits the therapeutic power of RDoC-organized psychotherapeutic projects in addressing categorical psychopathologic entities, as some implicated deficits go unaddressed while focusing on others.

In contrast, ODD has been proposed to be best defined through its collapse onto the single neural deficit of emotion regulation (Cavanagh et al. 2014). This reorganization of pathology from behavioral models to those of affect reflects a broader transition towards understanding the role of emotions in behavioral disorders and linking these models with defined neural systems. This approach originated in the birth of affective neuroscience in the last decade of the twentieth century through the work of Damasio, Panksepp, and LeDoux (Panksepp 1998; Damasio 1994; LeDoux 1996) and has driven advances in identifying the neurophysiologic biomarkers of affect. This premise applies to many childhood disorders manifesting with disruptive and externalizing behaviors as well as those with aggressive behaviors (see Chapter 1).

As demonstrated in the tight association of "irritable" and "headstrong" symptom clusters within the ODD construct (as discussed in Chapter 1), variations of which have been verified by multiple research groups (Stringaris & Goodman 2009; Rowe et al. 2010; Burke et al. 2010; Leibenluft et al. 2006; Drabick & Gadow 2012; Gadow & Drabick 2012), disruptive behaviors are intimately linked with affect and emotion regulation deficits. In the framework of RFP-C, they are the secondary product of a primary deficit emotion regulation.

Emotion regulation: neurophysiology and development

Emotion regulation is an established focus of study (Gross 1998) that has long been in conversation with cognitive developmental research (Tamir 2011). The neurocircuitry of this regulative process has been established within the neuroanatomic framework into implicit and explicit processes (Gyurak et al. 2011). Though this division is not without controversy (Moors & De Houwer 2006), it enables a foothold in the exploration of the neural underpinnings to the construct of defenses against painful affect. There are other similar schemas, including organization into effortful and automatic regulation (Bargh & Williams 2007). As not all conscious activity is effortful, the implicit/explicit schema of Gyurak and Etkin organizes the RFP-C approach.

Implicit regulation, or implicit self and environmental evaluations with immediate response tendencies, is dependent upon the ventral prefrontal cortex (vPFC), which includes the orbitofrontal cortex (OFC), ventromedial PFC (vmPFC), and ventral anterior cingulate cortex (vACC) (Etkin et al. 2013). Explicit regulation, or deliberate or effortful conscious cognitive manipulations that monitor, adjust, and select responses from a range of options, is dependent upon the dorsal anterior cingulate cortex (dACC) and the dorsolateral PFC (dPFC). There is likely great overlap within the neurophysiology of both symptoms.

These two divisions of cerebral cortex both modulate lower brain structures, including the amygdala, hypothalamus, and brainstem nuclei through their respective regulative pathways. The successful modulation of these visceromotor centers by the PFC regulators leads to decreased sympathetic arousal and increased parasympathetic/vagal tone (Lane et al. 2009). This results in a measurable neurochemical state which promotes calmness and inhibits behavioral dysregulation. Unsuccessful modulation as may occur through an underdeveloped implicit ER system affects the autonomic nervous system and predisposes children to disruptive behaviors; it may also influence immunological and hormonal systems implicated in psychosomatic pathology. Internal physiological effects include diminished metabolic and immunologic control as evidenced by increased fasting glucose and hemoglobin A1c levels, overnight urinary cortisol, and proinflammatory cytokines and acute-phase proteins (Thayer & Sternberg 2006). Externally, we see the agitated, disruptive behaviors of children with externalizing behaviors.

Emotion regulation develops early in infancy (Kopp & Neufeld 2003). Prior to age three months, children either turn towards or turn away from stimuli in their attempts to self-regulate. By age three months, children begin to self-soothe through thumb sucking, starting to move away, or by reflexive social signaling via crying or social smiling. This culminates by age six months in the ability to self-distract through focusing attention on neutral objects in lieu of distressing stimuli. Notably, this work mirrors that of Phebe Cramer who postulated the importance of denial in early childhood (Cramer 2006).

Successful regulation requires extrinsic influence through flexible and supportive parental interactions (Calkins & Hill 2009). The toddler years mark the initiation of the organization of neural connectivity required for emotional regulation (Lewis et al. 2006; Rothbart et al. 2011). Thereafter, toddlers learn a variety of specific strategies to manage affective states. Clinically, a diversity of defense mechanisms emerges. Suboptimal organization of this development may be hypothesized to result in deficient emotional regulation.

Neuroanatomic and functional correlates involve the concept of sensitive periods of development (Lourenco & Casey 2013). Both progressive (myelination) and regressive (synaptic pruning) brain changes that occur in childhood and adolescence enable the RFP-C clinician to intervene at a moment of cognitive, behavioral, and emotional malleability afforded by neural plasticity. The creation and implementation of therapeutic interventions designed to profit from these time-sensitive periods of neural plasticity are in alignment with the goals of the National Institute of Health Blueprint for Neuroscience Research Workshop (Cramer et al. 2011), as has been noted by authors of alternate emergent RDoC-oriented psychotherapeutic approaches to child and adolescent psychopathology (Blom et al. 2014).

During these sensitive periods of childhood, subcortical areas including brainstem and limbic areas develop earlier than higher order cortical levels (Gogtay et al. 2004). This may be particularly relevant to self-regulation and emotion regulation in particular (Fjell et al. 2012). As amygdalo-cortical connections develop (Cunningham et al. 2002) there may be specific implications for the development of emotion regulation processes with defined functional biomarker correlates (Arnsten & Rubia 2012; Rubia 2013). Shortcomings in neural network development, through constitution or environmental stress, may result in an underdeveloped implicit emotion regulation system. This may manifest in the affected child or adolescent's preponderance of use of maladaptive defenses. Its crystallization in adulthood into defined patterns of regulation may be a significant signature of adult psychopathology.

Domain constructs and levels of analysis

With well-defined neural correlates, the emotion regulation system is particularly well suited for incorporation into the RDoC model. The recent ability to differentiate an implicit emotion regulation subsystem, with its similarities to the concept of defense mechanisms (Rice & Hoffman 2014), enables the incorporation of lessons from a long and rich clinical history of caring for children with externalizing behaviors (Hoffman 2015). To secure the incorporation into RDoC, it is of benefit to define and specify the relevant domain construct of function and levels of analysis.

These terms may be best understood within the organization of the RDoC structural matrix. Using the language of Insel et al. (2010), the structure is "a matrix in which the rows represent various constructs grouped hierarchically into broad domains of function. The columns of the matrix denote different levels of analysis, from genetic, molecular, and cellular levels, proceeding to the circuit-level to the level of the individual, family environment, and social context" (page 749). Within each domain of function, exist constructs and subconstructs that comprise the domains of function. It is of benefit to RFP-C to define its approach into domains of function and its evaluation in various levels of analysis.

Through the equivalency of ODD with the emotion regulation deficit concept (Cavanagh et al. 2014), we hypothesize that the RFP-C approach is best understood as operational within the sub-construct of response selection, inhibition, or suppression.[1] This subconstruct falls within the construct of cognitive control within the domain of cognitive systems. Despite the apparent incongruity of an affective process within a cognitive organization, the preceding discussion has attempted to demonstrate the dissolving boundaries between cognition and emotion. Rather than an irrational system intended to be controlled through the rationality of cognition, developed emotionality is rather a high-evolutionarily selected system of homeostatic organization (Panksepp 1998). There is no dichotomy between emotion and reason (Damasio 1994). The approach of RFP-C, through the descriptions outlined above, is hypothesized to address deficits in this domain construct via engagement in the implicit emotion regulation subsystem of the subconstruct.

Other domains of function may be secondarily affected in children with externalizing behaviors through dysfunction in the response selection, inhibition, or suppression. For example, the hyperactivity, irritability, and hyperarousal seen in these children may be understood as dysfunction within the sustained threat construct within the negative valence domain.[2] This construct shares a neural signature in its amygdalo-cortical connections, wherein sustained limbic hyperreactivity and dysregulation is salient. The sleep/wake disturbances frequently seen in these children may be understood as deficits within the arousal and regulatory functional domain. This may originate via the brainstem and autonomic connectivity of the limbic system, as we have discussed.

Our foundation in the evidence supporting the primacy of emotion regulation capacities in the development of ODD psychopathology (Cavanagh et al. 2014) enables us to focus on the negative valence domain of the RDoC. This precision targeting offers an advantage over alternative RDoC-oriented psychotherapeutic programs for childhood and adolescent psychopathology (e.g., Blom et al. 2014) where therapeutic interventions are dispersed to address multiple domains by virtue of heterogeneous DSM clinical entities. The organizational simplicity of ODD via an emotion regulation orientation provides an unparalleled opportunity for the development of an RDoC compatible approach in RFP-C. Whereas this approach is different from other RDoC approaches, it is also different from traditional psychodynamic psychiatry where there is a more nonspecific targeting of issues.

By virtue of the construction of RFP-C, we have opened the evaluation of its effect upon the negative valence domain and its constructs: Acute threat ("fear"), Potential threat ("anxiety"), Sustained threat, Loss, and Frustrative nonreward. RDoC identifies genes, cells, circuits, physiology, behavior, self-reports, and paradigms on a linear hierarchy of biological to behavioral. Of most importance to the RFP-C approach, it identifies impulsive behaviors, particularly "physical and relational aggression," as part of the construct "frustrative nonreward within the behavioral level of analysis. Clinically relevant self-report measures are listed, all of which RFP-C is capable of via the structure of its short-term therapeutic orientation with built-in opportunities for standardized clinical rating scale administration and evaluation. In the manual portion of this work, we describe the various relevant rating scales to emotion regulation in specific and negative valence domain in general (see Chapter 6).

The efficacy of RFP-C may be measured via symptom reduction within categorical diagnostic systems. It may also be measured by improvement in measures of improved emotion regulation, including both rating scales and questionnaires as well as via biomarkers. Pupilometry and electroencephalography are listed as physiological manifestations of dysfunction in this domain. The literature has already witnessed the careful application of EEG to demonstrate the benefit of an anger management cognitive behavioral protocol to improve explicit emotion regulation in order to address these target behaviors in children with externalizing behaviors (Woltering et al. 2011; Granic et al. 2012).

The study of Woltering et al. (2011) merits discussion as a model example. In this study, 71 children, aged 8–12 with clinical levels of externalizing behavior, and their families completed a three-month behavioral program that targeted the explicit emotion regulation system by reviewing explicit, conscious means to control angry and negative affects. Techniques of the program included cognitive restructuring, reappraisal, problem solving, and role-playing. These authors found a normalization of emotional regulation neural correlates among treatment responders: Specifically, these children showed an increase in prefrontal electroencephalographic activity in the dACC, the portion of the PFC associated with explicit emotional regulation. Simultaneously, there was a decrease in activity in the vmPFC, the portion of the PFC associated with implicit emotional regulation.

These children appear to have benefited through the teaching of explicit emotion regulation skills. Conscious, effortful cognitive-behavioral strategies that have been investigated include cognitive reappraisal (McRae et al. 2010; Goldin et al. 2008; Ochsner et al. 2002), suppression (Goldin et al. 2008; Dunn et al. 2009), and effortful distraction (Van Dillen & Koole 2007). In fMRI studies, these processes have demonstrated a hierarchy of effectiveness in the attenuation of limbic, hormonal, and sympathetic autonomic activity through midline prefrontal control in response to painful emotions (Goldin et al. 2008). Demonstration of comparable findings through RFP-C may be of clinical significance as deficits in implicit emotion regulation have greater association with functional impairment (Gyurak et al. 2011), a fact which has already been demonstrated in the mood (Ehring et al. 2010) and anxiety (Etkin et al. 2010) disorders.

Functional neuroimaging studies are also emergent (Bellani et al. 2012) and may enable investigation into the circuitry level. Levels of analysis within the cellular, molecular, and genetic layers is beyond the scope of this chapter but is discussed elsewhere in discussions of testosterone and the serotonin syndrome. As research investigation methods improve in the field of neuropsychiatry, the future holds many possibilities.

Benefits and promise

Transdiagnostic approaches through emotion regulation may be of particular benefit to the future of the field (Joormann & Goodman 2014). These approaches may very well present an opportunity for psychiatry to gain greater relevance as a medical specialty as correlations with mental health and physical dysfunction via neurology, endocrinology, immunology, and other homeostatic fields become more defined. In the present, these approaches may already be of benefit in tailoring approaches to target populations in need. For example, this approach may be very relevant in boys where androgen influences may greatly impair the emotion regulation system in this age group (Nolen-Hoeksema 2012). Above, we have already discussed the developmental wisdom of tailoring an intervention to children in this age group.

Psychodynamic psychiatry additionally gains an opportunity to build relevance in a contemporary mindset that has increasingly left it behind (Wolpert & Fonagy 2009; Salkovskis & Wolpert 2012). Following several decades of shift from theoretical understandings of human nature to the objective descriptive, there are now the beginnings of a return from behavioral descriptions to theory-driven models (Kupfer & Regier 2011). We have seen that these models are rooted in neuroscience. Descriptive, categorically defined disorders with an emphatic disregard for underlying mechanisms seem to be on the way out (Bradshaw et al. 2012). There is great interest in both academic and broad culture communities to reinvest mental health care with etiological substance.

The time is ripe to support the reinvestment of interest in psychoanalytic thought through its linkage with the brain-based etiologic theory of great contemporary favor. Some (e.g., Fertuck 2011) have advocated for this, and already great progress has been made in broad domains of the Freudian unconscious (Berlin 2011).

This chapter has explored the biological underpinnings to RFP-C and demonstrated the feasibility of its integration with the RDoC concept. The objective has been to align the theoretical basis of RFP-C with empirically originated models of contemporary neuroscience (Fertuck 2011). It is well established that psychotherapy can similarly provide neuroanatomical restoration (Kandel 2006). We have already referenced the value in a recent study of cognitive-behavioral therapy that affected the neuronal correlates of children with externalizing behaviors through an address of emotional regulation (Woltering et al. 2011). We have aimed to create a channel of communication between academic research and a psychotherapeutic clinical practice founded upon over a century of careful, developmentally informed research.

In the practice manual that follows, we demonstrate how such an approach may be implemented in a 16-session paradigm. The following chapter summarizes the structure and individual steps with component individual sessions are described.

Notes

1 For more information, see http://www.nimh.nih.gov/research-priorities/rdoc/rdoc-constructs.shtml#response_selection
2 For more information, see http://www.nimh.nih.gov/research-priorities/rdoc/research-domain-criteria-matrix.shtml

Bibliography

Arnsten, A.F.T. & Rubia, K., 2012. Neurobiological circuits regulating attention, cognitive control, motivation, and emotion: disruptions in neurodevelopmental psychiatric disorders. *Journal of the American Academy of Child and Adolescent Psychiatry*, 51(4), pp. 356–67.

Bargh, J. & Williams, L., 2007. The nonconscious regulation of emotion. In J. Gross, ed. *Handbook of emotion regulation*. New York, NY: Guilford Press, pp. 429–45.

Bellani, M., Garzitto, M., & Brambilla, P., 2012. Functional MRI studies in disruptive behaviour disorders. *Epidemiology and Psychiatric Sciences*, 21(1), pp. 31–3.

Berlin, H.A., 2011. The neural basis of the dynamic unconscious. *Neuropsychoanalysis*, 13(1), pp. 5–31.

Blom, E.H., Duncan, L.G., Ho, T.C., Connolly, C.G., LeWinn, K.Z., Chesney, M., Hecht, F.M., & Yang, T.T., 2014. The development of an RDoC-based treatment program for adolescent depression: "Training for Awareness, Resilience, and Action" (TARA). *Frontiers in Human Neuroscience*, 8(August), pp. 1–19.

Bradshaw, C. P., Goldweber, A., Fishbein, D., & Greenberg, M. T., 2012. Infusing developmental neuroscience into school-based preventive interventions: implications and future directions. *Journal of Adolescent Health*, 51(2 Supplement), pp. S41–S47.

Burke, J. D., Hipwell, A. E., & Loeber, R., 2010. Dimensions of oppositional defiant disorder as predictors of depression and conduct disorder in preadolescent girls. *Journal of the American Academy of Child and Adolescent Psychiatry*, 49(5), pp. 484–92.

Calkins, S. D. & Hill, A., 2009. Caregiver influences on emerging emotional regulation: biological and environmental transactions in early development. In J. J. Gross, ed. *Handbook of Emotion Regulation*. New York, NY: Guilford Press, pp. 229–48.

Cavanagh, M. et al., 2014. Oppositional defiant disorder is better conceptualized as a disorder of emotional regulation. *Journal of Attention Disorders*, pp. 1–9.

Cramer, P., 2006. *Protecting the self: defense mechanisms in action*, New York, NY: Guilford Press.

Cramer, S. C. et al., 2011. Harnessing neuroplasticity for clinical applications. *Brain: A Journal of Neurology*, 134(Pt 6), pp. 1591–609.

Cunningham, M. G., Bhattacharyya, S., & Benes, F. M., 2002. Amygdalo-cortical sprouting continues into early adulthood: implications for the development of normal and abnormal function during adolescence. *The Journal of Comparative Neurology*, 453(2), pp. 116–30.

Damasio, A., 1994. *Descartes' error: emotion, reason, and the human brain*, New York, NY: Grosset/Putnam.

Drabick, D.A.G. & Gadow, K. D., 2012. Deconstructing oppositional defiant disorder: clinic-based evidence for an anger/irritability phenotype. *Journal of the American Academy of Child and Adolescent Psychiatry*, 51(4), pp. 384–93.

Dunn, B. D. et al., 2009. The consequences of effortful emotion regulation when processing distressing material: a comparison of suppression and acceptance. *Behaviour Research and Therapy*, 47(9), pp. 761–3.

Ehring, T. et al., 2010. Emotion regulation and vulnerability to depression: spontaneous versus instructed use of emotion suppression and reappraisal. *Emotion (Washington, D.C.)*, 10(4), pp. 563–72.

Etkin, A. et al., 2010. Failure of anterior cingulate activation and connectivity with the amygdala during implicit regulation of emotional processing in generalized anxiety disorder. *The American journal of psychiatry*, 167(5), pp. 545–54.

Etkin, A., Gyurak, A., & O'Hara, R., 2013. A neurobiological approach to the cognitive deficits of psychiatric disorders. *Dialogues in Clinical Neuroscience*, 15(4), pp. 419–29.

Fertuck, E. A., 2011. The scientific study of unconscious processes: the time is ripe for (re) convergence of neuroscientific and psychoanalytic conceptions. *Neuropsychoanalysis*, 13(1), pp. 45–8.

Fjell, A. M. et al., 2012. Multimodal imaging of the self-regulating developing brain. *Proceedings of the National Academy of Sciences of the United States of America*, 109(48), pp. 19620–5.

Gadow, K. D. & Drabick, D.A.G., 2012. Anger and irritability symptoms among youth with ODD: cross-informant versus source-exclusive syndromes. *Journal of Abnormal Child Psychology*, 40(7), pp. 1073–85.

Gogtay, N. et al., 2004. Dynamic mapping of human cortical development during childhood through early adulthood. *Proceedings of the National Academy of Sciences of the United States of America*, 101(21), pp. 8174–9.

Goldin, P.R. et al., 2008. The neural bases of emotion regulation: reappraisal and suppression of negative emotion. *Biological Psychiatry*, 63(6), pp. 577–86.

Granic, I. et al., 2012. Emotion regulation in children with behavior problems: linking behavioral and brain processes. *Development and Psychopathology*, 24(3), pp. 1019–29.

Gross, J.J., 1998. The emerging field of emotion regulation: an integrative review. *Review of General Psychology*, 2(3), pp. 271–99.

Gyurak, A., Gross, J.J., & Etkin, A., 2011. Explicit and implicit emotion regulation: a dual-process framework. *Cognition & Emotion*, 25(3), pp. 400–12.

Hoffman, L., 2015. Berta Bornstein's Frankie: the contemporary relevance of a classic to the treatment of children with disruptive symptoms. *Psychoanalytic Study of the Child*, In press.

Insel, T. et al., 2010. Research domain criteria (RDoC): toward a new classification framework for research on mental disorders. *The American Journal of Psychiatry*, 167, pp. 748–51.

Insel, T.R., 2014. The NIMH research domain criteria (RDoC) project: precision medicine for psychiatry. *The American Journal of Psychiatry*, 171(4), pp. 395–7.

Joormann, J. & Goodman, S.H., 2014. Transdiagnostic processes in psychopathology: in memory of Susan Nolen-Hoeksema. *Journal of Abnormal Psychology*, 123(1), pp. 49–50.

Kandel, E., 2006. *In search of memory: the emergence of a new science of mind*, New York, NY: Norton.

Kopp, C. & Neufeld, S., 2003. Emotional development during infancy. In R.J. Davidson, K.R. Sherer, & H. Hill Goldsmith, eds. *Handbook of affective sciences*. Oxford, UK: Oxford University Press, pp. 347–74.

Kupfer, D.J. & Regier, D.A., 2011. Neuroscience, clinical evidence, and the future of psychiatric classification in DSM-5. *The American Journal of Psychiatry*, 168(7), pp. 672–4.

Lane, R.D. et al., 2009. Neural correlates of heart rate variability during emotion. *NeuroImage*, 44(1), pp. 213–22.

LeDoux, J., 1996. *The emotional brain: the mysterious underpinnings of emotional life*, New York, NY: Simon and Schuster.

Leibenluft, E. et al., 2006. Chronic versus episodic irritability in youth: a community-based, longitudinal study of clinical and diagnostic associations. *Journal of Child and Adolescent Psychopharmacology*, 16(4), pp. 456–66.

Lewis, M.D. et al., 2006. Neurophysiological correlates of emotion regulation in children and adolescents. *Journal of Cognitive Neuroscience*, 18(3), pp. 430–43.

Lourenco, F. & Casey, B.J., 2013. Adjusting behavior to changing environmental demands with development. *Neuroscience and Biobehavioral Reviews*, 37(9 Pt B), pp. 2233–42.

McRae, K. et al., 2010. The neural bases of distraction and reappraisal. *Journal of Cognitive Neuroscience*, 22(2), pp. 248–62.

Moors, A. & De Houwer, J., 2006. Automaticity: a theoretical and conceptual analysis. *Psychological Bulletin*, 132(2), pp. 297–326.

Nolen-Hoeksema, S., 2012. Emotion regulation and psychopathology: the role of gender. *Annual Review of Clinical Psychology*, 8, pp. 161–87.

Ochsner, K.N. et al., 2002. Rethinking feelings: an FMRI study of the cognitive regulation of emotion. *Journal of cognitive neuroscience*, 14(8), pp. 1215–29.

Panksepp, J., 1998. *Affective neuroscience: the foundations of human and animal emotions*, New York, NY: Oxford University Press.

Rice, T.R. & Hoffman, L., 2014. Defense mechanisms and implicit emotion regulation: a comparison of a psychodynamic construct with one from contemporary neuroscience. *Journal of the American Psychoanalytic Association*, 62(4), pp. 693–708.

Rothbart, M.K. et al., 2011. Developing mechanisms of self-regulation in early life. *Emotion Review: Journal of the International Society for Research on Emotion*, 3(2), pp. 207–13.

Rowe, R. et al., 2010. Developmental pathways in oppositional defiant disorder and conduct disorder. *Journal of Abnormal Psychology*, 119(4), pp. 726–38.

Rubia, K., 2013. Functional brain imaging across development. *European Child & Adolescent Psychiatry*, 22(12), pp. 719–31.

Salkovskis, P. & Wolpert, L., 2012. Does psychoanalysis have a valuable place in modern mental health services? No. *BMJ (Clinical research ed.)*, 344(7845), p. 18–19.

Stringaris, A. & Goodman, R., 2009. Longitudinal outcome of youth oppositionality: irritable, headstrong, and hurtful behaviors have distinctive predictions. *Journal of the American Academy of Child and Adolescent Psychiatry*, 48(4), pp. 404–12.

Tamir, M., 2011. The maturing field of emotion regulation. *Emotion Review*, 3(1), pp. 3–7.

Thayer, J.F. & Sternberg, E., 2006. Beyond heart rate variability: vagal regulation of allostatic systems. *Annals of the New York Academy of Sciences*, 1088, pp. 361–72.

Van Dillen, L.F. & Koole, S.L., 2007. Clearing the mind: a working memory model of distraction from negative mood. *Emotion (Washington, D.C.)*, 7(4), pp. 715–23.

Wolpert, L. & Fonagy, P., 2009. There is no place for the psychoanalytic case report in the British Journal of Psychiatry. *The British Journal of Psychiatry : The Journal of Mental Science*, 195(6), pp. 483–7.

Woltering, S. et al., 2011. Neural changes associated with treatment outcome in children with externalizing problems. *Biological Psychiatry*, 70(9), pp. 873–9.

Section 2

Practice manual

Chapter 5

Foreword to practice manual

Despite the pervasiveness of problematic externalizing behaviors in children (disruptive and aggressive), there are very few well-established, evidenced-based individual psychotherapeutic approaches for children with chronic irritability and externalizing behaviors. Helping parents *manage* the behavioral disturbance is currently the predominant therapeutic path to helping these children (Eyberg et al. 2008; Steiner & Remsing 2007). Division 53 of the American Psychological Association considers Individual Parent Management Training as the only well-established treatment for these children.[1] In addition, the most recent practice parameter from the American Academy of Child and Adolescent Psychiatry states that "current recommendations regarding the use of modalities such as individual therapy are based on clinical wisdom and consensus rather than extensive empirical evidence" (Steiner & Remsing 2007, page 136). It is noteworthy that both the Division 53 and American Academy of Child and Adolescent Psychiatry treatment recommendations have not been updated since 2007 and 2008.

Case studies, series of cases, and other descriptions of individual, dynamically oriented clinical work with disruptive children are common. This psychodynamic clinical history includes, among innumerable others, Bornstein (1945, 1949), Fonagy and Target (1994a, 1994b), Hoffman (1989, 2007, 2013a, 2013b, 2015), Karush (2006), and Yanof (1996a, 1996b, 2005). It is important to stress that despite the large clinical literature, to our knowledge, dynamically oriented works have not been systematically empirically evaluated with a level of methodological rigor to permit this approach's classification as an evidenced-based treatment for children with disruptive disorders or with externalizing behaviors, who in fact are difficult to treat (Eresund 2007 and Midgley & Kennedy 2011). As a result, there has been an increasing use of psychotropic medications especially because of the difficulties these children pose for themselves and those who care for them (Olfson et al. 2012). Palmer et al. (2013) argue that behavioral problems are more resistant to a classical, insight-oriented psychodynamic approach, while CBT has real limitations in the treatment of severe disorders in comparison to psychotropic medications.

In addition to the dearth of empirically validated or empirically supported psychotherapies (other than parent management training and limited success with variations of cognitive behavioral techniques) for children with disruptive disorders, there is a substantial amount of literature documenting the large dropout rates in child psychotherapy (Kazdin et al. 1997, Kennedy & Midgley, 2007). There are practical and emotional barriers that lead parents to discontinue their children's therapy prematurely. Thus, any systematic individual psychotherapy for children has to include supportive work with parents and/or guardians.

A systematic dynamic approach consistent with RDoC

Given this state of affairs, it seems timely to provide clinicians with a systematic individual psychotherapy as an alternative to Parent Management Training (PMT), Cognitive Behavioral Therapy (CBT), and psychotropic medication for children who exhibit disruptive behavior problems.

This psychotherapy manual was developed for use by mental health professionals who work with children who have externalizing behaviors. The treatment approach may be used as a primary or as an adjunctive treatment with children who meet criteria for a variety of DSM-5 diagnoses including Oppositional Defiant Disorder (ODD), Disruptive Mood Dysregulation Disorder (DMDD), Attention Deficit/Hyperactivity Disorder (ADHD), and Conduct Disorder (CD) when an ability to empathically relate to another person remains (i.e., those children without callous-unemotional [CU] traits). Additionally, children with disorders classically conceptualized as internalizing often manifest with co-occurring oppositional and defiant symptoms, which may render them malleable to this approach. This includes Obsessive Compulsive Disorder (OCD) and Tourette's Disorder (TD), where a rich clinical history dating back to Margaret Mahler and beyond describes efforts to address "affect-motor outbursts" (Mahler 1944, 1949) that in the current literature are described through the phenomenon of "rage attacks" (Budman et al. 2003). Indeed, increased attention to the disruptive emotional components of these (Stewart 2012) and other disorders is currently in vogue as we have previously described (Chapter 1).

From the perspective of the NIMH Research Domain Criteria (RDoC; Insel 2014), children with externalizing behaviors exhibit deficits primarily in two domains: Negative Valence Systems (i.e., systems for aversive motivation) (NIMH 2014a) and Systems for Social Processes (NIMH 2014b). They manifest problematic behaviors in the construct of "Frustrative nonreward," which is manifested by physical and relational aggression. In the domain Systems for Social Processes, children manifest problematic behaviors as a result of difficulties with their perception and understanding of themselves; they do not manifest a developmentally appropriate perception of their competences, skills, abilities beliefs, intentions, desires, and/or emotional states. As we have noted previously (Rice & Hoffman 2014), we propose that the modern neurocognitive concept of implicit emotional regulation (ER) is equivalent to unconscious automatic defense mechanisms. Therefore, we have chosen the term "Regulation-Focused Psychotherapy" instead of "Defense-Focused" for our therapeutic intervention because the term, "regulation," is more descriptive and theory-neutral than the term, "defense." And, in fact, as described in the RDoC domains noted above, a key feature in children with externalizing behaviors involves an inability to regulate their affective responses to negative stimuli.

The goal of defining a systematic and operationalized individual approach for children with externalizing behaviors and their parents is to allow for reliable implementation by a wide variety of clinicians. This manual will also aid in empirical evaluation of RFP-C's impact on children, in particular their main area of deficit, implicit affect regulation. With this approach, the clinician observes the child's disruptive symptoms and conceptualizes them as a way of avoiding an awareness of painful emotions. Over time, the clinician identifies and addresses *in the psychotherapy session* this pattern of avoidance of painful emotions. Over time, the clinician works with the child to identify the protective, yet maladaptive, coping devices and helps the child become able, in time, to discuss the painful emotions themselves. This process of gradual exposure to painful emotions thus shares similarity with Exposure with Response Prevention (ERP) treatment strategies. This gradual process allows for the development of more effective mastery, control, and modulation of disturbing emotions. Over time, developmental delays in the implicit emotion regulatory system can be resolved (see Chapter 4).

Working with parents

In working with the child's parents, the clinician first empathizes with the difficulty parents experience in parenting a child with poor affect regulation. The clinician tries to communicate that their children's disruptive behavior has meaning (e.g., there is a reason for the disruptive behavior) and helps parents identify situations that provoke negative emotions and trigger disruptions for the child. Over time, the clinician discusses methods that parents may employ in order to set behavioral limits while appreciating the child's difficulties complying with such limits.

Roots of RFP-C

Regulation-Focused Psychotherapy for Children with Externalizing Behaviors (RFP-C) owes a debt to the original work of Berta Bornstein (1945) and Paulina Kernberg (Kernberg & Chazan 1991) with children and adolescents, as well as other authors of dynamic treatment models such as Barbara Milrod and colleagues (2007). Another important source of ideas comes from Leigh McCullough and colleagues (2003) and their conception of affect phobia in adults. Affect phobia refers to a phobia about feelings (an internal phobia in contrast to an external phobia). In their manual (page 38), these authors discuss the Triangle of Conflict derived from Malan (1979); the three poles of the triangle are as follows:

1   Feeling (the feared feeling). What is the activating feeling that is being avoided?

2 Anxiety (inhibitory affects). Why is that feeling being avoided? What is the excessive inhibitory affect?
3 Defense (a phobic avoidance reaction). How is the adaptive feeling being avoided?

An experience-near approach

The avoidance of thoughts, feelings, and behaviors can be conceptualized to be similar to avoidance of external phobic situations. Similar to the response-prevention component of ERP, the child is prevented from engaging in avoidance mechanisms, or established "responses." The clinician achieves this through recognizing and commenting on the avoidance (defense) and thus disempowering their function. The emphasis remains on observed behaviors and emotions within the clinical encounter; naming of inferred instinctual drives and intellectualized "deep" interpretations are avoided. It is important to stress that RFP-C is an "experience-near" treatment whereby the clinician mainly speaks with the child about the "in-the-moment" interaction between child and clinician and minimizes discussion of what he/she heard from the parents and/or school. This technique allows the clinician to help the child observe and discuss the inevitable repetitions in the sessions of the maladaptive problematic externalizing behaviors. In addition, since this technique does not require the clinician to infer the children's motivations that are not observable, it is a technique that allows for ease of replicability and facilitates RFP-C's capability for empiric studies of treatment efficacy.

Additionally, this style of engagement in emotion and behaviors also allows for a synchrony of language with the implicit ER system in which these children have deficits (Rice & Hoffman 2014). It is the premise of RFP-C that these children's reliance on avoidant and externalizing behaviors result from developmental delays in implicit emotion regulation (ER) capacities. Children remain unable to tolerate dysphoric affects through dissipation of the painful or intolerable aspect of the emotion, and they thus avoid it. Their disruption occurs not only as a manifestation of autonomic arousal wrought by the undigestable/unregulatable emotion, but also as a self-reinforcing tactic to influence the environment away from the painful content. By addressing the externalizing behaviors as methods of avoidance, the RFP-C clinician does not allow this diversion tactic to continue endlessly.

Implicit emotion regulation dysfunction

To develop this concept further, an underdeveloped implicit ER system results in heightened prolonged limbic, hormonal, and autonomic nervous system arousal when these children are challenged with strong and painful emotions. These biochemical changes promote impulsive action and, when coupled with the cognitive distortions and errors in judgment afforded by their denials and projections, they cause major and multiple problems in these children's lives. RFP-C removes roadblocks to normative development by safely exposing children in the sessions to their feared affects and thereby promoting the maturation of ER processes. When introducing the process of therapy to parents with children who are experiencing maladaptive externalizing behaviors, the clinician should be mindful of these principles as a way to explain the nature of the child's symptoms as well as the nature of the treatment.

Some children may require more specialized interventions than those described in this manual. These include children with clinically significant disturbances in their capacities to relate to other people and children with significant problems in their sense of reality. They will thus be excluded as "good candidates" for RFP-C, unless it is clear to the clinician that the child's problems with relatedness and sense of reality are manifestations of a maladaptive coping strategy (as opposed to a psychotic or autistic spectrum disorder).

A short-term approach

RFP-C is a short-term, 16-session approach to irritable and disruptive children who frequently have tantrums. The psychotherapy has been designed to target the specific functional deficits in these children, that is, deficits in their implicit emotion regulation capabilities. RFP-C's foundation, within the RDoC approach, can be hypothesized to target circuit-level processes between prefrontal, limbic, and sympathetic/parasympathetic systems. Affective neuroscience has shown that persistently irritable children have deficits within this emotion regulation system (Deveney 2013), and that targeted interventions may correct aberrant neural signatures in children with externalizing symptoms (Woltering 2011). For example, Bebko et al. (2014) found that "reduced left ventrolateral prefrontal cortex activity to win may reflect reward insensitivity in youth with disruptive behavior disorders" (p.71).

The first step is to systematically implement RFP-C and determine whether it is clinically effective via the application of systematic empirical clinical rating scales and other measures (e.g., The Affective Reactivity Index [ARI; Stringaris et al. 2012]). Because of its hypothesized theoretical basis within the brain-based ER system, attempts at correlating results of RFP-C with biomarkers may be later considered.

Some of the children who will be treated with RFP-C will have symptoms consistent with ODD, especially those who experience a great deal of irritability (Stringaris and Goodman 2009). Based on existing literature on the neuroscience of externalizing behaviors, we hypothesize that a central mechanism leading to the disruptive behavior in these children is a result of the utilization of a variety of psychological mechanisms (defense mechanisms), explicit and implicit, to avoid the experience of painful emotions.

Central features of RFP-C

There are three central features of RFP-C:

1 By following the child's play and verbalization, the problematic symptoms that lead to disruption at home and/or at school will inevitably be repeated with the clinician.

> The clinician, thus, has the opportunity to observe directly the child's maladaptive behavior and the trigger to the child's maladaptive behavior (for example, in a situation, when the clinician says, "No" to a child's attempts to hit the clinician).

2 The child's difficulties regulating his/her emotions may become manifest at such moments.
3 From the beginning of psychotherapeutic work in RFP-C, the clinician addresses the sequence of events with the child as they occur and are experienced in the session, with the goal of helping find more adaptive emotion regulation mechanisms, such as avoiding explosions when faced with a "No," even if he/she feels angry and hurt.

A child can automatically, without conscious deliberation, utilize the mechanism of *avoidance of painful emotions*. At other times, a child can consciously avoid addressing a painful topic, such as parents' divorce by saying: "Let's not talk about that anymore; let's go back to our chess game."

RFP-C works through an integrative therapeutic approach that combines elements of behavioral therapy (limiting dangerous behavior in the therapy room) with those traditionally termed *psychodynamic* (allowing the child to lead the play and discussion in order to understand the meaning of the child's symptoms and behavior). In RFP-C, it is useful to conceptualize:

1 The child's emotions that are avoided;
2 How the emotion is being avoided; and
3 Trying to understand why that emotion is being avoided in a maladaptive way.

Malan's (1979) "Triangle of Conflict" and its utilization by McCullough et al. (2003) in the treatment of adults has influenced the development of this manual. Parents may be provided with material that discusses the process of therapy (see Appendix A).

In children with externalizing behaviors, one can observe their difficulties experiencing negative emotional responses (to a "No," for example). Such a child may want to leave the playroom immediately upon hearing the word "No." By so doing, the child masks the emotional-response-to-be-avoided by becoming angry at the clinician, wanting to leave him (a maladaptive response). The goals of RFP-C are to try to understand why that original emotion had to be avoided so dramatically and to help the child find more adaptive emotional regulation devices. When introducing the process of RFP-C to parents with children who are experiencing maladaptive oppositional symptoms, the clinician needs to bear in mind this "triangle of conflict" as a way to explain the nature of the child's symptoms as well as the nature of the treatment.

The manualization of this approach permits hypothesis testing and empirical study of this approach for these children. In addition, utilization of this manual may one day enable the study of the impact of RFP-C on the neurobiology of these children through the examination of biomarkers and their responsivity to treatment. For example, these youth show increased limbic activation with frustrating stimuli (Deveney et al. 2013), and they are hypothesized to have commensurate deficits in the prefrontal regions which modulate limbic responsiveness. The explosion of interest in the ER concept (Gross 2013) and the increasing transition to a transdiagnostic, brain-based dimensional system (Insel et al. 2010) means not only that biomarkers may be increasingly developed when the time for evaluation presents, but that such efforts will be accessible to a wide range of academic clinicians and researchers.

Procedure of RFP-C

The procedure for RFP-C will encompass three steps:

Step 1: An introductory meeting/s with the parents, two initial sessions with the child, and a feedback meeting with the parents. Ongoing check-ins and meetings with parents are crucial in order to develop a therapeutic alliance with the parents as well as with the child. As described in the manual, the clinician needs to carefully listen to parents, empathize with their plight, and carefully explain the process, as well as help them understand the nature of the problems at home and school and help them develop more effective interactions with the child.

Step 2: Sessions 3–11 (the bulk of the treatment) consist of the clinician addressing how the child responds to situations that trigger unpleasant emotions in the sessions with the clinician. In the language of psychodynamics, the clinician will address the defenses the child utilizes to ward off painful emotions in the transference. By directly addressing the child's maladaptive coping mechanisms that the child manifests explicitly and directly, the clinician does not have to guess what is on the child's mind. These sessions will be conducted twice weekly. Throughout the treatment, the clinician will recommend to the parents that they meet regularly and contact him/her whenever they need to report some event. The clinician will meet with the parent briefly every week in order to maintain a therapeutic alliance with them, provide support, and discuss with them the ongoing progress of the child, helping them understand the child and helping them find ways to deal with the child's externalizing behaviors. In the middle of the treatment (after about session 10), the clinician will meet with the parents in an in-depth way to review the progress and to prepare for the termination which will occur.

Step 3: Termination Step during sessions 12–16.

In Appendix B, we delineate adherence scales for these various steps in the treatment.

Goals of RFP-C

Finally, it is crucial to note that the focus of this treatment is not to promote cognitive (intellectual) change in the child (classical insight) ("Oh, now I understand") but to promote implicit awareness in the child that

1. The emotional state being avoided by the child is not as overwhelming as he/she thinks it is and that it will not destroy him/her.
2. There are better ways to manage those emotions than to fight.
3. That the clinician will not be hurt by those feelings and those feelings will not destroy the clinician.

The clinician, by understanding that the behavior has meaning, is always implicitly communicating to the child that his/her externalizing behaviors have meaning as well as implicitly communicating a nonjudgmental attitude towards the child.

Note

1. For information, see http://effectivechildtherapy.com/content/disruptive-behavior-problems-odd-cd

References

Bebko, G. et al., 2014. Parsing dimensional vs. diagnostic category-related patterns of reward circuitry function in behaviorally and emotionally dysregulated youth in the Longitudinal Assessment of Manic Symptoms study. *JAMA Psychiatry*, 71(1), pp. 71–80.

Bornstein, B., 1945. Clinical notes on child analysis. *Psychoanalytic Study of the Child*, 1, pp. 151–66.

Bornstein, B., 1949. The analysis of a phobic child-some problems of theory and technique in child analysis. *Psychoanalytic Study of the Child*, 3, pp. 181–226.

Budman, C. L., Rockmore, L., Stokes, J., & Sossin, M., 2013. Clinical phenomenology of episodic rage in children with Tourette syndrome. *Journal of Psychosomatic Research*, 55(1), 59–65.

Deveney, C. M. et al., 2013. Neural mechanisms of frustration in chronically irritable children. *The American Journal of Psychiatry*, 170, pp. 1186–94.

Eresund, P., 2007. Psychodynamic psychotherapy for children with disruptive disorders. *Journal of Child Psychotherapy*, 33, pp. 161–80.

Eyberg, S. M., Nelson, M. M., & Boggs, S. R., 2008. Evidence-based psychosocial treatments for child and adolescent with disruptive behavior. *Journal of Clinical Child & Adolescent Psychology*, 37, pp. 215–37.

Fonagy, P. & Target, M., 1994a. The efficacy of psychoanalysis for children with disruptive disorders. *Journal of the American Academy of Child & Adolescent Psychiatry*, 33(1), pp. 45–55. Retrieved from http://www.sciencedirect.com/science/article/pii/S0890856709641447

Fonagy, P. & Target, M., 1994b. Who is helped by child psychoanalysis? A sample study of disruptive children, from the Anna Freud Centre retrospective investigation. *Bulletin of the Anna Freud Center*, 17, pp. 291–315.

Gross, J. J., 2013. Emotion regulation: taking stock and moving forward. *Emotion*, 13(3), pp. 359–65.

Hoffman, L., 1989. The psychoanalytic process and the development of insight in child analysis: a case study. *The Psychoanalytic Quarterly*, 58, pp. 63–80.

Hoffman, L., 2007. Do children get better when we interpret their defenses against painful feelings? *The Psychoanalytic Study of the Child*, 62, pp. 291–313.

Hoffman, L., 2013a. Single case archive of In M. Desmet et al., eds. *Psychoanalytic Single Cases Published in ISI-Ranked Journals: The Construction of an Online Archive. Psychotherapy and Psychosomatics*, 82, pp. 120–21.

Hoffman, L., 2013b. The analyst as auxiliary ego/superego: discussion of "to analyze or not to analyze: the treatment of a severely disturbed four-year-old boy." *Psychoanalytic Inquiry: A Topical Journal for Mental Health Professionals*, 33(4), pp. 416–423.

Hoffman, L., 2015. Berta Bornstein's Frankie: the contemporary relevance of a classic to the treatment of children with disruptive symptoms. *The Psychoanalytic Study of the Child* 68, pp. 152–76.

Insel, T. R., 2014. The NIMH research domain criteria (RDoC) project: precision medicine for psychiatry. *The American Journal of Psychiatry*, 171(4), pp. 395–7.

Insel, T. et al., 2010. Research domain criteria (RDoC): toward a new classification framework for research on mental disorders. *The American Journal of Psychiatry*, 167, pp. 748–51.

Karush, R. K., 2006. The vicissitudes of aggression in a toddler: a clinical contribution. *The Psychoanalytic Study of the Child*, 61, pp. 3–19.

Kazdin, A. E., Holland, L., Crowley, M., & Breton, S., 1997. Barriers to treatment participation scale: evaluation and validation in the context of child outpatient treatment. *Journal of Child Psychology and Psychiatry*, 38(8), pp. 1051–62.

Kennedy, E. & Midgley, N., 2007. *Process and outcome research in child, adolescent and parent-infant psychotherapy: a thematic review*, London, England: North Central London Strategic Health Authority.

Kernberg, P. F. & Chazan, S. E., 1991. *Children with conduct disorders: a psychotherapy manual*, New York, NY: Basic Books.

Mahler, M. S., 1944. Tics and impulsions in children: a study of motility. *Psychoanalytic Quarterly*, 13, pp. 430–444.

Mahler, M. S. 1949. A psychoanalytic evaluation of tic in psychopathology of children—symptomatic and tic syndrome. *Psychoanalytic Study of the Child*, 4, pp. 279–310.

Malan, D. H., 1979. *Individual psychotherapy and the science of psychodynamics*, London, UK: Butterworth Heinemann.

McCullough, L., Kuhn, N., Andrews, S., Kaplan, A., Wolf, J., & Hurley, C. L., 2003. *Treating affect phobia: a manual for short-term dynamic psychotherapy*, New York, NY: Guilford Press.

Midgley, N. & Kennedy, E., 2011. Psychodynamic psychotherapy for children and adolescents: a critical review of the evidence base. *Journal of Child Psychotherapy*, 37, pp. 232–60.

Milrod, B. et al., 2007. A randomized controlled clinical trial of psychoanalytic psychotherapy for panic disorder. *The American Journal of Psychiatry*, 164(2), pp. 265–72. Retrieved from http://www.ncbi.nlm.nih.gov/pubmed/17267789 (Accessed December 15, 2012).

NIMH (2014a). RDoC Constructs: Domain: Negative Valence Systems. Retrieved from http://www.nimh.nih.gov/research-priorities/rdoc/rdoc-constructs.shtml#frustrative_nonreward (Accessed August 19).

NIMH (2014b). RDoC Constructs: Domain: Social Processes. Retrieved from http://www.nimh.nih.gov/research-priorities/rdoc/rdoc-constructs.shtml#selfknowledge (Accessed August 19).

Olfson, M., Blanco, C., Liu, S.-M., Wang, S., & Correll, C. U., 2012. National trends in the office-based treatment of children, adolescents, and adults with antipsychotics. *Archives of General Psychiatry*, 69(12), pp. 1247–56.

Palmer, R., Nascimento, L. N., & Fonagy, P., 2013. The state of the evidence base for psychodynamic psychotherapy for children and adolescents. *Child and Adolescent Psychiatric Clinics of North America*, 22, pp. 149–214.

Rice, T. R. & Hoffman, L., 2014. Defense mechanisms and implicit emotion regulation: a comparison of a psychodynamic construct with one from contemporary neuroscience. *Journal of the American Psychoanalytic Association*, 62(4), pp. 693–708.

Steiner, H. & Remsing, L., 2007. Practice parameter for the assessment and treatment of children and adolescents with oppositional defiant disorder. *Journal of the American Academy of Child and Adolescent Psychiatry*, 46, pp. 126–41.

Stewart, S. E., 2012. Rage takes center stage: focus on an underappreciated aspect of pediatric obsessive-compulsive disorder. *Journal of the American Academy of Child and Adolescent Psychiatry*, 51(6), pp. 569–71.

Stringaris, A. & Goodman, R., 2009. Longitudinal outcome of youth oppositionality: irritable, headstrong, and hurtful behaviors have distinctive predictions. *Journal of the American Academy of Child and Adolescent Psychiatry*, 48, pp. 404–12.

Stringaris, A., Goodman, R., Ferdinando, S., Razdan V., Muhrer E., Leibenluft E., & Brotman M. A., 2012. The affective reactivity index: a concise irritability scale for clinical and research settings. *Journal of Child Psychology and Psychiatry*, 53(11), pp. 1109–17

Woltering, S., Granic, I., Lamm C., & Lewis, MD., 2011. Neural changes associated with treatment outcome in children with externalizing problems. *Biological Psychiatry*, 70(9), 873–879.

Yanof, J. A., 1996a. Language, communication, and transference in child analysis I. Selective mutism: the medium is the message II. Is child analysis really analysis? *Journal of the American Psychoanalytic Association*, 44, pp. 79–99.

Yanof, J. A., 1996b. Language, communication, and transference in child analysis I. Selective mutism: the medium is the message II. Is child analysis really analysis? *Journal of the American Psychoanalytic Association*, 44, pp. 100–16

Yanof, J. A., 2005. Technique in child analysis. In E. S. Person, A. M. Cooper, & G. O. Gabbard, G. O., eds. *The American Psychiatric Publishing textbook of psychoanalysis*, Washington, DC: American Psychiatric Publishing, Inc., pp. 267–80

Chapter 6

Step 1: introductory meeting with the parents

(May require two meetings)

OUTLINE

A. Goals of the encounter
   1. Establishing a relationship between clinician and parents
      a. Empathic listening as a structuring agent
   2. Receiving the "chief complaint"
      a. Common parental anxieties and empathic listening
      b. Common parental protective measures and clinician responses
      c. Navigating divergences in parental perspectives
      d. Special issues in nontraditional parent families
      e. Role of educational providers and collaterals
      f. Restatement and recapitulation of the chief complaint
   3. Organizing and developing parental concerns
      a. Emphasizing family and child strengths
      b. Discussing areas of difficulties
         i. The parents' ideas of the child's symptoms: "Why now?"
         ii. The parents' conception of the child's ideas about the problem
         iii. The nature of the child's interaction with other people
            1. Inventory of relationships
            2. The "best friend" question
         iv. The nature of the child's cognitive, language, and motor development
         v. Review of clinical psychiatric examination
         vi. Review of symptom inventories
   4. Conclusions
      a. Recapitulations within the model of Malan's Triangle of conflict (provide parents with a copy of Appendix A)
      b. Scheduling two child sessions and a second meeting with parents

        c. Helping the parents to approach the child about the treatment
           i. Structuring within the history of prior discussions with the child
           ii. Professional titles
B. Global goals

A. Goals of the encounter

1. Establishing a relationship between clinician and parents

As in any initial clinical encounter between a patient and a clinician, the major goal of the first encounter is to establish a collaborative relationship between clinician and patient. Having surpassed the hurdles of initial contact, introductions, and scheduling, the first session presents an opportunity for a face-to-face encounter in which the parents are comforted and made confident by the security of this relationship. Following the initial moments of warm social greetings and welcoming to the consultation room, the clinician quickly moves to try to understand why the parents are seeking treatment for their child today.

a. Empathic listening as a structuring agent

Whereas active and directive interventions with parents are avoided as much as possible in RFP-C, interested listening and gentle clarifications are crucial interventions. The parents' experience of the clinician's empathic understanding and contemplation of the parents' concerns further establishes and models the structure of RFP-C.

As the listening proceeds, the clinician conveys the attitude of *trying to understand* what the parents are communicating while restraining from actively judging the nature of the parents' descriptions of their child rearing and interactions with their child or rushing to judging the nature of the child's problems. This approach reinforces the pattern for the parents that the clinician is nonjudgmental, which forms the groundwork for the course of RFP-C.

The clinician will have to pay close scrutiny to how he/she interacts with parents who have problematic attachments as a result of their early traumatic episodes. In such situations, the clinician models an empathic attitude towards the parent (usually the mother) with the aim of helping the mother develop an empathic and mentalizing attitude towards her child. More than two initial meetings with the parents may be required to enable the parents to provide the support necessary for their child to engage in RFP-C.

Dyadic or individual parent work may be invaluable for parents who have attachment difficulties with their child. This mirrors the commonsense statement that parents with major psychiatric (formerly Axis I) disorders may be immensely helped by their own active psychiatric care. In either of these two situations, the RFP-C focus remains on the child's intrapsychic world around defenses/implicit emotion regulation. This maintains the stance that any insult, be it disorganized attachment, major psychiatric illness, or otherwise, are invariably traumatic experiences to the child; empiric research suggests these insults directly impair implicit emotion regulation capacities (Marusak et al. 2015). Work with the parent in these situations is crucial but is outside the child-focused perspective of this manual and perspective. What is most important to the RFP-C is the child, while always remembering that there is no such thing as a child without his/her family and psychosocial context.

Parent work is discussed in greater detail in Chapter 11.

2. Receiving the "chief complaint"

A crucial element in these very first moments of meeting is for the clinician to be totally cognizant of the meaning of the consultation for the parents. This is especially crucial if this meeting is the parents' first encounter with a mental health professional, regardless of whether the parents sought help on their own or a teacher, professional, friend, or relative communicated to them that their child was in trouble and needed professional help.

a. Common parental anxieties and empathic listening

As Martin Silverman (1993) describes with great sensitivity, parents who seek help for their children may feel a great deal of shame, humiliation, anxiety, and concern for themselves and their children in the present and in the future. They may blame themselves, their partner, their child, or their genetic history. In that first encounter, the clinician needs to be mindful that whenever a parent is told by anyone that their child is in some kind of emotional trouble, parents may have a variety of intense reactions. Parents may feel frightened, anxious, and puzzled; they may not even know what questions to ask.

> **Parents who seek help for their children may feel a great deal of shame, humiliation, anxiety, and concern for themselves and their child in the present and in the future.**

b. Common parental protective measures and clinician responses

Parents may communicate a sense of denial, feeling that their child is not the problem. The parent may attribute the problem to a class that is too big, to a teacher who is too strict or too lenient, or to the other children in the class who are "bullies." Since the RFP-C clinician is not omniscient, he/she should not engage in arguments such as: "But the teacher said such and such." Instead the clinician must listen respectfully and try to understand the parents' version of the situation. Certainly, when parents feel coerced to seek help, the RFP-C clinician must be able to establish a collaborative bond with them without appearing to be an adjudicator between the parents' version and that of the school or other social service agency. This discussion of a variety of perspectives about the child may be an opportunity to discuss sources of potential differences between the perspectives of the child, the parents, and any third party. Often, there may be differing perspectives between the parents (see 6.A.2.c). The clinician and the parents can then collaborate on why there may be differing perspectives.

This approach, of *trying to understand*, lays the groundwork for modeling to parents the work of RFP-C, where the clinician tries to understand the nature and origin of the child's maladaptive behavior. By trying to understand the nature of the parents' communication, the clinician models how he/she will try to understand the child and help the parents understand the nature and source of the child's externalizing behavior.

The parents may feel defensive and make comments such as: "But he seems so happy at home," "He plays so well with his best friend," and "She is such a good girl with us." The parents may seem puzzled, asking: "We don't know what the teachers are talking about." They may also blame themselves through statements such as "What did we do wrong?" "Is it because of our divorce?" "Is it because of my illness?" "Is it because I went back to work?" or, "Is it because I travel too much?"

On the other hand, parents may blame the child through statements such as "Why can't he listen?" or "Why does she bully the other girls?" They may blame their own or their partner's genetic inheritance; they may blame the birth process or the activities during pregnancy or early childhood, e.g., "It is because I worked too late."

The nonjudgmental attitude of the RFP-C clinician allays the parents' guilt and anxieties. Negative affects and anxieties are accepted from the parents, metabolized, and returned to the parents in a nonthreatening, processed form: The clinician's calm, warmth, and receptiveness models for the parents the effective emotion regulation capacities that will be helped to developed. Instruction and interpretation of the meaning of the parents' activities are to be avoided; instead, acceptance, emotional validation, reassurance, and a focus on the child organizes and strengthens the parents while allowing the clinician access to consider the underlying parent–child relational problems. Development of the clinician's understanding of such problems enables greater informed listening to the clinical material of the child in later child sessions.

c. Navigating divergences in parental perspectives

The most difficult situations may occur when only one parent feels the need for consultation and the other parent feels that there are no problems or feels that the only problem is with the partner or ex-partner. It is unlikely that a treatment with a young child will succeed if there is active and contentious dissention about the treatment among the primary caretakers, unless the clinician forms a very strong alliance with the one parent who is supportive of the treatment and will proceed with the treatment regardless of the other's objections, which the engaged parent can override though at great cost. With few exceptions, clinicians should make every effort to engage both parents in a positive relatedness towards their child's treatment. Parents may disagree, may blame one another, or may be separated or divorced; however, they must at least try to collaborate for their child's wellbeing, even if they have to meet with the clinician independent of one another. It is important for parents to try to separate their own relational problems from their concern for their child. The clinician can encourage the parents to try to avoid placing the child in a position where he/she is a pawn in parental fights.

RFP-C clinicians need to emphasize that both parents are important for the child regardless of the degree of parental discord. Clinicians should, when needed, wonder out loud how their conflicts with one another can be put aside for the child's benefit. The majority of families are receptive to such gentle guidance. Some parents may not be receptive to such helps, e.g., such as those embroiled in legal conflicts over custody. This may lead to an ongoing impediment to the child's treatment, perhaps making it very difficult, if not impossible for treatment to occur.

d. Special issues in nontraditional parent families

In the United States, 41% of babies are born into families of unmarried parents, a fourfold increase since 1970, and only 63% are raised by two married parents (Angier 2013). Multigenerational families in which maternal or paternal grandparents provide childcare are increasingly common. Four percent of the United States' 1.6 million adopted children live in lesbian, gay, bisexual, or transgender families (Gates et al. 2007). Additionally, one of every 28 children is born to a family in which one parent is incarcerated, up from one in 125 in 1990 (Angier 2013).

The RFP-C clinician must be both familiar with and accepting of these demographic trends. Respect for the family regardless of its form must be communicated verbally and nonverbally whenever the clinician meets with the parents. With single parents, one may observe differences and conflicts between the child's parent and the parent's mother or father or other relative or friend or partner whose emotional and/or financial support is important for the child's parent.

e. Role of educational providers and collaterals

Often, parents may introduce and discuss significant areas of disagreement between their perspectives and those of professionals involved in the child's care, including teachers, school administrators, after-school activity leaders, or social system and legal professionals, including, at times, child protective service professionals. The parents' wishes and expectations for the clinician to discuss their child's care with these collateral informants should be explored and, if parents are supportive of outreach, written consent should be received. If parents can collaborate with the clinician, differences in perspectives that may emerge between the parents and the school or the other third parties may provide an avenue for the clinician to discuss the family constellation and potential areas of stress.

f. Restatement and recapitulation of the chief complaint

At the conclusion of this active process of receiving, organizing, and formulating the chief complaint, the RFP-C clinician should restate the chief parental concerns to the parents in order ensure that he/she has "got it right." While addressing the parent's perception of his/her role in the problem, it is crucial to communicate that problematic symptoms do not arise simply from a parent doing this or that. All behavior and emotion, it should be explained, is a result of complex interactions among a variety of factors: The child's inborn endowment, the parents' responses elicited by the child, the interactions among the various family members, and most importantly the *meaning* imbued on these interactions by the child and parents. The clinician's mode of listening will nonverbally communicate this message; however, explicit statements when helpful are encouraged. These discussions can be an avenue to talk about the stigma parents may feel for seeing a mental health clinician, both for themselves and for their children.

All behavior and emotion are a result of complex interactions among the various family members, including the meaning imbued on these interactions by the child and parents.

---

3. Organizing and developing parental concerns

The clinician's explicit introduction of this central tenet of RFP-C allows the discussion to move beyond initial manifest concerns and into a discussion of the layers of meaning beneath the chief complaint. To support the parents' sense of mastery and accomplishment, the clinician should begin the discussion by emphasizing the child and parents' strengths.

a. Emphasizing family and child strengths

In order to ally with the parents and to create a balanced mental picture of the child, it is crucial that the clinician understand the strengths of the child and the family, and not just the problematic areas. Understanding strengths is important because one goal of any treatment is to promote the parents' and child's coping mechanisms to adapt to stressful states. Eliciting and recognizing areas of strength may provide the clinician with clues as to how to promote the family's resiliency. For example, genuinely empathizing with the difficulties involved in being a single parent can have a profoundly positive impact on the clinician's relationship with the parent. The clinician has to be careful not to be judgmental in situations where the parent exhibits maladaptive defenses to the child's behavioral difficulties, such as thinking that the child's misbehavior is cute. Such parental responses should be mentally noted without comment during the introductory period and stored for later discussion at a time when it would be more helpful for the parent, e.g., when initial anxieties have been allayed and trust in the therapeutic relationship is strong.

The RFP-C clinician should directly ask about the child's activities, his/her likes and dislikes, what he/she enjoys most, activities that the family does together, as well as the child's social interactions, academic interests, and leisure-time interests. Similarly, one should elicit information about the parents' interests and activities. The RFP-C clinician then needs to stress to the parents the importance of positive descriptions of the child, despite the obvious difficulties. For example, the clinician may say: "It sounds like he is a very sociable child." Or, the interviewer may say: "She really loves to play games," or "Most of the time he is so friendly," or "he sounds so smart." Similarly, the clinician needs to elicit and recognize the parents' strengths with comments such as: "You try very hard to deal with the problems," or, in the case of a divorce, "The two of you have really been able to work together for your child's benefit."

Parent and child strengths:

1 In what areas does the child excel?
2 How have the parents coped with problems?
3 What are potential areas that can help promote resiliency?

b. Discussing areas of difficulties

The development and consolidation of the child's strengths serve as segue into the more painful discussion of the child's areas of difficulties. During this initial discussion, there are six general areas that need to be addressed by the clinician as he/she helps the parent think about the child's issues.

I. THE PARENTS' IDEAS OF THE CHILD'S SYMPTOMS: "WHY NOW?"

In trying to understand parental concerns about the child, it is important to try to decipher the question that every RFP-C clinician must ask him/herself: "Why now?" It is important to consider and explore what has triggered the current difficulties in managing the situation. This line of questioning can be very helpful in trying to understand the origin, the child's development, and the particular triggers to the child's maladaptive behaviors.

For example, a teacher may have noted chronic difficulties earlier in the school year, yet the parents may have only sought consultation later in the year. By asking the question "Why now?" the clinician may be able to understand the nature of the situation in the home in the context of recent changes (e.g., illness, marital discord). This discussion may promote the therapeutic alliance and allow parents a way to address the issues in a nondefensive manner. For example, a single parent requested a consultation for her five-year-old boy who had increasing behavioral difficulties. In response to a question about recent changes at home, she responded that her mother, who had helped care for the child, died a few months earlier.

This example illustrates how the clinician may learn of events that parents do not automatically connect to the eruption or exacerbation of a child's symptoms. The clinician's empathic response to the parents' reactions to these events can promote further discussion about the impact on the family and the child.

Care should be given regarding direct interpretation of the nature of the parental reaction since the parent is not the primary patient. For example, in the illustration above, if the clinician senses a depression in a parent and hypothesizes that this reaction of the parent to the grandparent's death is one of several precipitating factors to the child's disruptive behaviors (or perhaps to the decision to seek care as a displaced means of healing hurt and satisfying wishes for gratification), the clinician should ask before make a mental note of this thought and store it for later discussion if and when it would be helpful for the parent to discuss these personal feelings. However, in this introductory session, it is important to discuss with parents that, even though a child may have chronic temperamental difficulties, symptoms often become noticeably worse and therefore unmanageable in response to difficult situations. This highlights the fact that the child's difficulty is associated with managing painful emotions, such as the withdrawal of a depressed parent or the birth of a new sibling.

II. THE PARENTS' CONCEPTION OF THE CHILD'S IDEAS ABOUT THE PROBLEM

What do the parents think is their child's perception of the problem? Parents can be helped to understand the nature of a child's mind and how the child deals with emotion and conflict. Often, children carry fantasies concerning their misbehaviors and their misbehavior's relationship to their inner world. Children's fantasies may reflect internalized messages from parents, teachers, peers, or others and may become tightly intertwined with problems of self-esteem and mood (e.g., as one child said who was the victim of recurrent and insidious abuse, "because I am evil"). Children of various culture backgrounds may understand themselves to be bewitched, cursed, or possessed. Some children with prior exposure to academic psychiatry may build their fantasies upon vague references to neurotransmitters, brain pathways, or brain disease. Some may think they are "crazy," "damaged," or "no good." All these fantasies that the children may share with their families – but which may take many hours before being openly reported to the clinician in session – may be heard in order to understand co-occurring problems in the children. They then can be used to help the parents understand how children's fantasies may be understood as means of coping with the burdens wrought by their disruptive behaviors. Negative or self-derogatory conceptions should be gently redirected and the parents helped to understand that the goal of the treatment will be to help the child cope with their behavioral burdens in more effective, adaptive means.

Broadly and perhaps most importantly, however, parents may find it helpful to consider that most children communicate their complicated feelings indirectly and perhaps in a disguised fashion. Parents should be reminded that unlike adults, most children do not complain directly.

It may be explained that in young children, the kinds of games and play they choose can provide clues as to what is troubling them most. Some children who are very anxious will complain about their worries. Children who are depressed may very well say that they feel sad. Children who express their problems through activity will usually not feel like they have problems and will instead misbehave. This is one of the primary differences between children with internalizing versus externalizing disorders. For example, a six-year-old boy with aggressive behaviors never complained that he was disturbed by his younger sister's birth, yet each time she walked into a room, he drew a line on the floor and insisted that she could not cross over the line to his side of the room. He became uncontrollably enraged whenever she even touched one of his toys.

When eliciting such material from parents, the RFP-C clinician should encourage the parents to develop the material by explicitly asking the parents to consider how the child communicates his/her feelings in the context of such behaviors. In the above example, the clinician might ask: "When your son drew a line, what do you think he might have been feeling or trying to express?" Such explorations by the clinician model reflective functioning skills for the parents that build a foundation for later exploration of the nature and source of oppositional and disruptive behaviors as reactions to uncomfortable or even painful emotional states. As another example, parents may be asked: "Are there any unusual or new behaviors that indicate that he/she is troubled by something, even though he/she does not speak about that directly?"

These gentle clarifications and expansions of the parents' ideas about the child's manifest difficulties lead to greater understanding of the clinical themes to both the clinician and the parents. It models a collaborative sense of exploration, strengthens the alliance when performed gently and empathically, and models for the parents an interchange that may be continued outside of the consultation room for ongoing progress and development.

III. THE NATURE OF THE CHILD'S INTERACTION WITH OTHER PEOPLE

Another area for exploration and development of these capacities may be reached through a discussion of the details of the child's interactions with others.

1. Inventory of relationships Relationships with parents, siblings, relatives, other children, and significant adults may be explored. It is very important to understand the variety of ways a child interacts with different people in his/her life. Are the problems related to specific people, to parents, to teachers, to friends, to siblings? These questions will assist the clinician towards establishing an "inventory of relationships" wherein the clinician may familiarize him/herself with relevant and meaningful external and internal objects in the child's life. A temporal course of the rise and fall of meaningful relationships in the child's life will permit another venue into the introduction of potential triggers to the child's presentation that parents may not recognize prior to their collaborative exploration of these themes. A social and emotional developmental history marked with particular milestones may be developed through this strategy.

2. The "best friend" question A question that should always be considered and asked explicitly is whether the child has a best friend. The parents' answer is one of the most important global indicators of satisfactory emotional health and adjustment. Wilkinson (2010) notes that "the general view is that friends, and best friends in particular, are important to current psychological and relational functioning," especially as children reach middle school and beyond (page 709). Information pertaining to the child's attachment security, the family's permeability to extrafamilial relationships, and the presence of supportive age-appropriate interest and behaviors may be elicited. If parents reply that "everyone is his/her best friend," the RFP-C clinician should inquire further as to the nature of the relationships. Vague responses should trigger the clinician's attention to potential parental anxieties or poor attunement to the child's age-appropriate developmental needs; acceptance, comfort, validation, and clarification will permit more meaningful material to be produced.

IV. THE NATURE OF THE CHILD'S COGNITIVE, LANGUAGE, AND MOTOR DEVELOPMENT

The construction of a social developmental history promotes the transition into the collaborative production of a cognitive and motor developmental history. Parents often have a difficult time understanding the nature of their children's cognitive and motor development. This includes understanding the child's language development, memory, fund of knowledge, ability to understand social situations, and fine motor and gross motor development. Parents do have a sense whether their child's development proceeded smoothly or unevenly as well as how the development compared to the development of siblings or friends. If there is a pediatrician involved with the family whom the parents feel warmly towards and whom they can trust, parents often can be helped to recall significant problems by helping the parents to think back to their well-child visits and revisiting any prior conversations regarding strengths and areas of needed improvement. Parents may be helped to construct the timeline by anchoring specific developmental events to meaningful events in the family, such as the passing of a pet or the celebration of a sibling's graduation. Any histories of involvement with early intervention, speech and language therapy, occupational therapy, physical therapy, or counseling should all be directly inquired about. The clinician has to be very sensitive to the parents' feelings and be aware that these questions may feel like stinging blows, especially if there are some developmental delays.

Additional specific questions may be of use in identifying emotional milestones. These questions may be particularly useful in understanding the presence of anxiety in children of a young age. The clinician may ask whether the child slept with a nightlight or had fears of the dark, and if so, at what age was the nightlight able to be discontinued? With these questions, no affirmative answer is indicative of maladaptive anxiety or emotional immaturity on its own; however, prolonged retention of these anxiety-mitigating childhood objects can be a concrete way to identify deviations in expected development. A child's use of an imaginary friend or friends beyond the early school age years, for example, can be illustrated. Additional items to be asked include whether the child uses a transitional object, such as a blanket or stuffed animal, beyond expected years. Some children may bring such objects into schools and be the target of ridicule, causing social exclusion and missed opportunities for development in other domains. Asking whether the child sucked, or continues to suck, his/her thumb is another helpful question. The clinician has to be sensitive to the cultural mores and the socioeconomic status of families who seek treatment. This is especially true when it comes to understanding the nature of the sleeping arrangements in the family and the weaning and toilet training practices. It is crucial that the clinician not automatically assume that one practice or another is indicative of family psychopathology. Following a review of the milestones, parents should be explicitly asked whether they have any concerns about the endorsed material. Even when deviations from normative development are not appreciated, parents may produce fears and worries over real and imagined losses that provide material for exploration.

V. REVIEW OF CLINICAL PSYCHIATRIC EXAMINATION

In a summary way, the initial meeting with the parents includes the standard format of a clinical psychiatric examination. Material not yet collaboratively produced in the above discussions should be systematically retrieved through adherence to the below formulaic approach to a clinical interview:

Identifying data: This will include living situation, school, and interactions within the family. Identifying the socioeconomic status of the community in which the child lives as well as the physical location of the dwelling in proximity to community resources can be revealing. Understanding the number of bedrooms in an apartment is helpful as well as the number of siblings, extended family members, or frequency of extrafamilial member contact in the child's home. Asking how siblings get along can be helpful. Understanding the child's school, its place in the community, and his/her services at the school can be productive. Is the child in regular or special education? In America, does the child have an Individualized Educational Plan (IEP) under the national Individuals with Disabilities Education Act (IDEA); if so, for what indications? What services are to be provided?

Chief complaint: This will include an understanding of why the parents came at this moment and whose idea it was.

History of present illness: This will include the brief story as to what led to major symptoms leading to the consultation. What were the stressors, triggers, and associated crises?

Past history: This will include a history of medical, psychological, psychiatric, substance use issues, as well as the history of use of any medications (both for physical and for psychiatric problems).

Family history: This will include a question to the parents (if possible), "Can you describe what you were like at your child's current age?"

History of abuse/Administration for Children's Service (ACS) involvement: This should include a discussion of any precipitating events and outcomes. The current status of open cases should be determined, as well as whether parents have been mandated to engage in any remedial action plans. How the family handled any allegations may be illustrative, as well as asking the parent's conceptions of their child's understanding of the events.

Legal/disciplinary history: Any history of expulsions, suspensions, and even detentions should be elicited as a way of gauging functional impairment attributable to disruptive symptoms. In older children, legal charges and convictions may be revealing. When concern for Conduct Disorder is sufficiently elicited, reviewing its constitutive criteria may be revealing and identify significant clusters or patterns of antisocial behaviors.

VI. REVIEW OF SYMPTOM INVENTORIES

As discussed, RFP-C targets children with primary difficulties in affect regulation. These children present with irritability and disruptive behaviors. In categorical systems, they often meet criteria for Disruptive Mood Dysregulation Disorder (DMDD) and Oppositional Defiant Disorder (ODD) (American Psychiatric Association 2013). Dimensionally, these children score high on the Affective Reactivity Index (ARI; see Appendix C; Stringaris et al. 2012). RFP-C clinicians should track the respective constitutive symptom criteria dimensionally. For DMDD, in the contemporary void of specific reliable and valid scales, unmodified DSM-5 diagnostic criteria should be used, with dimensional sampling afforded by the ARI. For ODD, the Oppositional Defiant Disorder Rating Scale

(Hommersen et al. 2006) is recommended. This parent self-report instrument uses a four-point Likert scale for each ODD constitutive criterion to indicate to what extent each of the eight DSM-IV-TR ODD symptoms is specific to the child.

Additional broad range scales, such as a modified version of the clinician-administered Target Symptom Rating Scale (TSRS; see Appendix C; Barber et al. 2002) may be used clinically to monitor symptoms resolution in various domains of functioning. Target symptoms are expected to decrease as a reflection of the broad symptom reduction and as a result of improved affective regulation and implicit emotional regulation. Additional broad-range scales, such as a modified version of the TSRS, may be used to monitor symptoms in various domains of functioning. Target symptoms are expected to decrease as a result of improved affective regulation and implicit emotional regulation. These domains include the degree of Family Conflict (from none to serious); the nature of Peer Relationship Problems (from good to no peer relations); School Difficulties (from none to severe); Depression (from no signs to severe and debilitating); Anxiety (from none to pervasive); Psychosomatic Problems (none to severe, such as asthma); Suicidality (from none to serious plan or attempt); Self-destructive/dangerous Behaviors (from none to severe); Aggression (from none to severely hurting others); Substance Abuse (unlikely in young children but possible in preadolescent children); Psychotic Symptoms (none to serious); Runaway/out of control/legal Problems (unlikely in young children but possible with preadolescents); and Impulsivity (from well controlled to severe and pervasive).

In administering these scales, parents should be informed briefly about their purpose in the context of the total treatment framework. Parents should be made aware of the anticipated readministration of the scales at the conclusion of treatment.

4. Conclusions

The first parent meeting (or second meeting if it is necessary) concludes with a recapitulation of the expressed parental concerns within the model of Malan's Triangle of conflict (Malan 1979). The clinician may then transition to matters of scheduling and structuring the follow-up check-ins and meetings with the parents after the clinician meets the child. He/she concludes with interventions intended to facilitate the transition to the first child session.

a. Recapitulations within the model of Malan's Triangle of conflict
(provide parents with a copy of Appendix A)

At the conclusion of the interview/s, the RFP-C clinician will review the child and family's strengths and formulate the child's difficulties in the language of Malan's Triangle of conflict (see Appendix A for a review of Malan's Triangle that can be given to parents and discussed with them). This model forms the basis of RFP-C, in which the clinician understands disruptive behaviors as maladaptive defenses against painful affects. This will begin with an elicitation from the parents of their ideas about the child's feelings/emotional state at the time of disruptive behaviors. Can the parents conjecture or definitively identify which feeling the child is trying to avoid? For example, is there a feeling of shame if he/she gets a poor mark or does poorly on the athletic field? Can the parents imagine why this feeling is so intolerable for the child? And finally, can the parents understand that the child's disruptive symptoms are ways to cope or deny or avoid the feeling? It would be helpful to understand whether either parent or other important person utilizes the same avoidance pattern.

Malan's Triangle of conflict:

1 WHAT: Feeling (the feared feeling). What is the activating feeling that is being avoided?
2 HOW: Defense (a phobic avoidance reaction). How is the adaptive feeling being avoided?
3 WHY: Anxiety (inhibitory affects). Why is that feeling being avoided? What is the excessive inhibitory affect?

b. Scheduling two child sessions and a second meeting with parents

At the end of the meeting/s, the RFP-C clinician should ask parents for their ideas and further questions. Finally, the clinician will summarize the ideas that emerged in this meeting and arrange for two sessions with the child. The clinician should explain to the parents that he/she will discuss the important issues that emerged in the sessions with the child and then will proceed with the planned treatment.

c. Helping the parents to approach the child about the treatment

Prior to meeting the child, the clinician needs to review with the parents how to present the initial consultations to the child. This is an important step because parents often enough will simply say to the child on the day of the meeting: "Let's go, we have to go someplace." Shame, anxiety, or depression about the situation, or, alternatively, parental anger towards either the child, themselves, one another, or professionals can contribute to the difficulty most parents experience in figuring out what to tell the child about the upcoming meeting with a mental health clinician. It is as if parents' emotional conflicts about the evaluation process interfere with their cognitive and communication skills.

Regardless of the parent's level of sophistication, it is crucial to review with parents how they will approach the child about the consultation. This maxim remains applicable even in cases where parents are themselves mental health clinicians. The clinician will have to be more explicit with the parents with a younger child.

I. STRUCTURING WITHIN THE HISTORY OF PRIOR DISCUSSIONS WITH THE CHILD

It is best to ask parents what words they have used when discussing the child's problems with the child him/herself. One can then guide the parents to use similar words to the child to describe the upcoming meeting with the child.

For example, they can say: "You have seemed very upset recently, so we went to talk with someone who knows about children and their parents" or "We seem to fight so much that we went to see someone who knows how to help children and parents with those kinds of problems" or "Your teacher told us that you are having problems with the other children; we went to speak with someone who knows about children and the problems they have." Each of these examples communicates a reassuring invitation to the child to proceed with the treatment. Parents should be encouraged to communicate as directly and as nonjudgmentally as possible, even if they are very angry or depressed.

II. PROFESSIONAL TITLES

Parents should know that most children will ask: "Who is this person?" The main theme that should be communicated to the child is that the clinician is a person who listens to parents and children in order to help them with any problems that they may have. The parents can then describe how they got to the clinician: From their pediatrician, from a relative, from a friend, or from their clinic doctor, being as specific as possible using names the child might or should know. The parents then need to add, especially with younger children, that so-and-so is a nice person and spoke very nicely with them. Parents can explain that the clinician has toys and a playroom and that he/she plays and talks with children. With older children, parents should use direct descriptions, such as therapist, psychiatrist, psychologist, or social worker. Some parents use the appellation "talking doctor," "worry doctor," or "play doctor." With young children, it may be important to add that the clinician is not the kind of doctor who examines children nor give shots to them.

Some parents will automatically call the clinician by his/her first name to their child; others by title and last name; others by title and first name or last initial. The clinician needs to identify him/herself in a way that feels comfortable as well as professional. The clinician should limit calling parents by their first names, but the clinician should always agree if parents want to use the clinician's first name and/or they want the clinician to use their first names, being clear about professional boundaries.

B. Global goals

The key to the initial meeting is that the parents need to feel comfortable with the clinician. They need to feel reassured with his/her competence, and most importantly that the clinician seems to understand the nature of the child's problems. The specific goals of the initial encounter listed in this manual are designed to foster this sense of security and structure at the outset of the treatment.

Additional "global goals" describing warm and empathic characteristics of the RFP-C clinician must be met. Their attainment and maintenance throughout the treatment is of primary importance. Their achievement should not be compromised in an attempt to meet all of the above specific goals in one parent meeting. When indicated, the RFP-C clinician may postpone or defer a specific goal when concerns are evoked about the quality of the clinician–parental relationship. An additional parental meeting to accomplish the specific goals should then be scheduled prior to the first session with the child.

The first global goal entails the pursuit of a nonjudgmental manner with parents. When clinicians experience judgmental feelings towards parents, often there are countertransference issues at play. These feelings should not be verbalized or introduced into the treatment. Instead, the clinician should acknowledge their presence to him/herself, accept the feelings, and use them to better understand the contributing factors to their development as well as strategies to correct any underlying relational issues. When immediate solutions cannot be found, the RFP-C clinician should hold on to these feelings for later consideration through the use of various professional supports (see below).

A second global goal entails the establishment of a strong alliance with parents. In RFP-C, an alliance is best fostered when the value of the real relationship between the parents and the clinician is acknowledged and respected. As role models and emotional guideposts for the child, parents are crucial to the child's life and are needed to maintain the treatment. Just as crucial as the alliance with the child, the parental alliance is needed to help support their child in the treatment.

The presentation of a warm, collaborative attitude is a third global goal. Applications of concepts of anonymity, neutrality, and abstinence must be limited and not set the tone for the encounter. Parents' contributions and needs must be taken into account in the formulation of a collaborative treatment plan.

A fourth and fifth global goal involves empathy. The RFP-C clinician must empathize with parents' feelings about the child's difficulties in a nonjudgmental manner. These will often include frustrations and other negative feelings. Similarly, the clinician must empathize with the parents' feelings about seeking consultation for their child. As aforementioned, various emotions may be experienced at intense levels by the parents, including shame, guilt, and rage. The clinician must be able to tolerate these strong feelings and help the family to process them effectively.

RFP-C clinicians develop these comforting capacities through clinical experience and introspection. Consultation with colleagues, supervision, study groups, and one's own personal work in psychotherapy may be of additional help.

> "When we left your office, we felt so hopeful because 'you got it.'"
> A therapeutic connection between clinician and parents is essential in order to promote a therapeutic connection between clinician and child.

Bibliography

American Psychiatric Association, 2013. *Diagnostic and statistical manual of mental disorders*, 5th edition., Washington, DC: Author.

Angier, N., 2013. The changing American family. *The New York Times*. November 26. Retrieved from http://www.nytimes.com/2013/11/26/health/families.html?_r=0

Barber, C.C. et al., 2002. The target symptom rating: a brief clinical measure of acute psychiatric symptoms in children and adolescents. *Journal of Clinical Child and Adolescent Psychology : The Official Journal for the Society of Clinical Child and Adolescent Psychology, American Psychological Association, Division*, 53, 31(2), pp. 181–92.

Gates, G., Lee, M.V., Badgett, J.E, & Macomber, K.C., 2007. *Adoption and foster care by gay and lesbian parents in the United States*, Washington, DC: Urban Institute.

Hommersen, P. et al., 2006. Oppositional defiant disorder rating scale: preliminary evidence of reliability and validity. *Journal of Behavioral and Emotional Disorders*, 14, pp. 118–25.

Malan, D., 1979. *Individual psychotherapy and the science of psychodynamics*, London: Butterworth.

Marusak, H.A. et al., (2015). Childhood trauma exposure disrupts the automatic regulation of emotional processing. *Neuropsychopharmacology: Official Publication of the American College of Neuropsychopharmacology* (epub before print).

Silverman, M., 1993. Working with parents at the beginning of treatment. In H.M. Etezady, ed. *Treatment of neurosis in the young: a psychoanalytic perspective*. Northvale, NJ: Jason Aronson, pp. 9–17.

Stringaris, A. et al., 2012. The affective reactivity index: a concise irritability scale for clinical and research settings. *Journal of Child Psychology and Psychiatry, and Allied Disciplines*, 53(11), pp. 1109–17.

Wilkinson, R.B., 2010. Best friend attachment versus peer attachment in the prediction of adolescent psychological adjustment. *Journal of Adolescence*, 33, pp. 709–17.

Chapter 7

Step 1: sessions 1 and 2
Initial sessions with the child

OUTLINE

A. First session with the child
1. Initial moments of meeting: creation of atmosphere, child unburdening, clinician listening
2. First question
3. The play environment
   a. Suitable toys
   b. Internet and computer activities
4. Unstructured techniques
   a. The stylistic contrast with social play
   b. Finding meaning in the play (What is the communicative intent of the play?)
      i. Caution against uncorroborated readings of the meaning of the play
   c. Attending to patterns, repetitions, and play disruptions
      i. Play disruptions as attempts at implicit emotional regulation
   d. Performance in relation to goals
   e. Theoretical organization and importance of the early encounters
   f. Setting the rules of the space
   g. Recognizing other defensive maneuvers
5. Structured techniques
   a. Draw anything and dictate a story to the clinician
   b. Draw a family
   c. Draw a person
   d. When the child declines
   e. Three wishes
   f. Lost in a forest and going to the moon
   g. Born over again
6. Summary
7. Clinical example 1: Brenda: a girl reticent to communicate
8. Clinical example 2: Henry: an overtly negativistic boy

B. Second session with the child
  1. Rationale and goals for the second session
  2. Clinical example 3: Stacy: a child whose externalizing behaviors could not be explored until the second session
     a. Rationale and when to allow a parent into the consultation room
     b. Attend to communication in displacement
     c. Attend to separation anxiety manifestations
     d. Attend to punishment anxiety manifestations
     e. Refrain from giving direction
     f. Attend to repetitive themes
     g. Identify moments of obsessive play
     h. Identify moments of discontinuity in the play
     i. Attend to interactions surrounding wanting to leave or to stay
     j. Put limits on disruptive behavior when safety becomes threatened
     k. Identify moments of transference
C. Conclusions
D. Global Goals
  1. Approaching in a nonjudgmental manner
  2. Establishing an alliance with child
  3. Presenting a warm, collaborative attitude
  4. Empathizing with child's feelings about the child's difficulties
  5. Empathizing with child's feelings about coming to consultation

A. First session with the child

The atmosphere created by the clinician, the clinician trying to touch on the patient's wish to unburden him/herself, and the clinician's careful listening often results in a revelatory first meeting with a child. As with adults, the clinician conveys a tone of respect and acceptance, allowing the child to communicate stories in his/her own way and her/his own pace with the clinician paying close attention and listening carefully. This atmosphere of safety and acceptance allows the child's concerns to emerge spontaneously. In addition, the parents' comfort with the clinician, with whom they have discussed the child's problems are inevitably communicated to the child by the parents (verbally and/or nonverbally). This greatly improves the chances that the child will develop a positive alliance with the clinician.

1. Initial moments of meeting: creation of atmosphere, child unburdening, clinician listening

Some children may be frightened to come into the playroom or office and speak with a stranger. Others will insist that a parent enter the playroom or consulting room with them. Some may enter the playroom or consulting room easily. This point of separation between parent and child allows the clinician to observe the nonverbal communications that occur between parent and child. Does the parent encourage autonomy or implicitly encourage greater clinginess on the part of the child? Does the parent communicate comfort or anxiety to the child? It is best for the clinician to greet the child in the waiting area, introduce him/herself, and shake the child's hand both as a greeting as well as a sign of respect. The handshake suggests that the clinician considers and treats the child the way one adult would greet another adult (regardless of the age of the child). This act by the clinician communicates an important message to the parents and child: The clinician thinks of the child as his/her own person and not simply an extension of the parents. The clinician may say to a young child: "Come in and I will show you the toys I have." Once in the play/consultation room, the clinician shows the child the toys in the room, invites him/her to play and/or sit and talk, at first chatting about familiar and neutral topics, such as how he/she came to the office, where does he/she live, or what fun things the child has done recently? It is important to note that, throughout the treatment, it is important for the clinician to interact with a child in a friendly supportive manner, including playing games or activities and chatting about everyday neutral topics to solidify the bond between clinician and patient.

> **Throughout the treatment, it is important for the clinician to interact with a child in a friendly supportive manner, including playing games or activities and chatting about everyday neutral topics to solidify the bond between clinician and patient.**

2. First question

Early in the interaction, even with the most disruptive children, the clinician can ask the child what the parent/s said about the clinician and the reason for coming to the session. If the child responds affirmatively and factually to these questions, the clinician can then ask about the child's opinion about these ideas and invite the child to talk about them, with the clinician following the child's lead.

Many children, particularly very young ones, respond to this question by saying that no one told them why they were coming, nor did they know who the clinician was. The clinician could then say "Your mom/dad told me . . ." Or, "I am the kind of doctor/person who helps children with . . ." (With either phrase, the clinician should name a problem that the parents have reported in developmentally appropriate language, e.g., "worries" or "anger.") Younger children will often avoid any discussion and immediately turn to a play activity. Older children may engage in a discussion. The clinician needs to follow the child's lead and make mental notes of many things, including the nature of the child's language and communications, the nature of his/her play and activity, the closeness and distance from the clinician, the openness with which the child communicates, and his/her ability to tolerate separation from the parents, who usually wait in the waiting area. During the initial meeting, the clinician evaluates the child's mental status through a formal mental status examination, including how the child appears, the level of impulsivity and hyperactivity of his/her behavior, his/her affect state and how this state affects behavior, how developed is his/her play as a manifestation of thought content, and how organized and logical is his/her thinking.

Most importantly, in evaluating the thought content, the clinician notes to him/herself whether there are any topics that are deliberately avoided by the child. For example, does the child refuse to say anything about his/her school or home life, parents or siblings, or friends? Such avoidance may be a sign of implicit emotional regulation (that the child is avoiding a topic that would cause too much discomfort).

It is important to note that during sessions with a child it is more useful not to take notes. Towards the end of the first couple of sessions, it may be valuable to spend a couple of minutes with the child reviewing with the child the important areas covered and jotting them down together, noting which topics would be valuable to discuss further, which to share with the parents and which not. In contrast, during the early consultation with the parents, note-taking is valuable to ensure that important issues are noted and not forgotten. Usually all patients are much more revelatory during early sessions with a clinician and more defended in subsequent sessions. Thus, although the clinician may not appreciate fully the nuanced significance of the early communications from parents and children, most often, central psychological themes are clearly outlined which direct the course of the treatment.

Early in the interaction, even with the most disruptive children, the clinician needs to ask the child what the parent/s told him/her about the clinician and what they said about why he/she is coming to see the clinician.

The clinician could say, "Your mom/dad told me . . ." or, "I am the kind of doctor/person who helps children with . . ." (With the clinician naming some problem that the parents reported.)

A key element in the technique of RFP-C is following the child's lead: Important themes will emerge in the early sessions.

When a child avoids a topic, the clinician should consider that the child is avoiding a topic that would cause too much discomfort. This may be a sign of implicit emotional regulation.

3. The play environment

Children, of course, communicate through play and activities and not just with words. Play is fun, not only for children, but for parents and children to share – a means by which children develop skills critical to their development. Through play, children learn how to interact with other people, express their emotions, master conflicted feeling states, and cultivate a variety of developmental skills (sensory, motor, and cognitive) (e.g., Pellegrini & Smith 1998 and Chazan 2002). Although often overlooked, play is especially effective in helping children develop their capacities to symbolize – that is, to be able to represent one thing (such as an image or an idea) by another. These capacities to symbolize are critical to enable children to learn to cope with emotions and situations that they are trying to master.

As with adults, children react to trauma in their own personal way. Play allows them to assimilate an event and master its potential traumatic effects. However, one has to bear in mind that inferences about the meaning of play can only be tentative unless corroborated. Sometimes the symbolic meaning is transparent and at other times it is not. By observing young children play over a period of time, one may recognize patterns, repetitions, and play disruptions. Repetitive themes and/or moments of disruptions in the play, in particular, provide clues to those emotional issues that children are trying to cope with and master. These issues may be personal, such as feeding, toileting, or mastery of separation; environmental (i.e., events that occur in the child's daily life); or, as often is the case, a mixture of various issues.

a. Suitable toys

Children four to eight years of age often play imaginative games, such as with a family doll or superhero games. Children in the later elementary school years and early middle school years play more structured games (e.g., board, computer, art, or ball games) while chatting. Older children are more likely to focus on talking.

It is, therefore, important to have a supply of toys and games available: Paper, pencils, crayons or markers, playing cards, a small selection of board games, dolls (both genders), superheroes, soft balls, cars, blocks and Legos, as well as a version of a doll-house where the child has an opportunity to set up family scenes.

b. Internet and computer activities

Computer and internet activities can be too engrossing and distracting for the child, and therefore should usually be avoided. Some children bring their handheld computer games. The clinician can engage with the child through his/her device in order to form a bond with the child. If the child's focus on the handheld device becomes entrenched, the clinician should address with the child how his/her focus on the device protects him/her from difficult thoughts and feelings. This technique may effectively reduce the amount of focus on the video game.

4. Unstructured techniques

a. The stylistic contrast with social play

The nature of the play and verbal interaction between a clinician and a child is very different from the play with other adults or with the play in a school or after-school setting. In these latter situations, the child is more or less accustomed to follow certain social convention, including turn-taking, reciprocation, sharing, and, in older children, abiding to rules. Most children enter the play space with the clinician having the idea that the play and verbal interaction will be similar to his/her play interactions with other adults. In the clinical setting, the clinician may want to ascertain the level of the play activity by the child. However, the goal of the play/activity interaction *is not* to directly help the child play more adaptively or more developmentally appropriately. This is a critical point. At times, the child may want to play in an interactive way, directing the adult as to what to do. At other times, the child will expect the adult to simply sit and watch the child play, without the adult's active participation. In RFP-C, the clinician utilizes the child's play activity for ***its communicative intent***, to learn about the child and the issues that are most important for the child. The primary clinical goal is to ***ascertain which issues are too emotionally difficult for the child***.

Play in the therapeutic setting:

It is not social play.
What is its communicative intent?
What issues are too emotionally difficult for the child?

It is important to stress that play and activity are both the work and the language of childhood. Through play, children interact with other people, express their emotions, master conflicted feeling states, and master various developmental skills: Sensory, motor, and cognitive. Play is fun as well as central to a child's development.

It is crucial to bear in mind that all behavior, including play, has meaning. For example, children play out themes that refer to their lives. As with adults, children react to potential traumatic experiences in their own personal way. Play allows them to assimilate the event and master its potential traumatic effects.

b. Finding meaning in the play (What is the communicative intent of the play?)

I. CAUTION AGAINST UNCORROBORATED READINGS OF THE MEANING OF
THE PLAY

However, the clinician has to be aware that conclusions about the meaning of the play for a particular child at a particular time can only be a conjecture unless corroborated. It may be very difficult to corroborate that a play sequence has a particular personal symbolic meaning for the child. For example, children love to build blocks and knock them down. When this play occurred repetitively after 9/11, one could tentatively hypothesize that the play was an attempt to master the fears provoked by the Twin Towers being knocked down. At other times, one would have to get corroborating evidence to understand the symbolic meaning, if any, of the play. If a child plays with two dolls fighting with one another, one could surmise that the child is repeating some fighting that he/she observed, but, one can never be sure. The clinician has to be extremely careful about labeling the conjectured symbolic meaning of the play.

> **The clinician has to be extremely careful about labeling the conjectured symbolic meaning of the play.**

When observing a child depict fighting between two characters, the clinician can be curious about it ("Oh, what's going on?"), while being cautious about either asking the child about real-life fighting that he/she has observed or participated in or translating arbitrarily that the play has some meaning connected to the child's life. Rather, the clinician can observe the evolution of the child's play to ascertain if there are patterns, repetitions, and disruptions, which may provide a clue as to the real-life or internal issue with which the child is trying to cope and master.

c. Attending to patterns, repetitions, and play disruptions

By observing young children play over a period of time, one will recognize patterns, repetitions, and play disruptions. Repetitive themes and moments of disruptions in the play provide clues to those emotional issues with which children are trying to cope and master, such as by avoiding particular play scenes. This technique of observing patterns eliminates the dangers of guessing the meaning of the child's play and other communication.

> **Observing the patterns of the child's play, especially disruptions in the play, provides clues about the important issues for the child and eliminates the dangers of guessing the meaning of the child's play and other communication.**

This is the central tenet of RFP-C – observing the pattern of the child's verbal and nonverbal productions and, in particular, the times when there is a disruption in the flow of the child's communication are the key to understanding which emotions are being avoided.

> **Repetitive themes and/or moments of disruptions in the play, in particular, provide clues to those emotional issues with which children are trying to cope and master.**

I. PLAY DISRUPTIONS AS ATTEMPTS AT IMPLICIT EMOTIONAL REGULATION

By observing when disruptions occur (in the child's play, in his/her words, and/or in his/her behavior), the clinician begins to decipher:

1. The *topics* of discussion or play that provoke a disruption.
2. The *emotion* inherent in the topic that provokes a disruption.
3. The *nature* of the child's activity, play, or verbalization when he/she changes the topic.
4. And, over time, *why* the avoided emotion is so disturbing that it always needs to be circumvented.

> **In RFP-C, the clinician tries to observe instances when the child tries to distance him/herself from topics that provoke potentially painful emotional states.**

Throughout the treatment, in RFP-C, the clinician tries to understand when and how the child shifts away from topics that provoke potentially painful emotional states. Children with a variety of externalizing behaviors often utilize behavioral disruptions as mechanisms to avoid elaborating on play, behavior, or verbalizations that may provoke unbearable emotions, such as sadness or shame. In RFP-C, the clinician tries to observe instances when the child tries to distance him/herself from or avoid potentially painful emotional states.

A basic premise discussed earlier in this volume is that a central task in development is the regulation of emotions that help the child adapt to his/her environment, particularly coping with those situations that inherently provoke stress. Children with externalizing behaviors do not have sufficient internal strength to tolerate the pain and anxiety of disturbing emotional states. Without the ability to tolerate pain and anxiety, they have a difficult time mastering the stressors of everyday life and may not be able to master the usual demands of childhood. Events with even greater emotional valence such as separations, the birth of siblings, and parental discord will be even more difficult for the child to effectively manage.

All people at various times in their life, especially during very stressful moments, utilize the defense mechanism of denial. In fact without a certain amount of denial it would be impossible to successfully respond to many of the everyday challenges of one's environment. Children with externalizing behaviors, from early life, are highly reactive and easily frustrated and difficult for parents to aid in the development of their emotion regulation capacities. Thus, they continue to primarily utilize denial in preference to more mature defense mechanisms when confronted with events that others would not be experienced as overwhelming.

d. Performance in relation to goals

An important goal of RFP-C is to increase the child's ability to tolerate and adaptively process painful emotional states (in our model, to facilitate the developmental maturation of implicit emotion regulation capacities). By so doing, the child experiences greater mastery and feels more confident in his/her abilities.

From the very first contact with the child, the clinician should attempt to ascertain:

1 Which areas the child feels comfortable discussing or playing.
2 Which areas the child wants to avoid.
3 How the child avoids discussion or playing out of those scenes that are too painful to address.

From the beginning of the treatment, the clinician needs to attend to instances when the child disrupts the flow of the play, behavior, and speech. The goal is to increase the child's ability to tolerate and process the painful state precipitating the disruption, thereby minimizing disruptive and violent behaviors.

e. Theoretical organization and importance of the early encounters

The best defense is a good offense.

This is the motto, in one way or another, of most children with externalizing behaviors. These are children who are frightened but cannot show it to themselves or others. They fear humiliation or communicating weakness, and they are anxious about being shamed if they expose vulnerable parts of themselves. All of these feelings are difficult for them to tolerate consciously. When discussions with the clinician threaten the children's feelings of omnipotence or omniscience, they may experience the discussions as attacks because they provoke feelings of humiliation, shame, and weakness. Thus, when they feel signs that these feelings may emerge in their consciousness they may attack or disrupt proactively. For example, when called on by a teacher and the child is concerned that he/she will appear "stupid," the child can immediately become disruptive rather than answer the question or simply say, "I don't know." Or, he/she may act like a clown.

Coming to a clinician for the first time engenders a significant amount of anxiety in a child who is prone to feel humiliated because he/she is concerned that the areas of weakness (*which the child needs to deny*) will be revealed to the clinician. From the discussions with the parent/s, the clinician gleans the areas that are potentially problematic for the child. When those areas first emerge in discussion with the child, the child will undoubtedly deny any problems in that area. This protective device of denial allows the child to maintain a false sense of grandiosity, but it is certainly maladaptive because it prevents the child from effectively responding to the demands of his/her life. The child must instead resort to maladaptive defensive maneuvers, such as disruptive behaviors, or fall into a state of disorganized dysregulation in lieu of more activating and more developmentally advanced implicit or explicit emotion regulation capacities, such as humor, reappraisal, or sublimation.

The child needs to deny signs of weakness, failure, humiliation.

Early in the treatment, it is important not to interfere with the child's denial because the child may experience attempts by the clinician to discuss the patient's denial as an attack. Instead, the clinician should promote the development of a solid therapeutic alliance with the child by chatting about nonthreatening areas and allowing the child to play and interact with the clinician in a positive manner.

f. Setting the rules of the space

Most children enter the first session in a calm way. Only the most frightened will immediately express disruptive behaviors in the first meeting. Such children pose a challenge to the clinician since he/she will have difficulty fully understanding the nature of the internal trigger to the disruptive behavior when it occurs so quickly. The most important task at those early moments in the treatment is to ensure that no harm comes to the clinician, to the child, or to the materials in the office and that the clinician communicates to the child that his/her **disruptive behavior has meaning**.

Disruptive behavior has meaning.

If a disruption occurs, the clinician needs to explain the rules of the space while addressing the child's behavior:

"In this space you can play with any of the toys and you can tell me in words any thoughts and feelings you have. I guess it is hard for you to tell me in words the feelings you have about being here for the first time. Maybe you can later. But here we are not allowed to do things that are hurtful to either of us or to the things here. If things get out of hand, I will help us to keep safe."

At times, children may respond to such a comment. They may say, for example, that they did not know why they have to come to the clinician. In response, the clinician might remind them of their discussion in their first moments of meeting. Or, they may say that they were afraid that something bad was going to happen. In response, the clinician might remind them that they will help the child to help keep things safe. At other times, they may not respond at all but continue in a safer activity or discussion.

> **When a child is disruptive during the first session, the clinician needs to set limits while also communicating that the disruptive behavior has meaning.**

g. Recognizing other defensive maneuvers

From the first session, children may also use a variety of other maneuvers to avoid addressing topics that may provoke painful emotions: Silence, screaming, putting their hands over their ears, turning their back to the clinician, burying their faces, falling asleep, making fun of the clinician, or walking out of the session.

When these actions occur, the clinician should simply say something like: "You are showing me how hard it is to talk about . . .", or, "how hard it is to listen to me talk about . . ." A child may respond by saying: *"That's enough talking about that. Let's go back and just play."* The clinician might simply say at that moment, *"It's too hard to talk about [naming the actual subject]"* and engage in the activity or discussion desired by the child.

> **Children use a variety of maneuvers to avoid addressing topics that elicit painful emotions.**

As one listens and plays with the child during the first meeting, the clinician can ask questions to fill in the story in order to ascertain a picture of the central dynamics operative in the child's mind, including a global sense of the child's strengths and difficulties. However, by following the child's lead and the child's responses to a clinician's intervention, the clinician will observe those topics and situations that provoke disruption.

> **Throughout RFP-C, from the very first session, the clinician must be aware of disruptions in the play and/or verbalizations.**

5. Structured techniques

In the first or second session, as the clinician is getting to know the child, a variety of potential avenues of exploration may be utilized. If a child is conversing freely about him/herself and his/her life or openly playing out clear themes about his/her life, such structured questions may not be necessary. However, if in doubt, with children who either do not play spontaneously or are slow to talk very much about themselves, it is better to err on the side of asking some structured questions in order to come to a better understanding about the issues that are troubling to the child.

a. Draw anything and dictate a story to the clinician

Ask the child to draw a picture of anything he/she wants. Most children eagerly draw a scene from their lives, a movie, or video game. Some are puzzled and may need prompting about possible scenes. Some negativistic children will draw a dot, a squiggle, or a line and say, teasingly: "That's it." Whereas the clinician may wish to defer naming this defensive maneuver in the early work of the treatment, he/she may wish to take a mental note of the defense and proceed with other structured techniques to which the child may produce additional material (see this chapter, A.5.d). The clinician may ask the child to put his/her name and the date on the paper and have a valuable means of attaining a sense of the child's fine motor capacities, orthography, fund of knowledge (knowledge of left and right, months, years, and calendar conventions), and orientation to time. The clinician may ask the child to dictate a story about the picture that the clinician writes down in front of them, regardless of what they drew. Often times, the stories are revealing of the issues of concern to the child, such as:

"A child is about to fall with a hand reaching out for him but unable to grab and protect the child."

b. Draw a family

The clinician may ask the child to draw a picture of a family. Often, the directive to restrict the content of the drawing from "anything" to "a family" is conducive to mitigating the child's anxiety and effecting a production of material. If the child asks whether it should be his/her family, it can be useful to say, "Any family." Some children draw their own family, others a make-believe family, a family of animals or robots, or a family from a movie or TV show. One can learn about the child's perceptions of his/her family from the placement of the figures, which member the child draws first – an admired older sibling, a protective parent, or a teacher. Isolated children may simply draw themselves. Where each family member is placed on the page can be revealing. Who is next to whom? Are there members of the family missing? Is the father absent? Is the hated sibling omitted from the drawing? Who is the largest figure? Who is the smallest? When asked to tell a story about the family, some children tell a benign, happy story, some a dark story. Many children may actually communicate some critical issue from their lives.

c. Draw a person

At times, it might be valuable to ask a child to draw a person ("any person"). Most children will draw a person of the same gender and age. One then asks the child to draw a person of the opposite gender and ask the child to label how he/she distinguishes male from female. The most common response in young children is the amount of hair. If there are issues surrounding gender dysphoria, this drawing may provide valuable clues.

Observing how a child draws a person can provide the clinician with a rough estimate of the child's mental age, depending on the number of body parts and details (Goodenough 1926). A rating scale and manual (Harris 1963) can be used to reliably rate drawings and give a rough indication of the child's intelligence. Other rating scales and manuals, such as that of Koppitz (1968), can be employed to explore developmental and emotional indicators to supplement the material derived from the clinical encounter.

d. When the child declines

If a child declines to do any of these activities, the clinician should demur and go on, while hypothesizing *only* in his/her mind why the child declined. Is it a result of some cognitive difficulty that the child is embarrassed to expose? Is the child frightened? Is the child being negativistic, refusing to follow instructions? This information in the clinician's mind can be useful in the ongoing work to generate hypotheses to be corroborated or discarded as the work proceeds.

e. Three wishes

Asking the child some standard questions can generate important emotional material about the child. Ask the child if he/she had three wishes, what would he/she wish for? Frequently, the responses are standard responses connected to some present that the child wants. However, often enough, the child will wish for peace or no war (perhaps communicating that there is too much fighting in his/her environment), the child may wish for a father to return home, or a mother to get healthy. Some children get into an obsessive loop of wanting a million and a million more wishes. Such children may feel very needy or may have a difficult time revealing private thoughts.

f. Lost in a forest and going to the moon

Two additional and related useful questions entail "If you could pretend that you were lost in a forest, who would come look for you?" and "If you could pretend that you had to go to the moon and could take one person with you, who would you take?" Some concrete children answer "an astronaut because he can fly me there." Some children who feel unprotected would say that no one would come to look for them; if a parent does not come looking for a younger child or the parent does not call the police but someone else, one has to question the child's feelings about the parents' reliability. Some children say that they would find their way out by themselves or with the help of a compass, perhaps indicating grandiosity and intellectualization, respectively. The person the child takes to the moon is often the person to whom the child feels closest. If a child says he/she would take no one to the moon, the clinician, of course, has to wonder about the nature of his/her relationships to other people, whether the child has a genuine friendship, or whether the child needs to deny any close connections.

g. Born over again

With young children, the clinician might ask, "Pretend you were born over again. What would you like to be born as?" Most children say themselves, giving their current age. Some say they would like to be a baby, the opposite gender, some an older age, or an animal (a powerful one like a tiger or a placid one like a sweet kitten). All of these answers can provide a clue as to the child's sense of him/herself as well as what he/she wishes he/she could be. The clinician may want to ask follow-up questions in response (e.g., "What would life be like if you were a tiger?").

6. Summary

A. The clinician, implicitly and/or directly, communicates a welcoming, respectful demeanor, ready to play with and listen to the child.
B. The child may present him/herself in a variety of ways – anxiety about coming to meet a stranger; reluctance to play with the stranger; needing an adult to enter the playroom; eagerness to play with particularly toys; or, less commonly, immediate direct expression of oppositional disruptive symptoms.
C. During the initial meetings, the clinician allows the child, as much as possible, to take the lead in choosing activities and topics for discussion.
D. At times, it may be necessary to have a structured part of the interview to elicit salient emotional issues and to elicit a global impression of the child's cognitive functioning.

E. Throughout the free play, the clinician observes for repetitive themes – repetitive themes indicate central issues in the child's mind.
F. The clinician tries to observe shifts in the play – from one activity to another; stopping play; wanting to leave the session.
G. The clinician observes shifts in topics of conversation – when the child no longer wants to talk about a particular topic.
H. From these very first sessions, the clinician could point out to the child the shifts that occur.
I. The clinician should be particularly cognizant of behaviors occurring with the clinician him/herself, especially if they are similar to the disruptive interactions that occur at home or at school; for example, getting into a fight with the clinician or trying to hurt him/her, or wanting to leave the play room.
J. Addressing those interactions – simply pointing them out – from the beginning sets the stage for the later central work of addressing in an in-depth way the patterns that occur between the clinician and the patient.

7. Clinical example 1: Brenda: a girl reticent to communicate

A five-year-old girl, Brenda, lived with her mother, older sister, and baby brother. The mother felt overwhelmed by Brenda's not listening at home, and reports from the school stated that Brenda was obstinate and disruptive.

At the first meeting, Brenda was clearly shy and was hesitant to come into the playroom, but after a short time was able to leave her mother in the waiting room. The clinician waited, allowing the child to take the lead. Eventually, the clinician reached out with two decks of cards, a regular deck and an UNO deck. The clinician showed the cards to her, and she nodded that she would play UNO. Even when a reticent child resists making a first choice, subsequent behavior by the clinician may allow the child to express some initiation of activity, as occurred here.

Brenda and the clinician sat on the floor and started to play cards; it was clear that she did not know the rules of the game and instead, they made piles of the various colors. Unlike with conventional play, the aim here was not to adhere to the games rules, nor teach the child the game, nor the rules of reciprocal social play. She identified all of the colors and placed them into correct piles of colors. There were three piles with an obvious space for the fourth color. When the fourth color came up she wondered where to put that pile; and put it outside of where one would naturally put the fourth pile. In the square-like construction below, the card with the fourth color is labeled "Y."

X   X
x   X   Y

The clinician asked her where else she might have put it, and she said further to the right. The clinician responded that she could have put it in the more symmetrical place (small x); Brenda did not respond.

The inference from this interaction was that Brenda saw herself outside of a group, perhaps unprotected. It was difficult to imagine that the spatial set-up was a result of some neurocognitive problem, or even a creative solution to a constitutional impairment, but of course such possibilities have to be considered if further evidence can be obtained. The clinician always has to remain vigilant and consider potential inherited contributions, such as temperamental and neurocognitive considerations, in understanding the play behavior.

After they played with the cards for a while, with very little verbal communication, the clinician asked her to draw a picture of anything she liked, the clinician's usual routine in the first session as described above. She drew a happy face. And, the clinician asked her to tell a story about it; instead of speaking, Brenda drew a girl. The clinician asked her to tell a story about the girl and Brenda drew a boy.

As there was a history about being seductive in school, the clinician wondered to himself, without saying anything, whether the immediate connection between a girl and a boy implied the presence of sexualized fantasies. At this point, the clinician was applying the RFP-C protocol by observing patterns, without communicating conjectures to the girl.

The clinician asked Brenda to tell a story about the girl and the boy, and Brenda drew a geometric figure. The clinician kept asking Brenda to tell stories about whatever she drew, and Brenda kept drawing figures or letters, getting increasingly excited, bordering on the out-of-control behaviors described by the teachers. Eventually her pencil accidentally flew out of her hands, and she said it was a rocket ship and she drew a rocket ship.

The clinician took this opportunity to ask her the standard structured questions, starting by asking Brenda who she would take to the moon on a rocket ship. Brenda said that she would take a boy from her class and then said the whole class; that that same boy/class would come looking for her if she were lost in a forest; and that if she had three wishes, she would ask for "everything" but would not be specific. She did not respond to the question about being born over again. The absence of parental figures in any of these images was notable.

The clinician asked who lived at home. She said, she, her mom, and dad. Since the clinician knew that the father and mother were separated and that there was an important babysitter and different men in the house, as well as a baby brother and older sister, the clinician asked for the first names of the people. Brenda did not respond.

The clinician, therefore, shifted from what seemed threatening questions about her family to what the clinician thought would be a more neutral activity and asked her to copy figures, which she could do very easily, even calling the diamond a parallelogram and then self-correcting to a diamond. These constructions made the presence of a significant neurocognitive problem unlikely. In doing so, the clinician recognized the importance of a graded approach to affectively intense material; the child's resistance necessitated a sensitive pause in the discussion of such material, with the more neutral material used both to effectively rule out any neurocognitive problem while allowing the child comfort.

The clinician then returned to the theme of the family, this time asking Brenda to draw a picture of a family, without asking her to use words. In other words, the clinician was attuned to Brenda's difficulty discussing the family, but thought that, perhaps, something could be learned from the drawing. Brenda, at first, did not want to draw but responded quickly to mild encouragement.

She drew a family of ghosts: a mother, father, and child. The father and child were clearly defined figures but the mother ghost was a scribble, without any detectable form to her. As she was doing this, she made scary noises like a ghost. The clinician noted with some exaggerated emotion the ghost noises Brenda was making. He said: "That sounds like a scary ghost." Brenda agreed. The clinician then said: "It was more fun for her to make scary ghost noises than to feel scared about ghosts." With this intervention, the clinician pointed out Brenda's coping mechanism of avoiding awareness of her fear by being the one who makes the scary noises. This mechanism is common with children: Turning passive into active (that is, instead of feeling helpless and scared she becomes the scary one). Or, in the words noted above, Brenda was communicating that "The best defense is a good offense."

Brenda eased up in her facial expression. The clinician asked her who protected her from scary stuff. She said her older sister. She said that when the sister was home the sister slept in the upper bunk bed and she on the bottom. When the sister was not home she slept in her mother's bed. At other times her older brother protected her.

As can be seen from this brief vignette, by trying to connect with a child at her level, one can often elicit emotionally salient information about the child's inner life. Even in a situation like this one where the child is scared to engage with a stranger, gentle interactions, trying to follow her lead eventually allowed for important material to emerge. Her first nonverbal communication through her play was seen by the clinician as a communication of her sense of isolation and perhaps feeling unprotected. This was verified by the nature of her responses to the standard questions.

In her drawing of her family, she certainly communicated that the mother was not as coherent a person as the child and father ghost. It was very important that the clinician listened closely to her sounds and picked up her scary ghost noises. This allowed the clinician to communicate to Brenda that the clinician understood that making those noises was a way of protecting herself from being scared. The inference, of course, is that the externalizing behaviors in school and at home serve that same function – to prevent feeling frightened in an environment where she feels alone and unprotected.

> **It is very important for the therapist to listen closely to a patient's verbalizations to ascertain their meaning and what protective purpose they serve. The inference, of course, is that the externalizing behaviors in school and at home serve that same function – to prevent feeling frightened in an environment where the child feels alone and unprotected.**

8. Clinical example 2: Henry: an overtly negativistic boy

Henry, a six-year-old boy with a younger sister, came because he was angry and fought with friends and his younger sister. In the first session with the clinician, he was difficult to engage; he had an angry demeanor and complained about his teacher and the kids in school. Interestingly, when the clinician asked him the routine questions, in response to the question, "What he would be if he could be born over again," he said that he would be God ("like God in heaven"). The clinician asked him why and he said that then he could control everything that happens to him. In drawing a picture of the family, it was notable that he omitted his sister from the family. In response to questions about a picture he drew of a robot, he said: "The robot's main problem is anger." The clinician asked him why the robot was angry. He responded that he did not know but then drew a picture of a bug that pushed a little girl, making her bleed.

From this exchange, one can surmise that the little boy's aggression was a result of his anger at his sister's birth; he wished that she was not part of the family. If he were God, he could have ensured that she had not come into his life. Her presence made the robot (representing himself) angry and he wished to hurt the girl as the bug did in the picture.

> **When children speak in the voice of a doll, animal, or any other figure, such as a robot, one assumes that they are communicating something about their own lives: Events and feelings (happy ones or worries).**

B. Second session with the child

1. Rationale and goals for the second session

Whenever one evaluates a patient, one needs to see the patient at least twice. This is particularly true of a child, who will often attend a first meeting with a stranger in a heightened state of anxiety and defensiveness. Externalizing behaviors are the most common reasons for parents to bring a child for a consultation with a clinician, even if anxiety symptoms are present. Unless the child's anxiety symptoms are overwhelming, most parents will not seek help for them. Children with mixed anxiety and externalizing behaviors will often first present to the clinician with anxiety and only once they feel comfortable will the externalizing behaviors manifest themselves in the sessions with the clinician.

> **Because disruptive behaviors are less socially sanctioned, when children interact with adults for the first time, the externalizing behaviors may not manifest themselves immediately.**

2. Clinical example 3: Stacy: a child whose externalizing behaviors could not be explored until the second session

Five years old, Stacy was brought for an evaluation because of a variety of fears. Most importantly, her parents reported she had been fighting a great deal in nursery school and at home. In contrast to the little girl discussed above, Stacy was verbal and communicative with her play and words so that there was no need for a structured section during the first session. Most importantly, for our purposes, her externalizing behaviors did not become manifest until the very end of the first session and in her second session.

a. Rationale and when to allow a parent into the consultation room

In the first session, the little girl wanted her mother to come into the play room with her. The clinician did not prevent this and the mother came into the play room with the little girl, who was clearly frightened. The mother sat back in the play room while the clinician and Stacy played with a doll that she had brought with her.

b. Attend to communication in displacement

Children will often communicate their distress in a displaced manner, through the voice of a doll or a toy. In this case, Stacy told the clinician that the doll came to see him because she (the doll) could not sleep on account of hearing mommy and daddy talking. Immediately, the clinician observed, from this behavior, that this was a girl who had some trouble separating from her mother; in addition, her initial communication (via the play) was that she was curious or worried about what was going on in the parents' room at night.

The girl continued to tell the clinician that her doll's problem began when she was in her old room, but that it also happens in her new room. She drew a picture of her doll's bed on wheels in the old room and then drew two rooms next to one another. The new room was bigger. She then switched to her own voice and told the clinician that she (Stacy) gets up at night to check on her parents.

In this brief sequence one sees how a child communicates, how she may find it much easier to express her issues via the voice of a doll. As we see, it is relatively easy for a young child to fluidly shift from talking in the voice of the doll to her own voice. By this point in the session, Stacy was consciously talking about herself.

> **With play, one sees how a child communicates; the child may find it much easier to express his/her issues via the voice of a doll or another toy. It is relatively easy for a young child to fluidly shift from expressing the voice of the doll to her own voice.**

c. Attend to separation anxiety manifestations

Stacy went on to play with many different toys. She put on a puppet show in which various characters said "hello" and "good-bye." One of the puppets was shy. This game, one in which the child attempts to master separation anxiety, was likely connected to worries resulting in difficulty separating from the mother.

d. Attend to punishment anxiety manifestations

The girl shifted to an operation game and gave her doll injections. She said that her doll was being punished for being bad. Towards the latter part of the session, she became more verbal and more direct about herself. She stressed that she had three problems: She could not sleep well, she whined when her parents punished her, and she worried that something bad would happen to someone. Since she had already communicated that her doll was bad, the clinician assumed that there was something about Stacy that "was bad." In response to a question whether anything bad ever happened with her, she described a scene where she was bad, whining, and her father held her firmly and fell on top of her and hurt her.

She then reported a bad dream where her mother's leg was cut off; she went to the hospital but the doctor operated on her (Stacy) instead. It was scary. Towards the end of the session she became excited, teased the clinician with the toy telephone – calling to say "hello–good-bye." She hung up repetitively. In general, she was very verbal and related well, but became more and more agitated as the time neared the end of the session, after the clinician said that there were only a few more minutes. She wanted to continue playing and did not leave the play room easily.

The sequence of this initial session demonstrated that there was a *connection between the child's misbehavior and her fears*. She punished her doll with an injection and revealed how her daddy similarly hurt her. Stacy also reported a fear of being severely punished with a shot and operation in her dream.

> **It is important to observe the sequence of a child's activity and play. One can then infer a connection between fears and misbehavior.**

e. Refrain from giving direction

In her second visit, Stacy came into the playroom without any problem but wanted Mommy to come into the playroom with her. The clinician asked if Stacy was ever away from her Mommy. Her mother responded: "Yes, when she had a sleepover at grandma's, but she had to go home early." After standing in the doorway where this conversation took place, the mother could stay out of the playroom. Stacy asked the clinician, "What do you want to do?" The clinician responded and said that it was up to her.

> **Whenever possible, one tries not to give the child directions.**

This maneuver is critical – *whenever possible, one tries not to give the child directions* – one wants to determine what the child chooses to play, how he/she chooses, whether there is difficulty in making a choice. In addition, the choice of play in young children is usually reflective of the important issues in the child's life and how they impact on his/her mind. By saying, "it is up to you," the clinician communicates permission to the child to freely communicate.

> **The choice of play the child makes can be indicative of the issues that he/she wants to communicate.**

f. Attend to repetitive themes

Stacy went out to the waiting room and retrieved her doll, which she had left outside. She told the clinician that her doll had a headache and they needed to operate on her.
   It is very important in an ongoing therapy to identify repetitive themes.
   By not giving the child instructions as to what to play, the child herself chose a play activity which revealed her underlying worries.

> **Repetitive themes in the play may indicate the central worries and conflicts in the child's life.**

The theme in the first session – and again in the second – involved some bodily hurt and some assault on her body (injections, operations). The clinician knew that this girl had a significant injury when she was about three – her grandmother had accidentally spilled hot water on her, resulting in a three-week hospitalization with a few small skin grafts. This was the same grandmother with whom she could not stay overnight.

In the play, the doctors could not find anything wrong with her doll and therefore they had to use a flashlight. Stacy once again shifted from a doll's voice to her own voice. In other words it was clear that Stacy had a solid grasp of pretend versus real. She was able to move fluidly from displacing her fears onto the doll to speaking about herself.

g. Identify moments of obsessive play

This very expressive fantasy play, which the clinician surmised was connected to her early trauma, did not continue. Instead she shifted to a variety of toys and games: The doll house, animals, and dominoes (she lined them up and pushed them down). In other words, Stacy left the realm of story-telling about her very personal life to a routinized obsessive play without seeming connection to her fantasy play or her real-life trauma.

h. Identify moments of discontinuity in the play

The clinician noted to Stacy the quick shift in her play, saying: "Oh, we are not playing the game with your doll anymore? Is that because she had a headache and needed an operation?" She responded: "That's a boring game." One conjecture is that this quick shift in her attention away from the play with her doll likely meant that the game got too close to her emotions about her own injury and clearly was not something to be pursued at the moment.

> **Early in a treatment, one has to be careful how to address how a child moves away from potentially painful subjects. The shift away from the doll game was simply noted to the child.**

Stacy took many turns lining up the various toys, playing in an organized way, likely to avoid spontaneous thoughts and feelings. Without being fully consciously aware, she may have felt that she was revealing too much.

i. Attend to interactions surrounding wanting to leave or to stay

She wanted to know how much time was left, and the clinician said that maybe today is different from last time. Last time she did not want to leave and today maybe "she wants to leave quickly." The clinician's focus on her desire to "get out of here" was met with defensiveness on Stacy's part. "No, I don't want to leave today either because I like to play." This is another example of Stacy's avoidance of difficult emotions. Her reluctance to leave in the first session and her eagerness to depart in the second both reveal some kind of vulnerability around separation. It is likely that these feelings provoke a sense of shame and humiliation when exposed; as a result, Stacy needed to deny them when the clinician inquired.

j. Put limits on disruptive behavior when safety becomes threatened

They proceeded to play together, throwing things to knock the animals down. At some point, she threw a toy too close to the clinician's head (an example of the disruptive behaviors that the parents reported). The clinician said to her: "Here we can play whatever you want and you can say whatever you think or feel, but we can't let anyone get hurt." The clinician suggested that Stacy throw the block in a different direction.

Stacy immediately wanted to leave the playroom, spoke in babyish tone, whiny voice, was angry with the clinician, turned over a chair and started to go out to her mother. As she was starting to leave the playroom, she said that she was angry with the clinician, using a much more infantile whiny voice, again like the parents reported.

k. *Identify moments of transference*

The clinician said to her: "Gosh, you are so upset. When else have you gotten this upset?" She said that at home when something happens that she doesn't like, she gets angry with her father; the father gets angry with her and a big fight starts. Shortly after, the session ended with her still being angry with the clinician.

From these initial two sessions, one can confidently conjecture that the little girl's negativistic behaviors in response to gentle redirection were closely connected to her worries about being hurt. We can see the dramatic difference between the first and the second session. It was only in the second session that the symptoms that had been reported by the parents became manifest in the playroom.

> **The little girl's negativistic behaviors in response to gentle redirection were closely connected to her worries about being hurt.**

Notably, in the first session, Stacy was quite open about her concerns through her play and report of a dream. In the second session, this theme of being hurt continued but was quickly curtailed by Stacy. This led to some obsessive, controlled play and then a disruptive act, nearly hitting the clinician in the head. In essence, the clinician and she got into a fight in the same way she fought with her father at home. Without needing to infer anything else, we can observe that it was safer to fight with the clinician (like father) than express her fears about being hurt, even in play. Importantly, in a good prognostic sign for treatment, Stacy was able to connect what happened in the office with what happened at home.

> **It was safer to fight with the clinician (like father) than express her fears about being hurt, even in play.**

COMPARISONS BETWEEN CHILDREN

When one compares Stacy with Brenda, the first girl described above, who protected herself from feeling scared by making scary ghost noises, one can observe a dramatic difference between the two children. Stacy's sessions were much more fluid, she was more verbal, and she revealed much more about herself. Yet, both children exhibited disruptive behaviors as ways of coping with problematic frightening feelings. Taken at face value, one would conjecture that Stacy would do better with psychotherapy than Brenda because of her ability to communicate as well as because Brenda's family was much more chaotic. However, discussions with Brenda's mother revealed, after two meetings, that she very much wanted to help her daughter and would be very engaged in a short-term treatment.

C. Conclusions

The reader will notice that the techniques of addressing the child's avoidance mechanisms (defense) during these first two sessions are very similar to the procedures that will be described in Step 2 of RFP-C. These techniques are very informative and will continue throughout the treatment, allowing for a smooth transition into the working-through portion. The protocol of these first two sessions may be extended into Step 2 when needed, underlying the fluidity of this treatment.

D. Global goals

As with the first meeting with the parents, there are global goals that the clinician must meet. The key remains to ensure that the child feels comfortable with the clinician and reassured about the clinician's competence. Most importantly, the child should feel that the clinician *understands* the nature of his/her problems. The specific goals of the initial encounter are designed to foster this sense of security and structure at the outset of the treatment.

Additional "global goals" describing warm and empathic characteristics of the RFP-C clinician must be met. Their attainment and maintenance throughout the treatment is of primary importance. Their achievement should not be compromised in an attempt to meet all of the above specific goals in any one parent meeting or child session. As a result, most clinicians will have two initial assessment meetings with the child. When indicated, the RFP-C clinician may defer obtainment of the above specific goals when concerns are evoked that the quality of the clinician-child relationship is not proceeding sufficiently to ensure their success. They may be revisited in Step 2 as needed.

The first global goal entails the pursuit of a nonjudgmental manner to the approach with the child. As mentioned in the introduction to the manual, a potential, major reason for the lack of individual treatments of children with externalizing behaviors may entail the negative countertransference issues these children can evoke with their disruptive behaviors. These feelings should not be verbalized or introduced into the treatment. As in the initial parent meeting, the clinician should acknowledge to him/herself their presence, accept the feelings, and use them to better understand the contributing factors to their development as well as strategies to correct any underlying relational issues. When immediate solutions cannot be found, the RFP-C clinician should hold on to these feelings for later consideration through the use of various professional supports for him/herself in either supervision or personal psychotherapy.

A second global goal entails the establishment of a strong alliance with the child. In RFP-C, an alliance is best fostered when the value of the real relationship between the child and the clinician is acknowledged and respected. The presentation of a warm, collaborative attitude is a third global goal. Applications of analytic concepts of anonymity, neutrality, and abstinence must be limited and not set the tone for the encounter.

A fourth and fifth global goals involve empathy. The RFP-C clinician must empathize with the child's feelings about his/her difficulties in a nonjudgmental manner. These will often include frustrations and other negative feelings. Similarly, the clinician must empathize with the child's potentially negative feelings about coming to treatment. Intense emotions may also be experienced by the parents, including shame, guilt, and rage. The clinician must be able to tolerate these strong feelings and help the family to process them effectively. Frequent check-ins and parent meetings will allow the clinician to assess parental emotions and to respond to them effectively.

In RFP-C clinicians should:

1   Be sensitive to the child's feelings that may be too painful to talk about right away.
2   Work out how to gently help the child to gradually become aware of and discuss how the child protects (defends) him/herself from experiencing those feelings.

As the child becomes aware of these protective devices, there will be less need for externalizing behaviors and the child may be more willing to share these previously disavowed feelings.

Throughout the treatment, chatting with the child about everyday activities, playing games and activities, and interacting spontaneously are important for the maintenance of a therapeutic alliance.

References

Chazan, S.E., 2002. *Profiles of play,* London, UK: Jessica Kingsley Press.
Goodenough, F., 1926. *Measurement of intelligence by drawings*, Chicago, IL: World Book.
Harris, D.B., 1963. *Children's drawings as measures of intellectual maturity*, New York, NY: Harcourt Brace Jovanovich.
Koppitz, E.M., 1968. *Psychological evaluation of children's human figure drawings*, New York, NY: Grune and Stratton.
Pellegrini, A.D. & Smith, P.K., 1998. Physical activity play: the nature and function of a neglected aspect of playing. *Child Development,* 69(3), pp. 577–98.

Chapter 8

Step 1: second meeting with the parents
Feedback

OUTLINE

A. Goals of the encounter
  1. Recognition and addressing common parental experiences and concerns
     a. Structure to reduce opportunities for discrepancies
     b. Begin with the clinician's impression of the child
     c. Emphasize the child's strengths
     d. Avoid judgmental statements, including good/bad descriptors
  2. Organize the discussion within a stress-diathesis model of understanding the child's problems
     a. Introduce sensory gating and temperamental contributions (diathesis)
     b. Introduce common childhood experiences as stressors (stress)
  3. Revisit the dynamic model: the importance of understanding
     a. Discuss generalization
        i. Clinical example: Stacy
     b. Discuss the meaning of behavior
        i. Reintroduce Malan's Triangle
        ii. Clinical example 1: Stacy
        iii. Clinical example 2: Josh
     c. Identify divergence in the handling of external problems
        i. Clinical example 3: Henry
  4. Conclusion
     a. Addressing parental concerns
     b. Revisiting treatment timeline
     c. Planning an individualized treatment plan
B. Global goals of the encounter
  1. A nonjudgmental stance
  2. Promotion of a parental alliance
  3. A warm, collaborative attitude
  4. Empathy with the parents' feelings regarding their child
  5. Empathy with the parents regarding the difficulty of proceeding with the sessions and meetings

A. Goals of the encounter

In the second parent meeting, the clinician meets with the parents or parent-surrogates to discuss with them his/her ideas about the child and his/her recommendations for further psychotherapeutic work.

1. Recognition and addressing common parental experiences and concerns

It is difficult to ascertain which meeting may be more anxiety-provoking to parents: The very first meeting with the clinician, which they may have entered with anxiety and shame about their child's problems, or the feedback session. In this session, parents may anticipate rebuke for their parenting skills, fear a report that their child is very disturbed, experience suspiciousness that the clinician will not understand their child, or experience a myriad of other feelings that provoke potential defensive responses in the parents. Parents may be obsequious on the surface but seething on the inside; or, on the other hand, they may present a negativistic façade yet feel relieved that the clinician understands them and their child. Far too many mental health professionals, especially those who have been engaged in this field for a long time, forget the potential negative impact on parents and their children of a well-meaning, but inadvertently insensitive, remark or gesture by the clinician.

> **Mental health professionals always have to be cognizant of the anxiety, shame, and concern parents may have (expressed or unexpressed) about the feedback session with the professional.**

a. Structure to reduce opportunities for discrepancies

Since a child's problems may often intensify whatever marital discord may already be present, if possible, it is valuable for the feedback session to include all of the primary adults in the child's life. This remains true even if, and especially when, parents are divorced and not living together so as to minimize inevitable situations where the clinician can find her/himself in the middle of the marital discord. A joint meeting also reduces the clinician's reliance on one parent to report back to the other, with the lapses and distortions that inevitably occur in everyone's memory. A similar problem occurs if an interpreter is needed or if the child becomes the translator for the parents. Some parents may remember the negative qualities addressed by the clinician and feel that their child is hopelessly disturbed. Others may only remember the positive qualities about the child and deny that there is any problem. In other words, parents, like all of us, come with their own coping devices that affect how they hear, interpret, and remember what the clinician says. Separate feedback sessions to each adult (because of profoundly difficult marital or divorce problems), though sometimes absolutely necessary, may easily result in distortions and differences in nuances as the clinician cannot possibly repeat him/herself in exactly the same manner. In addition, the clinician's actual report to a parent will be modified in the parent's mind as a result of the nature of the interaction between the parent/s in the room and the clinician.

b. Begin with the clinician's impression of the child

In speaking with parents, it is useful for the clinician to begin the discussion about the child by asking them if their child spoke about the meeting.

> **The parent should be asked what the child told them about the meeting/s with the clinician.**

Some parents report that their child described a game they played, a picture they drew, or a story they told. It is also possible that the child may not share anything at all.

c. Emphasize the child's strengths

The clinician can then reflect upon the information reported by the parents and begin with a positive statement about the child. For example, the clinician might say: "She certainly is very bright" or "She started out feeling nervous when she met me but she really expressed herself" or "He really knows his mind." These comments can form a bridge for the parents to discuss their perception of their child and how they view the child's adaptive and maladaptive reactions, including agreement or disagreement with the clinician's perspective. They can complement the strengths emphasized within the first parent session (see 6.3.a), which, reproduced here in modified form to emphasize the clinician's now first-hand experience of the child, include "He sure is a very sociable child," "She really does love to play games," "Most of the time he is indeed so friendly," or "He sounds so smart." Similarly to emphasizing the child's strengths, it is important to review the parents' strengths: "You try very hard to deal with these very difficult problems" or "It is even more clear now that the two of you have really been able to work together for your child's benefit." Parents will benefit from the continuity of perspective from the first to the second feedback session and may feel reassured that the clinician has kept them in mind in the intervening time.

d. Avoid judgmental statements, including good/bad descriptors

It is more effective to avoid the words "good" and 'bad" because those labels can intensify the judgmental perspective that parents have about their child and about themselves. If the clinician agrees that the child has "bad behavior" the parent may think: "What does the clinician think of my parenting? Does he/she think that I am a bad parent?"

> **Clinicians should avoid judgmental words like "good" and "bad."**

2. Organize the discussion within a stress-diathesis model of understanding the child's problems

Contemporary models of problematic behaviors that recognize the importance of both innate constitutional and environmental contributions to problematic behaviors can help structure the ensuing discussion.

a. Introduce sensory gating and temperamental contributions (diathesis)

There are two important physiological contributors to the development of irritability and externalizing behaviors: Sensory over- or underresponsiveness and temperamental variations. Both of these factors may contribute to an infant, toddler, or older child's difficulties in being soothed. These early difficulties may form a template for subsequent interactions with other people. By preschool age, both sensory and temperamental factors can contribute to a child's difficulties with his/her educational experience. These factors will influence and shape the child's academic functioning, stance towards teachers and other authority figures, and relationships with peers. They may affect the development of friendships and possibly prevent the child from having a best friend. The child may become the victim of bullies and/or bully others. He/she may simply be neglected by his/her peers.

Deficits in sensory processing are often characterized by a few common complaints and problems in social functioning. For example, does the child complain a lot about the clothes that he/she wears? Does the child look and act overwhelmed because of the numbers of people and loudness of noise when he/she goes to a birthday party or to a children's play? Is the child easily frustrated? These observations may help the parents to help the child accommodate to these situations, such as staying in the periphery of a party before entering. In circle time in school, the teacher may have to adjust their expectation of the child's full participation right near the other children. In other words, a highly reactive and easily frustrated child may develop externalizing behaviors.

It is important to stress with parents that the "effects of particular sensory and/ or temperamental characteristics can be modulated by the attention of a sensitive, responsive caregiver" (PDM Task Force 2006). This is sometimes referred to as "goodness of fit" – that is, the parents find a way to *fit* or match the child's needs as they arise. Parental sensitivity and supporting the child to become gradually autonomous promote executive functioning skills and self-regulatory capacities in the child (Bernier et al. 2010). The clinician and the parents together can find methods of responding to the child more effectively, while at the same time stressing to the parents that the clinician understands the challenges of parenting a child with such difficulties. In addition to sensory and/or temperamental characteristics, the child's academic progression and potential language and cognitive difficulties need to be considered. If significant deficits are evident or suspected, more formal evaluation (e.g., an educational and cognitive assessment with a psychologist) is recommended. In discussing these innate issues and the need for special parental responses, the clinician needs to be aware of parental guilt resulting in either self-blame or denial of emotional contributors. Self-critical comments such as "We should have treated him differently when he was younger" or "All she has to do is listen" need to be received, processed, and returned to the parents in a form that does not deny or dispute the parent's perspective but in one that recognizes and validates the strengths of the parents and their commitment to their child. Reminding the parents that they are currently taking the steps to find their child help now can be a helpful way to reorient from ruminations over missed opportunities in the past and redirect the emphasis back to the present where helpful changes can be made.

b. Introduce common childhood experiences as stressors (stress)

Many clinicians have observed that children with even mild to moderate difficulties with their temperament, sensory development, or language and general cognitive development may have difficulties adapting to stressors such as the birth of a sibling, a move, a nanny leaving, other separations, or parental discord and separation. These children have a difficult time mastering the aggression that is provoked by those stressors and which may result in a variety of behaviors. Some children withdraw into themselves, while others develop externalizing behaviors, particularly oppositional behaviors. These children have a very difficult time regulating their negative emotions, which then results in problematic externalizing behaviors. In the language of the NIMH Research Domain Criteria (RDoC), these children exhibit deficits in the domain of Negative Valence Systems (i.e., systems for aversive motivation). Specifically, they manifest problematic behaviors in the functional dimension of "frustrative nonreward," which often manifests with physical and relational aggression.

In short, these children have difficulties with their affect regulation, which may be a large contributor to externalizing behaviors, including severe oppositional symptoms. The clinician can review with the parents the sequence of events in the session that provoked a disruption by the child. These observations can then be compared with the parents' observations about the child's difficulties at home and that of the teachers at school. In this way, the clinician helps the parents understand potential antecedents to the disruptive symptoms. And, the clinician can help parents develop understanding that these behaviors have *meaning* as maladaptive, underdeveloped attempts at affect regulation. This awareness will also help parents recognize the value of a regulation-focused treatment. The clinician can then discuss with the parents how in the treatment, the clinician will be able to:

1   Discuss with the child the triggers for the child's aggressive outbursts,
2   Identify for the child how the child protects him/herself from emotional states that are difficult to tolerate,
3   Help the child find more adaptive strategies, and
4   Work collaboratively with the parents.

These four foci of treatment will help the child and the parents identify those triggers that lead to irritability and oppositional behavior in the child's daily life. This will help prepare the child for difficult situations that provoke disruptive responses and enable them to better navigate the interactions when outbursts do occur.

This work with parents and children is different from behavioral techniques in which parents are helped to modify their responses in order to help the child modify his/her responses so he/she interacts in a more socially adaptive and appropriate way. A common criticism of a behavioral approach is that it invalidates the child's individuality and needs by working only on the disruptive behaviors. Children may become "programmed" without addressing developmental issues that underlie the disruptive behaviors. The work that is described in this manual highlights the importance of understanding the triggers (stressors) of the irritability and the disruptive symptoms while maintaining attention upon the diathesis with which many of these children are burdened.

3. Revisit the dynamic model: the importance of understanding

The technique utilized in most behaviorally oriented therapies (either jointly with the parent or individually with the child) includes the proscribing or ignoring of nonsocial or antisocial interactions with the therapist, such as cursing or yelling, in order to try to extinguish the behavior. In a therapy such as RFP-C where the clinician is trying to understand the origins of the child's disruptive outbursts, openly hostile communications towards the clinician are not only allowed, but encouraged, as long as no one is hurt, nothing is damaged, and the behavior does not continue after the session.

Parents often come to treatment with an assumption of therapy as working within a behavioral model; that is, that the clinician's in-session goal is to reduce target behaviors in an attempt to generalize these gains to the outside world. This misconception may produce alarm when parents observe a treatment that deviates significantly from this model. As such, the differences between RFP-C and a behavioral model must be made explicit through a revisiting of the dynamic model as was introduced in the first parent meeting.

> **Parents are usually unaware that, in RFP-C, unsocial attitudes towards the clinician is helpful for the progression of the treatment (as long as no one is hurt nor is property damaged).**

a. Discuss generalization

Hearing their child's language or the "misbehavior" with the clinician can fill parents with anxiety, shame, or anger. They may say aloud or self-critically preoccupy themselves with the thought while in the waiting room: "A child should not talk in a disrespectful way to an adult." Thus, it is crucial that the clinician explain to the parents the actual technique of RFP-C. Parents are helped to understand differences between the play and the verbal communication in the therapy sessions and the play and communication in the child's everyday life and interactions. The permissive attitude and encouragement of uncensored communication by the child towards the clinician should not be replicated by the parents. It is valuable for the clinician to explain to the parents the rationale for the permissive attitude in the sessions, to allow access to the child's conflicts and maladaptive regulating mechanisms that underlie the externalizing behaviors. Outside the session, with parents and in school, the child is expected to follow the ordinary rules of social conduct.

It is important to make this distinction because parents can be embarrassed by the words and actions the child exhibits towards the clinician. The clinician needs to explain to the parents the process of therapy: A goal is for the major symptoms in the child's life to be replayed with the clinician. Neither hurting people nor property, of course, is allowed. The clinician can explain that by allowing full freedom of expression, even if it is not socially appropriate, the clinician will be able to observe in a firsthand manner the nature of the child's maladaptive actions and verbalizations as well as the triggers for these behaviors. By observing the sequence from the trigger event to the maladaptive behavior the clinician obtains information about the problematic emotion that the child cannot regulate. The clinician can provide examples from the child's interactions during the initial sessions that illustrate this process.

Some parents, particularly those who have a tendency to worry or may feel distrustful of therapeutic approaches that lack the disciplinarian structure of behavioral treatments, may be concerned that the permissive stance towards disruptive behaviors within RFP-C may undo or worsen all the efforts that the family and child have put towards improving or controlling his/her behavior, be it through interventions at home, in the school, or in behavioral therapy. The clinician can remind the parents that though interactions within the treatment may appear unstructured they are in fact a component of a time-limited, manualized treatment approach that is constructed upon time-proven interventions in the field of child psychotherapy and developmental pediatrics. The goal remains for the child to "transfer" the intensity of his/her emotional feelings and consequent maladaptive behaviors onto the clinician and the clinical setting and thereby reduce the pressure or need for these strong feelings to emerge in such disruptive means in the child's life at home or in the school. Parents may be advised to anticipate significant improvement in the relatively short time frequency of the standardized treatment, and the help to assist parents with patience often provides them with the support and reassurance to unburden themselves of their anxiety and place trust within the clinician. When there are difficulties in the emergence of this process, and the parents may continually push for medication and/or more directive techniques, a reminder that any safety concerns should they emerge in the course of the treatment (e.g., suicidal ideation or violence) would necessitate such maneuvers. However, given the relative time frame of many years over which the child's disruptive behaviors may have emerged, placed in comparison with the relatively much shorter 10-week, 16-child session time course, it is helpful to remind the parents that though help is now available, allowing it the time to develop and help the child in the most full manner possible is of greatest benefit to the child's development.

I. CLINICAL EXAMPLE I: STACY

In the previous chapter, we described the initial sessions with five-year-old Stacy who was brought for an evaluation for fighting in nursery school and at home. In the feedback session, the clinician described to the parents how Stacy wanted to leave the playroom, spoke in a whiny voice, and was angry with the clinician.

The clinician explained that Stacy had trouble mastering the fearful emotions that emerged in the interaction with the clinician and leaving the room became her only option. The clinician further explained that Stacy's behavior with the clinician was identical to the problematic behavior the parents experienced at home, where she would provoke and her father would get angry. The clinician explained that in the therapy, the clinician and Stacy would identify the connection between the anxiety and the disruptive behavior, helping Stacy cope more effectively with her anxiety and needing to be disruptive less frequently and less intensely.

Step 1: second meeting with the parents 153

b. Discuss the meaning of behavior

In the feedback meeting with the parents, the clinician needs to *lay the groundwork for the ongoing periodic parent meetings* where interactions between the parents and between the parents and the child are discussed. Since the parents are coming to the clinician *for their child and because of the child's symptoms*, focusing on family dynamics too extensively may increase the parents' resistance to the treatment as whole. At other times, the child's symptoms may be used by the family as a way to address complex family dynamics.

> **Clinicians should try to communicate what they understand about the meaning of the child's symptom: "When she is too conscious of her fears, she fights."**

The clinician can touch on trying to ascertain the impact on the child of the family's interactions with one another and with the child. The clinician should also determine which important events in the family may have had an impact on the child (e.g., family of origin, adoptive family, siblings, change in caretakers, moves, separations and divorce, illnesses, deaths). It is important to try to understand the impact of frightening or potentially traumatic events in the family prior to the child's birth that may have a continual impact on the parenting of the child. This history may, in some way, be internalized by the child and contribute to his/her difficulties. The family's coping styles, particularly in response to frightening or potentially traumatic events during the child's life, should be understood.

> **Laying the groundwork for the treatment.**

I. REINTRODUCE MALAN'S TRIANGLE

Malan's Triangle (See Appendix A), as was initially presented in the first family meeting, should be explicitly reviewed with the family. Externalizing behavior is reintroduced as a maladaptive phobic avoidance reaction or defense mechanism. Irritability and tension are reintroduced as the negative inhibitory affect. Parents are encouraged to develop in their own minds their understanding of the feared feeling. The following clinical examples present two separate feared feelings and the respective inhibitory and defensive reactions.

II. CLINICAL EXAMPLE I: STACY

In the case of Stacy, for example, when it seemed that Stacy was still trying to deal with a burn suffered at the hands of the grandmother at the age of three, it was challenging for her to communicate her suffering to the parents, without intensifying their guilt and anger at the grandmother.

In the second meeting, the clinician had an open discussion about Stacy's problems – that she had certain fears, worried about being hurt, and fought when these fears came too close to her conscious awareness. In fact, the clinician reiterated several times, as described above, that "She fought with me, the same way you described fighting with you at home; she fought with me when she became too immersed in talking about her worries. She fought as a way of avoiding the worries."

A direct statement about the nature of Stacy's fighting put Stacy's problems into perspective for the parents. ***There was meaning to her fighting.*** She was not fighting because she was a "bad" child. And, since Stacy also fought with the clinician like she did with her father, the father was not a bad parent. In reviewing with the parents some of the issues that frightened Stacy, the parents themselves went back to the burn and how scared they all were when it happened. They wondered themselves whether she still worried about it even though she did not talk about it.

Describing Stacy's interactions with the clinician as similar to her interaction with the father lay the groundwork for the treatment. Later on in the session, as the clinician and parents were planning out a treatment plan, the clinician referred back to this observation, noting that the RFP-C would consist of trying to delineate for Stacy those moments where she would try to fight with the clinician, when troublesome emotions would come too close to her consciousness.

The clinician should utilize his/her interactions with the child as an illustration of how the treatment will proceed: Trying to understand the nature of the triggers for the child's fighting with the clinician.

III. CLINICAL EXAMPLE 2: JOSH

In another situation, in thinking about the oppositional behavior of Josh, an eight-year-old boy, the clinician learned from the boy how his favorite babysitter left suddenly, about a year before. It seemed from the sessions with the child that his disappointment with this loss was very likely a trigger for his emotional angry outbursts at his parents, whom he blamed for the babysitter leaving. In talking with the parents, it was very hard to discuss this trigger with them because they themselves were raised by strict parents and were very "good" children, who kept their feelings to themselves. As children, it would never have dawned on them to complain about something the parents had done.

The parents had reported that they had let this person go a year before because they felt the boy and his older sister no longer needed a full-time nanny. They proceeded with this change very matter-of-factly, not even thinking that the children would have a reaction to this. The older sister was a rule-follower, without any temperamental difficulties, and had no overt reaction. Because of the parents' strong antipathy to emotional expression, the clinician did not make a connection in the feedback meeting with the parents between the boy's oppositional behavior and the babysitter's leaving. Instead the clinician focused in an abstract way on the boy's oppositional behavior as needing intervention to avoid social problems, with a goal of addressing the connection with the parents later in the RFP-C.

> **One has to be careful that one's comments to parents do not appear to them as "blaming" them for the child's problems.**

c. Identify divergence in the handling of external problems

The greatest difficulty in talking with parents often occurs when there is a disparity between the parents' descriptions of the child at home and the teacher's description of the child at school. In such a situation, one has to navigate a very fine line without adjudicating between the parents' perceptions and the teacher's perspective.

I. CLINICAL EXAMPLE 3: HENRY

With one little boy, eight-year-old Henry, who was reacting to his sister's birth, the teacher focused on his disruptive behavior at school. The parents and the clinician were able to discuss Henry's problems at home and what the clinician perceived in the session. The parents and the clinician discussed the teacher's observation as another piece of data to consider, including the idea that even if she were exaggerating the problems and even if she contributed to the exacerbation of symptoms, Henry had difficulty adapting to that teacher's expectations.

This is an important way of trying to help parents integrate information from teachers. Even if there were a bad match between their child and the teacher, the work of the therapy was to help the child develop more effective coping mechanisms to deal with stresses, whether the stress is the presence of a sibling or a teacher who is less attuned to his needs than another teacher or his parents would be. In other words, the more the clinician can communicate an understanding of the child's behavior, in very general terms, the more relief the parents will feel that there is a way of addressing the child's problems and the less focused they will be on good or bad behavior or whether he has a good teacher or a bad teacher.

The key factor that the clinician has to communicate to the parents is to help them understand that the child's irritability and oppositional behavior are maladaptive ways to try to cope with the intense negative emotions that have arisen and have interfered with ongoing development.

> **The key factor that the clinician has to communicate to the parents is to help them understand that the child's irritability and oppositional behavior are maladaptive ways to try to cope with the intense negative emotions that have arisen and have interfered with ongoing development.**

4. Conclusion

It is often clear after the initial evaluation that an ongoing relationship with the child would be of value to help the child master his/her unpleasant emotions more effectively by addressing the maladaptive coping mechanisms (e.g., externalizing behaviors). If the meetings proceed as planned, the parents at the end of this meeting would feel a certain amount of confidence of the plan for ongoing treatment to help their child address those conflicts that are interfering with his/her functioning and development.

By describing his/her interactions with the child, the clinician has given the parents a flavor of the nature of the work that can be accomplished. In Stacy's case, the clinician told the parents how they played a game where the doll was sick and suddenly the play was interrupted. The clinician described how pointing out this interruption led Stacy to want to leave the session, indicating that the subject of sickness provoked feelings that were too difficult to consciously experience, and she became disruptive.

Parents usually understand the sequence of events and the interventions that the clinician can provide. They can also see that such events will recur over and over with the goal of greater mastery of those emotions. Parents are also relieved to hear that usually as the disruptive symptoms get played out in the office with the clinician, they recede in intensity or disappear at home.

> **It is crucial to communicate to parents the process of the treatment and the nature of the clinician's interventions.**

a. Addressing parental concerns

Parents should be given the opportunity to express their concerns. These may include concerns about the treatment model, the treatment structure, or the clinician him/herself. Concerns should always be respected and addressed with care taken to understand the difficulty parents may be experiencing in accepting the need for treatment. Reassurance, comfort, structure, and kindness should be portrayed to the family in ensuring all questions have been answered to their satisfaction.

b. Revisiting treatment timeline

The timeline of treatment should be revisited. This will include a discussion of the 14 remaining child sessions as well as scheduled weekly brief parent meetings following sessions and fuller meetings with the parents following session 7 and before session 16. The goal is to build a strong alliance with the parents to support the child's therapy. Parent meetings can promote the process. Any request for additional meetings may warrant a discussion of the parent's needs and expectations for the parent meetings. Family concerns beyond the child may be verbalized, in which case the option for referral to a family therapist or an individual therapist for a parent may be considered.

c. Planning an individualized treatment plan

Following a discussion of the above, a detailed plan could be agreed upon that is specific to the child and parents' needs. Generally, child sessions are to be held twice a week, optimally spaced equally throughout the week (Monday and Thursday/Friday, for example). Contacts for interval urgent or emergent care are reviewed. Any documentation required by the parents may be discussed at this point and consideration of another clinician if additional family support is needed.

B. Global goals of the encounter

As in the first parent meeting, the clinician's adherence to global goals remains crucial. These include attention to:

1 A nonjudgmental stance,
2 Promotion of a parental alliance,
3 A warm, collaborative attitude,
4 Empathy with the parents' feelings regarding their child, and
5 Empathy with the parents regarding the difficulty of proceeding with the sessions and meetings.

Bibliography

Bernier, A., Carlson, S.M., & Whipple, N., 2010. From external regulation to self-regulation: early parenting precursors of young children's executive functioning. *Child Development*, 81(1), pp. 326–39.

PDM Task Force, 2006. *Psychodynamic diagnostic manual*, Silver Spring, MD: Alliance of Psychoanalytic Organizations.

Chapter 9

Step 2: sessions 3–11
Addressing child's avoidance of disturbing thoughts and feelings

OUTLINE

A. Introduction and specific goals
1. Initiation of each session
   a. Respectful demeanor
   b. Unstructured introduction
   c. Unstructured initiation of play
      i. What to do when a child won't play
2. Progression and main tasks of each session
   a. Identification of defenses and empathy
3. Goals and signs of improvement

B. Precautions
1. Imputing meaning to the child's activity and play without evidence
2. Continuous cathartic expressions of emotions
3. Simple reassurance
4. Thinking moralistically
5. Failure to reflect on one's own limits

C. Clinical examples
1. Case 1: Betty and the standard treatment process
   a. Interplay with genetic determinants
   b. Gradual address of defenses
   c. Initial sessions and intervention
   d. Indicators of progress
      i. New play activities with referents
      ii. Decreasing attacks on clinician
      iii. Transition from real to pretend attacks and defense
         a. The importance of interruptions, such as holidays
         b. The importance of remaining experience-near
         c. Setting and observing response to limits to the play
         d. Encouraging the pretend in play
      iv. Discussing real-life problems
         a. Encouraging gradual development of child's acknowledgement of life problems

Step 2: addressing child's avoidance   159

           b. Addressing boredom and other defensive affects in real life
           c. Addressing vacations and feelings of missing the play
           d. Continuing to address the child's problems gradually
        v. Clinician is allowed to score points
           e. Case conclusion
    2. Case 2: Stephanie and issues of countertransference
    3. Case 3: Pete and severe aggression
D. Review of the regulation-focused approach
E. Supportive interventions
    1. Examples of supportive interventions
    2. Balance between supportive and expressive interventions
F. Conclusion

A. Introduction and specific goals

In contrast to the initial evaluative sessions with the child, which, of necessity, have a certain amount of structure, the transition to Step 2 marks a transition to a more open-ended, unstructured style. In these sessions, sessions three through eleven, the child chooses what to talk about and what to play in his/her interactions with the clinician.

The rationale for unstructured sessions is that by allowing the child to take the lead and communicate, in his/her own way, *issues will spontaneously emerge* that are the most *emotionally salient* for the child at the moment, including, in a seeming paradox, his/her *need to avoid communication of painful emotions*, by either being silent or avoiding play and interaction.

Central features of RFP-C

a. **By following the child's play and verbalizations, the problematic symptoms that lead to disruption at home and/or at school inevitably will be repeated with the clinician.**

b. **The clinician has the opportunity to observe directly the child's maladaptive behavior and the trigger to the child's maladaptive behavior (such as a child's difficulties regulating her/his emotions when she/he hears the word, "no").**

c. **The clinician can observe the child's attempts to avoid disturbing emotions**

d. **From the beginning of the RFP-C the clinician addresses with the child the sequence of events which occur in the office, especially the child's avoidance.**

e. **The goal of this process is to help the child find more adaptive emotion regulation mechanisms (other than aggression) when faced with unpleasant emotions such as feeling hurt.**

> *Rationale for unstructured sessions:*
>
> *Emotionally salient issues emerge spontaneously.*
> *Child's need to avoid communication of painful emotions will be observed.*

1. Initiation of each session

a. Respectful demeanor

The RFP-C clinician must exhibit a respectful demeanor and be ready to play and chat about everyday activities with the child and listen for emotionally salient themes. Children can be very sensitive to any indication that the clinician is not emotionally present for the child. If needed, allowing oneself the time to refresh and realign focus from patient to patient by scheduling short intervals between cases may be of help.

b. Unstructured introduction

When greeting the child, the RFP-C clinician should allow the child the lead as to how to present him/herself. Large displays of affect on the clinician's part, such as spontaneously giving a warm, loud greeting, are counterproductive. The clinician must display a warm, accommodating stance but remain relatively neutral to allow the patient's mood and current circumstances to have the spotlight.

c. Unstructured initiation of play

If a child does not begin to talk or play after the passage of a bit of time, the clinician might address the child with a comment, such as: "How are things going?" or, the clinician might ask what they would like to play or do today or remind the child of what they were doing in the last session. If the child persists in not talking or playing, the clinician might say something like: "It's hard to decide what to do or what to talk about today."

In order to try to understand the nature of the child's emotions and the avoidant strategies the child utilizes, including maladaptive disruptive behavior, the clinician utilizes two techniques throughout all of the sessions:

1 *The clinician observes and addresses how a child's maladaptive behaviors enable him/her to avoid disturbing thoughts and feelings.*
2 *The clinician observes how the child's maladaptive behaviors and avoidance of disturbing thoughts and feelings emerge in the interactions with the clinician.*

The focus on these two elements continues from the beginning until the end of the treatment. The clinician's focus on what actually occurs between child and clinician is an experience-near technique that avoids the pitfalls of trying to guess the child's motivations for the maladaptive behavior.

1. WHAT TO DO WHEN A CHILD WON'T PLAY

In the example noted above, where the child does not talk or play, the clinician simply notes the child's withdrawal, without trying to guess what the child is avoiding and without trying to coerce the child to communicate. Guessing or cajoling the child, however gentle, can be felt as intrusive and as impositions and can lead to increased avoidance by the child.

2. Progression and main tasks of each session

In this chapter, we describe how the clinician recognizes and addresses the child's avoidance mechanisms. In the next chapter, we discuss the importance of addressing the interaction between clinician and the child. This interaction between clinician and child is the arena where the child's problems are played out. In-session interactions between clinician and child are valuable because they can be directly observed by clinician and discussed by clinician and child. This microscopic examination of an interaction that both clinician and child experience simultaneously in the immediacy of the moment does not rely on second-hand or third-hand reporting, such as the clinician saying: "I heard from your mother that the teacher told her that you had to leave the class today because you were disruptive." Most children will respond to such comments with denial or rationalizations, and usually it will cheapen the intimacy of the therapeutic relationship because the clinician, not protecting the child's sense of healthy pride or security, allows his/her parents or teacher to "tattle" on him/her. The child and the clinician are working together to try to help the child face and bear the problems he/she would rather avoid. In contrast to such "hearsay" discussions about problems, an examination of the presentation of the problems within the therapeutic relationship provides the clinician an opportunity for the clinician to communicate to child how the child attempts to avoid painful emotions within the session. This procedure will allow the difficult emotions to gradually become more tolerable and for maladaptive responses to be modified, allowing the child opportunities to develop more effective ways to interact.

Indicators of how a child avoids unpleasant feelings:

1   Silence and avoidance of play and activity.
2   Spontaneous change in the topic under discussion.
3   Abrupt change of play activity.

4	Actively resisting clinician's attempts to explore original topic.
5	Denial of feelings of discomfort or expression of opposite feelings.
6	In anxious children, engagement in integrative or defensive compulsions or rituals.

a. Identification of defenses and empathy

While utilizing the RFP-C technique, clinicians have to:

1 Be sensitive to the child's feelings that may be too painful to talk about right away.
2 Carefully address how the child is avoiding thinking about and expressing difficult emotions.
3 Work out how to gently help the child to gradually become aware of and discuss those feelings willingly.

The clinician listens empathically and respectfully, seeks clarification, and points out that not continuing with the original subject may reflect avoidance of an unpleasant feeling, e.g., *"It feels better to fight than to feel scared about mom and dad arguing with one another"* or *"It's easier to feel tired and fall asleep than to think about how uncomfortable you felt about the grade on that test."*

3. Goals and signs of improvement

Over time, the child feels more at ease openly acknowledging or playing out uncomfortable topics. The greater openness in their discussions allows children to reveal other awkward events in their life. In the interaction with the clinician, the child can become more playful, may use humor, and can become less aggressive to the clinician when he/she brings up painful topics. This allows the child to discuss (or play out) conflicts more adaptively, e.g., by using humor or playacting aggression rather than being really aggressive towards the clinician/analyst.

Indicators of improvement in the child

1 Greater comfort in sharing uncomfortable topics.
2 Revealing problematic events from his/her life.
3 More direct expression of feelings about the clinician.
4 Decreased aggression at home and at school.
5 Parents have greater comfort with child.

> 6 Reports of greater socially appropriate interactions at home and at school.
> 7 More direct discussion about aggression at home or at school.
> 8 Verbal attacks towards clinician replace physical attacks.
> 9 Playacting aggression towards clinician rather than direct attacks.
> 10 Verbalization by the child that interactions are pretend.
> 11 Ability to play games by the rules and allow the clinician a chance of making points or even at times winning.
> 12 Greater use of humor in the sessions instead of direct verbal attacks.
> 13 More direct elaboration of fantasy material.

All of these indicators of improvement in the child may be discussed with the parents in the intervening parent check-ins and meetings. These improvements may be relayed to the parents as part of the education regarding the RFP-C process. In tracking progress through the treatment, the clinician may want to informally review this list of indicators at the conclusion of each session. Any particular barriers to the attainment of these indicators may be identified and addressed as needed in the treatment. Such a review can reveal to the clinician areas requiring further attention and may also aid in hypothesis gathering concerning any potential defenses against progress in each domain.

B. Precautions

In RFP-C, the following principles should be kept in mind throughout the treatment:

1   The clinician should be careful about imputing meaning to the child's activity and play – for example, assuming that the child's anger at other patients is a result of aggression against a rival sibling – unless there is a great deal of evidence that such an inference is close to what the child is consciously experiencing.
2   Continuous cathartic expressions of emotions without trying to understand the origin of the emotion with the child may not be very helpful.
3   Simple reassurance often has only a transitory effect. Reassurance may be helpful in some situations, but in children with oppositional symptoms, the externalizing behavior prevents them from becoming aware of the emotional triggers. Therefore, reassurance of the underlying fears often may be met by intensification of the maladaptive protective externalizing behavior. For example, if a child came to a session following the death of his/her pet, and the clinician expressed his/her sympathies to the child in an effort to provide some empathic comfort and reassurance that he/she was not alone in his/her

experience of loss, it is anticipated that the child would only attack more in both an effort to ward off the closeness between the child and the clinician as expressed in his/her empathic reaching out to the child.
4 The clinician should be careful about becoming a moral compass for the child. Focusing on the do's and don'ts of socially appropriate behavior could lead to an increase in oppositional symptoms or total withdrawal. Only if there is danger to the child or to the clinician, or to property, should the clinician intervene directly.
5 Obviously every clinician will have a different tolerance level for what is allowed and what is not allowed; children will very quickly gauge that limit beyond which the clinician will respond with a direct interdiction. The clinician should try to judge his/her own tolerance for misbehavior and utilize limit setting in a neutral way with explanations.

Thus, as often as possible, the clinician should focus on the child's avoidance of the conscious experience of his/her unbearable affects

---

Cautions:

1 **Take great caution before imputing meaning to the child's actions.**
2 **Do not allow unlimited catharsis of emotion without addressing potential source of difficult affect.**
3 **Reassurance should be judiciously communicated.**
4 **Try to avoid judgmental comments such as "this is good or bad behavior."**
5 **Try to judge your own tolerance for misbehavior and utilize limit setting in a neutral way with explanations.**

C. Clinical examples

We provide three examples to illustrate the process of RFP-C. In the first example, we illustrate the importance of the diagnostic process as well as the ongoing therapeutic process throughout a portion of the treatment. In this child, a sensory problem contributed to the promotion of externalizing symptoms. Understanding the nature of the sensory problem allowed the therapy to proceed effectively. In this first example, we also illustrate how a child develops greater emotional regulation without directly verbally expressing her understanding. In the second example, we illustrate the impact of the clinician's feelings on the process of the psychotherapy and how the clinician has to bear in mind that his/her inner responses to the child may affect his/her interaction with the child ("countertransference"). In the third example, we describe a child with severe aggression.

We conclude this chapter with an overview of the techniques utilized in RFP-C, including the intermingling of supportive interventions by the clinician while addressing the child's avoidant mechanisms.

I. Case I: Betty and the standard treatment process

An important diagnostic issue with six-year-old Betty, who came for therapy because of disruptive behaviors, involved her capacities to relate and to interact. Betty's problems began with the birth of a younger sister when she was three. During the evaluation, it became clear that her maladaptive social responses (such as not always looking at someone's eyes when in a strange situation or when being reminded of a wrongdoing) were defensive responses and at least not solely due to social or cognitive deficits.

a. Interplay with genetic determinants

A prime example of this "retreat" from social situations occurred when Betty would feel overwhelmed by a large gathering or the close contact in circle time in school.[1] In these situations, Betty would occasionally remove herself from the close contact with others (adults and children). Most often, she became disruptive as a result of the purposeful or inadvertent physical contact with others. It became clear that Betty had a sensory oversensitivity to noises and touch, which were intensified when she was not fully comfortable with the situation. An important goal of the psychotherapeutic work was to help her translate her feelings and hypersensitivity into words so she could process the negative stimuli more effectively.

In the psychotherapy sessions, the dynamics of disruption and retreat became evident. These two responses were seemingly polar-opposite twin responses to "overwhelming" stress:

1. Betty shutting out the unbearable stimulus, or
2. Responding to the frightening environment in a maladaptive aggressive fashion (the "best defense is a good offense").

b. Gradual address of defenses

Occasionally, Betty's sister accompanied Betty and her mother to the sessions. Betty acted as if the younger sister did not exist and would come right into the playroom. If the clinician made a comment about the sister, Betty would ignore the clinician, acting as if she had no idea what the clinician was describing. In essence, trying to talk directly about her sister was much too threatening.

The clinician elected to be supportive at this stage and did not yet attempt to address her denial. It was clear to the clinician that Betty needed to consciously deny the impact of her sister on her. To address her denial at the early stage of the psychotherapy would have been too overwhelming. It is important for the RFP-C clinician to respect the presence of long-standing defenses as the child's best attempt to regulate overwhelming emotional stimuli. This is an example of the importance of the clinician not trying to impose his/her ideas on the child and respecting the child's avoidance, especially if it does not result in disruptive behavior. Material would eventually emerge where the clinician could more effectively address the denial.

> **The clinician should respect the child's avoidance mechanisms, especially denial, early in the psychotherapy.**

c. *Initial sessions and intervention*

In contrast to her manifest nonresponse to questions about her sister, inside the playroom there was a great deal of disruptive behavior for many sessions. This occurred whenever something disturbing, not related to her sister, would emerge, like the clinician asking what was happening at school, Betty would angrily tell the clinician to stop talking and throw whatever she was holding at her. Sometimes she would say: "It's none of your business," or she would threaten to leave the session and "never come back again." The clinician responded that it was hard for Betty to think about things that were upsetting and therefore she fought with the clinician. This was the major line of intervention for several sessions; at times, the clinician needed to limit Betty's attempts to hit the clinician directly. Gradually, Betty began to modulate her angry responses towards the clinician.

> 1 **Addressing denial directly is very difficult.**
> 2 **If the clinician addresses what the child does not want to hear, the child may shut down or attack.**
> 3 **Addressing the child's attack as defense will lead to modulation of responses.**

d. *Indicators of progress*

I. NEW PLAY ACTIVITIES WITH REFERENTS

An important turning point in the sessions occurred when Betty likened the playroom to a protective castle, saying to the clinician that in the playroom they were protected from her sister coming into the sessions and disrupting their play. Interestingly, Betty took one of the Barbie dolls, saying that the doll would be her playmate while they were in the castle. The clinician conjectured that the doll was a representation of her sister. But she did not tell that to Betty.

> **A new play activity with obvious reference to the problematic dynamics in the child's life is an indicator of progress.**

II. DECREASING ATTACKS ON CLINICIAN

Reporting that the playroom was safe was a totally spontaneous expression on Betty's part. She became happier to see the clinician and they played a variety of games. There were fewer episodes where she wanted to hurt the clinician and fewer threats that she would leave the sessions and never come back.

> **Decreasing attacks at the clinician and fewer threats to walk out are indicators of progress.**

III. TRANSITION FROM REAL TO PRETEND ATTACKS AND DEFENSE

At one point, they played a bomb game, throwing foam balls at one another. This is an example where there was shift from actually trying to hurt the clinician toward pretend play where they tried to hurt each another in a pretend fashion. Betty responded to the clinician's usual question on greeting her, "How are things going?" by telling the clinician to shut up and that she was not going to tell the clinician anything. In the pretend play, Betty protected the Barbie doll. The clinician did not interpret this act of reaction formation.

> **Indicator of progress: Switch from real attacks towards clinician to pretend attacks.**

a. The importance of interruptions, such as holidays A session after a holiday break illustrates the strength of Betty's denial. In that session, Betty was more agitated than she had been before the holiday break. The clinician commented that perhaps she was more wired up because of some feelings about missing a session because of the holiday. Betty denied that she longed for the session. The clinician continued saying that it was hard for Betty to tell the clinician what was on her mind. This was the usual interpretation of Betty's defensive avoidance. She did not continue the discussion but noticeably calmed down after that comment.

> **Importance of addressing interruptions in the continuity of the sessions such as holidays.**

b. The importance of remaining experience-near Betty then decided that both of them would go into the castle (a separate part of the playroom), but not near each other. The clinician said that in the castle Betty would be safe from the clinician and that Betty would not have to hear the clinician, because talking was too disturbing for Betty. It is important to note that the clinician did not conjecture to Betty that there may be a connection between her need to protect herself from the clinician and her need to protect herself from her sister as she had expressed in an earlier session, when talking about the playroom as a castle. Nor, did the clinician address the reaction formations involved in her play with the Barbie. Such symbolic translations of her play may have likely resulted in a disruption of her play. It is essential that the RFP-C clinician stay as close as possible to the at-the-moment material unfolding in the room; this is an in-vivo opportunity for the child to *feel* (and not simply *think*) about his/her feelings.

> **Avoid symbolic interpretations of the play.**
> **Sign of greater adaptation.**
> **Ability to be flexible and find a compromise between her desires and other person's desires.**

c. Setting and observing response to limits to the play Betty's face noticeably changed and she looked more comfortable as she rearranged the furniture in the castle. Instead of the two of them being together in the castle, she instructed the clinician to build her own castle and gave her some blocks, chairs, and a table to build it. She said to the clinician that she should move her chair to the other side of the room so the castles would be far apart. The clinician said that she really did not want to move the chair and inquired if they could just pretend that the clinician's castle was on the far side of the room. Betty thought about that and didn't think that was such a good idea. She said that she had never seen a situation where castles were so close to one another. The clinician commented again on pretending, but Betty did not buy that.

> **Signs of improvement:**
>
> 1 Acceptance of defensive avoidance.
> 2 Continuous collaborative play sequence.
> 3 Acceptance of limits set by the clinician about his/her actions.

d. Encouraging the pretend in play   They set up their castles and began to throw the various foam balls as bombs to one another. Again, the clinician did not provide a translation of the play, such as that the bombs represented the expression of her anger at the clinician for missing a session because of the holiday. At one point, Betty said she was going to shoot the clinician. The clinician looked at her with a raised brow (she was surprised by her tone – was it real?). Betty looked at the clinician and said, "Pretend." The clinician thought to herself that this communication of "pretend" was a sign of improvement; Betty was able to shift her aggressive interaction with the clinician from a real attempt to hurt to the pretend mode, where she could enact the fantasy of wishing to hurt the clinician through pretend play.

> **Importance of direct verbalization by the child acknowledging that interaction was pretend.**

Betty then went inside her castle and the clinician was on her chair, and they threw the balls back and forth. Betty added the wastepaper basket to the clinician's side for more protection for the clinician. Betty then explained that if her bomb fell into the basket, it would explode and it would then go to Betty's side and the ball would also be Betty's.

IV. DISCUSSING REAL-LIFE PROBLEMS

This play was continued during the next two sessions where Betty set up the castles once again. At one point, the ball went into the wastebasket and Betty brought it to her side and then said that she needed more protection. She got her school bag and put in the front of her castle. She said that the bag had her schoolwork, and the clinician could not explode it and besides, "The work was very boring." This was the first time that Betty spontaneously brought up school directly.

a. Encouraging gradual development of child's acknowledgement of life problems   Very careful and judicious interventions must be made trying to directly address the child's first tentative steps in discussing problems from their real lives.

> **One has to be very judicious in responding to a child's revelation of an important problem, e.g., schoolwork.**
> **Signs of improvement:**
> **1   Did not shut clinician out when clinician addressed missing feelings.**
> **2   Modification of denial: Did not deny fun in the sessions.**

b. Addressing boredom and other defensive affects in real life As they continued the game, the clinician said that schoolwork must surely be boring and that it was more fun to play their game. With this comment, the clinician addressed that the feeling of boredom was the conscious emotion that served as an avoidance mechanism to prevent painful affects provoked by schoolwork to emerge in Betty's consciousness.

> **The clinician did not ask, "Why is work boring?" That could have provoked increase in avoidance because it would force the child to address her painful emotions associated with difficulties with schoolwork before she herself was ready to do so. The clinician let her set the pace. Instead, the clinician acknowledged the emotional value of playing instead of talking about the boring schoolwork.**

Returning to Malan's Triangle of Conflict, the feared feeling or the activated feeling that is being avoided is the unpleasant emotion associated with schoolwork. The phobic avoidance reaction is maintained by the experience of boredom and trying to understand why the unpleasant emotion (about schoolwork) is so unbearable that it needs to be avoided, the goal of RFP-C. In this situation, the clinician addressed the power of the boredom as an avoidance mechanism of more painful emotions and play with the clinician as a further escape from the painful emotions.

c. Addressing vacations and feelings of missing the play When Betty did not deny the clinician's comment, the clinician continued, saying that since it was fun to play here, perhaps she missed the sessions during the vacation.

> **The clinician used this opportunity to directly address the importance of their relationship and directly addressing the "missing" feelings.**

Betty said that she had fun during the vacation too. In contrast to prior denials and attacks at the clinician, this was a matter-of-fact discussion without any overt anger. And she implicitly acknowledged that she was having fun in the sessions; she did find the work with the clinician valuable.

d. Continuing to address the child's problems gradually A couple of sessions later, as they continued to play the bomb game, Betty again mentioned that she was bored with schoolwork. Later in that session, the clinician said, "It's more fun to play here than to do boring work." Betty did not respond but did not deny the observation. They continued bombing each other with the foam balls in the game.

> **Another attempt by the clinician to open up the topic of schoolwork via her need to avoid discussion of the topic.**

V. CLINICIAN IS ALLOWED TO SCORE POINTS

In contrast to the past, the clinician was now able to score some points in the game as Betty followed the rules she had set up – e.g., the lines on the floor that they could not cross, where they could hit each other. At one point, she even gave the clinician five chances to be hit before she would lose her life and she gave herself only three. Of course, Betty won the game. It is important to note that the clinician allows the child to arrange the rules of the game and avoids thinking about whether there is "cheating" or not. The purpose of games in therapy, even competitive games, like checkers, is to elicit fantasy material from the child and how the child sets up the role of clinician. In fact, allowing the clinician extra chances was a remarkable development for Betty, who had never allowed that previously.

> **Sign of improvement: Clinician is allowed to score some points.**

e. Case conclusion

It is clear from this material that Betty was more comfortable with the clinician and was better able to tolerate listening to discussions. In the past, these would have provoked disruptive behaviors. In fact, the mother also reported improvement at home and at school. This development of greater emotional regulation within a session is often accompanied by parallel improvements for the children in their social world. It is also clear from this clinical material that Betty, like most young children, did not explicitly verbalize her understanding that there were emotions associated with schoolwork or with her sister that were unbearable.

One can infer that there was indirect or implicit recognition that in the safety of the playroom (such as closing the door on her sister or building the castles) she could tolerate expressing her conflicted feelings through behavior and play and then listening to the clinician address potentially painful states. Her increased ability to play cooperatively was an indication that she was developing new ways to regulate her emotions, or in other words, that her implicit emotion regulation capacities had developed and matured to an extent to enable increased tolerance and metabolism of negative affect without resorting to defensive disruptive behaviors. Through play, Betty attempted to master her emotional conflicts via an age-appropriate substitute for direct verbalization of conscious understanding.

2. Case 2: Stephanie and issues of countertransference[2]

One session with Stephanie, a seven-year-old girl, demonstrates a fundamental problem that must be addressed when considering children with oppositional symptoms. This active, athletic girl (a tomboy) with disruptive behaviors in school, requiring disciplinary action, had one parent who was anxious, overindulgent, and inconsistent and another who was rigid, punitive, and emotionally unavailable. The play with the clinician consisted of a variety of ball games, often kickball. As is typical with young children, for Stephanie, winning was of central importance. However, unlike with other children, the clinician's occasional point or occasional win led to dramatic hysterics and accusations that the clinician was cheating. Stephanie's accusation of the therapist helped her avoid any guilt or shame about his behavior. The parents exhibited a similar pattern.

Stephanie is a typical example of children with externalizing behaviors – they can demonstrate intense denial and projection so that they may not be able to integrate or usefully consider *direct verbal interventions* about their actions. This example illustrates how *premature direct verbal interventions about their actions* are at best not useful and at worst disruptive to the treatment.

At one point in the treatment with Stephanie, there was a great deal of tension at school as she had been threatened with suspension. The parents were dissatisfied with the treatment, and Stephanie was in a particularly cheating mode. As a result of countertransference feelings of which the clinician was unaware at the time, the clinician said to Stephanie, "You know I really don't understand why it's so difficult for you to ever lose a point, even though you win every game." You certainly can hear in the clinician's words her own disguised aggression and frustration and wish that she "shape up" so the treatment could proceed.

The clinician addressed Stephanie's actions directly and not her emotions that she was defending against by his action.

Undoubtedly, the clinician's tone and affect towards Stephanie was similar to the way teachers and his parents responded to her. Everyone was, in essence saying:

"If you would just stop it and shape up and act like other kids, everything would be OK."

Stephanie ran out of the playroom to her mother screaming inconsolably that Dr. X was cheating. "She wants to cheat all the time and stops me from winning!" The clinician, perhaps because of countertransference feelings, did not anticipate the impact of the interaction between them. Stephanie continued to refuse to come into the office alone, which led to an interruption in the treatment.

This brief vignette highlights a common clinical moment when a clinician may not be aware of his/her own affective response and communication to the patient. This type of impediment limits the clinician's ability to effectively address the child's emotional state. In this particular instance, the clinician was engaged in a communication in the cognitive sphere, without being aware of the child's emotional state affecting her cognitions. ***As a result, she did not address the patient's*** *affective experience or the self-protective role of the disruptive behavior.* This moment of therapeutic impasse provides us with a valuable lesson in how to address children with disruptive symptoms.

> **The clinician needs to be aware of his/her own countertransference. The clinician has to be aware that the main goal of the treatment is to understand the self-protective role of the disruptive behavior. Winning or losing games in the sessions is irrelevant to the therapy. The role of the clinician is not to teach the child prosocial behavior. More adaptive social behavior will emerge from the treatment not from education.**

3. Case 3: Pete and severe aggression

Pete, an eight-year-old boy came for treatment because of tantrums and nightmares. Within a short period of time, he became aggressive in sessions, trying to cut the analyst's beard off, going into the closet, and making noises to scare him. Pete alluded to his parents' fierce arguments in their bedroom and said he protected himself by building a fort around his bed. In sessions, he built a model fort with blocks and other toys, saying he wanted to play "hit the donkey on the butt." Pete presented his clothed butt to the clinician, asking him to throw a soft ball at it. Before the clinician could respond, Pete said he was tired, "Never mind, I don't want to play." The clinician said, "*Maybe you feel tired because you feel uncomfortable.*" Pete ignored this comment, but said his older half-brother could beat anyone because *he* was not afraid and came close to the clinician's face with a menacing expression. The clinician suggested "*Pete, you're acting tough so you don't have to worry about getting hurt*" and thought to himself that Pete seemed to be provoking him to hurt Pete. Pete's aggression subsided.

> **Two instances of addressing avoidance of recognition of unpleasant emotions:**
> 1 **Tiredness to avoid discomfort.**
> 2 **Acting tough to pretend to be not worried.**

A short time later, Pete missed a session because of illness. On returning, he threw lit matches toward the clinician and, in an off-hand barely audible whisper, said, "I'm going to the orthodontist right after the session." Pete calmed down when the clinician said, "*Oh, I understand, it's easier to attack me with matches than to worry about getting hurt by the orthodontist.*" Pete replied that he worried that *he* (Pete) would get hurt if he did not attack and jokingly asked if the clinician thought words could hurt him. Pete took a dictionary and playfully threw it at the clinician, who said: *"You get angry and attack when you worry about being hurt."* Pete became friendlier and demonstrated karate moves saying that the clinician should learn how to defend himself if he were mugged. The clinician said *"You're teaching me how to protect myself when you attack me!"* Pete laughed: "I get you angry, don't I?" The clinician replied, *"You know how to do that well."*

Continued interpretation of addressing the avoidance:

Attacking the other person feels better than worrying about being attacked.
(Turning passive into active).

Sign of improvement:

Could be playful and use metaphor instead of direct attack.

In the earlier session describe above, the clinician pointed out to Pete that he (1) warded off uncomfortable feelings by becoming tired and (2) acted tough to avoid scary feelings. In the later session, the clinician interpreted Pete's utilization of the mechanism of turning passive into active in order to avoid painful feelings about the orthodontist, after which Pete behaved more adaptively.

D. Review of the regulation-focused approach

Goal of treatment:

1   **Understand how the patient deals with unpleasant emotions usually by avoidance.**
2   **Determine how to communicate this understanding to the patient.**
3   **Help the child better tolerate the unpleasant emotions.**

The clinical example of Betty illustrates how we conceptualize the regulation-focused therapeutic approach. In everyday life, children, and adults for that matter, spend a great deal of mental energy attempting to avoid unpleasant emotions. This effort is often involuntary. In a psychotherapy session, avoidance of unpleasant feelings is inevitable. At times, this avoidance is manifested in maladaptive ways, such as oppositional symptoms, which not only cause grief to the people in the child's environment, but also to the child.

An important factor is that the patient makes an implicit equation in his/her mind: "The unpleasant feelings are so difficult to bear that I would rather fight or get into trouble than to allow myself to consciously feel those feelings." Therefore, as demonstrated in the clinical examples, an important goal of treatment of children with these maladaptive reactions is to:

1 Understand how the patient deals with unpleasant emotions, particularly avoidance.
2 Determine how to communicate this understanding to the patient.
3 And eventually, help the child better tolerate the unpleasant emotions.

In other words, the primary goal of RFP-C is to help the child develop more effective *__affect regulation__*.

E. Supportive interventions

I. Examples of supportive interventions

As we see in the treatment of Betty, all treatments have different degrees of supportive interventions and methods of directly addressing avoidance mechanisms. With supportive interventions, we attempt to curb the child's emotional reactions. The clinician may be encouraging, reassuring, set limits with explanations, and try to show the child a more realistic view of his/her life situation.

Examples of supportive interventions:
1 **Limit setting when play becomes dangerous.**
2 **Respect avoidance when emotions become too intense.**
3 **Respect denial.**

Many of these supportive interventions were present in the work with Betty. Most notably, limit setting occurred when her play became too dangerous; whenever she clearly and definitively wanted to avoid the expression emotions, this avoidance was respected. The most notable example of this technique occurred when she refused to address, or even acknowledge, her sister's presence in the office.

Supportive interventions, by their very nature, promote the child's reliance on the other person as the judge of danger or safety. For example, telling Betty that her sister will not hurt her and that she should not worry about her sister may deny the reality of Betty's emotions, which may lead to a negative outcome. This type of supportive intervention may also preempt the child's development of the autonomous recognition that reassurance comes from within, a more positive result than simply relying on continual support from other people. When the clinician directly addresses the child's avoidance mechanisms, the clinician implicitly facilitates the child's autonomous regulation of his/her unpleasant emotions and increases his/her awareness of how he/she needs to avoid recognition of those emotions, both positive outcomes.

In the situation with Betty, the most important and repeated intervention was trying to point out the need to avoid difficult emotions by either trying to hurt the clinician or trying to shut her up. It is important to note that the great majority of the interventions did not communicate a content that was hidden from Betty. Rather, the focus was on what was actually occurring between her and the clinician, and, most importantly, her avoidance of certain emotions.

> **Interventions aimed at avoidance mechanisms:**
> Pointing out how awareness of some unpleasant affect was avoided.
> Addressing avoidance against awareness of transference feelings.

2. Balance between supportive and expressive interventions

In the three clinical examples, we observe the impact of the interaction between the patient and the clinician. Discussing the nature of this interaction and pointing out the child's utilization of certain avoidance mechanisms promotes the emergence of more adaptive methods by the child. At the same time, the clinician is aware that when feelings are too intense, he/she may have to back away from interpreting avoidance mechanisms and take a more supportive stance with the child. A crucial element in RFP-C is trying to understand the mutual impact of the clinician–patient interaction and finding a balance between supportive interventions and those directed at the avoidance mechanisms.

> **Need to find a balance between supportive interventions and expressive interventions.**

This requires that the clinician understand the nature of the child's affective communication and the function of the avoidance mechanisms that children use to protect themselves from unpleasant emotions. The clinician then has to communicate to the child how he/she understands the nature of the child's avoidance of unpleasant emotions. This may be followed by identification of the child's emotions in a manner that is consistent with and respectful of the child's needs to maintain an avoidance of these difficult feelings. The clinician has to be sensitive to emotions that may be too painful to express directly. He/she must think about how to gently help the child gradually become aware of and discuss those feelings voluntarily.

By demonstrating sensitivity to the child's avoidance of unpleasant emotions (such as with Betty, being aware that talking directly about the sister would be too disturbing) the child will be more amenable to addressing the avoidance mechanisms as the alliance between clinician and patient is strengthened. It is important that, throughout the treatment, the clinician stay attuned to situations which indicate the activity of avoidance mechanisms. These include

1. Spontaneous change of topic under discussion.
2. Change of play activity.
3. Resisting clinician's attempts to explore topic.
4. Denial of discomfort.
5. Expression of opposite feelings.

Indications of avoidance activity
1. **Spontaneous change of topic under discussion.**
2. **Change of play activity.**
3. **Resisting clinician's attempts to explore topic.**
4. **Denial of discomfort.**
5. **Expression of opposite feelings.**

The clinician's empathic and respectful listening and careful attempts at clarifying what is happening will help the clinician recognize when to address shifts in the child's discussion and play. The child may be more amenable to hearing how the shifts may reflect avoidance of painful topics and this will lead to a gradual increase in affect tolerance.

Gradually, as the cases illustrate, the child has greater comfort discussing (or playing out) uncomfortable topics. The child will grow in his/her ability to discuss distress more openly and reveal other awkward events in his/her life, such as Pete revealing his fear of going to the orthodontist. In these situations, the children expressed their conflicts in a more adaptive fashion, including the use of humor and playacting their aggression instead of expressing overt aggression towards the clinician. At the same time, their disruptive symptoms at home and at school were very much improved.

F. Conclusion

In sum, the crux of the regulation-focused approach does not include the direct symbolic interpretation of the content of the child's expressions. The treatment is not simply catharsis and does not rely on simple reassurance. The clinician must be careful to not promote feelings of shame, guilt, or humiliation in the child. Children with oppositional symptoms may have bad feelings about their schoolwork or towards parents and siblings. As a result, there is a phobic avoidance of these feelings and they make comments that reflect this sense that "I am not afraid or I am not ashamed, I will fight instead." When the clinician addresses this sequence, more adaptive reactions follow.

What the clinician addresses by addressing defense

1 Externalizing behavior as a way to avoid certain thoughts and feelings (How).
2 What is the feared feeling (What).
3 Why is the feared feeling being avoided (Why).

Notes

1 Educators and parents often do not appreciate the stress-inducing situation of circle time when a child with temperamental difficulties may require special interventions such as individualized attention.
2 This example was discussed in Chapter 1. It is repeated here.

Chapter 10

Step 2: sessions 3–11

Examination of the clinician/patient relationship in the treatment of children

A. Introduction
 1. Similarities with Chapter 9
 2. Differences and unique aspects of the protocol contained in Chapter 10
 3. Key theme: the experience-near intervention and the avoidance of "hearsay"
B. The transference concept
 1. Mutative factor in a psychotherapeutic treatment
 2. Transference in plain language
 3. The use of transference in the clinical situation
    a. Neutrality
    b. The gradual communication of meaning
    c. The ideal therapeutic situation
C. Evidence in support of using transference as a key mutative factor
 1. Generalization
 2. Therapeutic realism
 3. An evolving process
 4. Displacement of externalizing behaviors to the clinician
D. Complications that may arise
 1. Confusion in the parents
 2. Suboptimal behavioral diminishment in the real-world environment
E. Countertransference
 1. Introduction to countertransference in children with disruptive behaviors
 2. Clinical example of problematic enactment of countertransference
 3. Means of addressing common countertransference issues
    a. Self-understanding
    b. Limit setting
    c. Positive regard
F. Clinical example 1: Sherlock Holmes and the vacation
 1. Accepting and discussing aggression in the child's language
 2. Addressing a break in the treatment
 3. Summary and a discussion of insight
G. Clinical example 2: refraining from making transference prematurely explicit
H. Summary and conclusions

A. Introduction

In RFP-C, the major focus throughout all sessions is on two aspects:

1. Addressing how a child's maladaptive behaviors enable the avoidance of disturbing thoughts and feelings (see Chapter 9).
2. Addressing how the avoidant behavior is experienced in the treatment interaction with the clinician.

The second focus will be the topic of this chapter.

1. Similarities with Chapter 9

Both of these aims continue from the beginning until the end of the treatment. As we have mentioned, observation of these behaviors occurs as early as the first child session in Step 1. In the examples noted in Chapter 9, where the child does not talk or play, the clinician simply notes the child's withdrawal, without trying to guess what the child is avoiding and without trying to coerce the child to communicate. These actions can be felt as impositions by the child and will almost always increase avoidance in the child.

2. Differences and unique aspects of the protocol contained in Chapter 10

In Chapter 9, we described how the clinician can recognize and address the child's avoidance mechanisms. In this chapter, we discuss the importance of addressing how the avoidance mechanisms occur within the interaction between clinician and child. The clinician's focus on what actually occurs between child and clinician is an experience-near technique that avoids the pitfalls of trying to guess the child's motivations for the maladaptive behavior.

3. Key theme: the experience-near intervention and the avoidance of "hearsay"

This interaction between clinician and child:

A. The arena where the child's problems are played out.
B. They can be directly observed by clinician.
C. They can be discussed by clinician and child.

An approach where the clinician helps the child understand the meaning of his/her actions and words cannot be conducted by an experience-distant practitioner whose aim is to read the patient's mind and decode the meaning of the child's behavior and words in a symbolic way and communicate this "guess" to the child. Throughout the work with the child in RFP-C, by focusing on what actually occurs between clinician and patient, and how the patient is protecting him/herself (defending) from the awareness of unpleasant emotions, the clinician engages in a respectful experience-near technique.

> ### Central features of RFP-C
>
> By following the child's play and verbalization, the problematic symptoms that lead to disruption at home and/or at school inevitably will be repeated with the clinician.
>
> The clinician has the opportunity to observe directly the child's maladaptive behavior and the trigger to the child's maladaptive behavior (such as a child's difficulties regulating his/her emotions when he/she hears the word, "no").
>
> From the beginning of the RFP-C, the clinician addresses with the child the sequence of events that occur in the office.
>
> The clinician's focus helps the child recognize the way he/she avoids unpleasant emotions.
>
> The goal of this process is to help the child find more adaptive emotion regulation mechanisms, such as avoiding disruptive explosions when faced with a "no," even when the child feels angry and hurt.

B. The transference concept

1. Mutative factor in a psychotherapeutic treatment

Clinicians always wonder: What is the nature of the mutative factor in a psychotherapeutic treatment (Rosenfeld & Terr 1994)? Is the improvement a result of the relationship that develops between the clinician and child? Or due to exploratory interventions that are proffered to the child by the clinician? Is the improvement in response to supportive interventions that are provided? Does a young child gain insight into his/her problems and thus explicitly understand that the symptoms are problematic and thus give them up? Or is the gain in insight more a result of implicit processes within the child's mind?

> **What are the mutative factors in psychotherapy?**

These questions are difficult to answer and there is variability with each child; however, what seems clear is that the interaction between the clinician and the child is a crucial vehicle whereby the child's problems are played out and enacted, addressed by the clinician, and processed by clinician and child. Thus, the interchange between clinician and child provides the child with an opportunity to modify maladaptive responses.

"Addressing the transference" is the technical term applied to the examination of the interaction between clinician and child. The examination of the interaction is important because of the human tendency to repeat and relive with others the interactions we have had or are having with the centrally important people in our lives, such as parents, teachers, and siblings.

What is transference?

The interaction between the clinician and the child is a crucial vehicle where the child's problems are played out and enacted, addressed by the clinician, discussed by clinician and child, and thus provide the child with an opportunity for maladaptive responses to be modified.

---

2. Transference in plain language

Why do patients repeat behavioral interpersonal patterns with their clinicians? How does this happen? This occurs because of the presence of "transference." In brief, transference is a universal psychological phenomenon in which a person's relation to another person has elements that are similar to and/or are based on his/her earlier attachments, especially to parents, siblings, and significant others. The presence of transference in everyday life has been demonstrated experimentally (Andersen & Chen 2002). In other words, a patient's relationship to teachers, club leaders, other grownups, as well as any other relationship, including the clinician, includes elements from his/her earliest parental relationships.

Transference is ubiquitous.

---

3. The use of transference in the clinical situation

As with any other relationship, the child not only sees the clinician objectively but also imputes qualities to the clinician that are derived from qualities of other important figures in his/her life. In real relationships, the other person directly expresses his/her needs or displeasures.

a. Neutrality

In contrast, in the relationship between patient and clinician, one member of this dyad, the clinician, attempts to be relatively "neutral." The clinician attempts to limit the gratifications of the patient's desires and attempts to control his/her own counterreactions (and tries to understand his/her own countertransference) as the patient attempts to provoke gratification or rejection. In the previous chapter, we described the problems that can arise when the clinician is not cognizant of his/her countertransference.

b. The gradual communication of meaning

The psychotherapeutic relationship, which becomes an important relationship for both patient and clinician, fosters the intensification of feelings, which for both patient and clinician can be accentuated. Thus, a major tool utilized in the therapeutic situation, with children, adolescents, and with adults, is trying to understand and address the meaning of the patient's transference relationship to the clinician. In this setting, the clinician attempts to understand the meaning of the patient's verbal and nonverbal communications, including the meaning of the interactions with and responses to the clinician by the patient. The clinician can then communicate his/her understanding to the patient in order to broaden the patient's view of him/herself. During this process, rather than gratifying or rejecting the patient, the clinician attempts to examine the nature of the patient's interactions with the clinician. Over time, the clinician communicates his/her understanding to the patient.

c. The ideal therapeutic situation

In an ideal therapeutic situation (which of course, we strive for but never fully realize), the clinician does not react in kind, especially when a patient disparages him/her or threatens to walk out of the room. Instead, the clinician tries to help the patient understand why his/her attacks and attempts at rejection feel necessary. Sometimes, the connection between the child's experience of the clinician and the child's experiences with his/her family may emerge spontaneously in this short-term treatment. The clinician's accepting attitude towards the child's emotional expressions promotes the emergence of these transference feelings.

C. Evidence in support of using transference as a key mutative factor

There has been an increased amount of empirical work demonstrating the power of transference interpretations in the psychotherapy of adults (Høglend 2014; Høglend et al. 2011; Høglend et al. 2008; Gerber & Peterson 2006). Unquestionably, the most effective way to help patients in a psychotherapeutic situation is to help the patient understand the nature of the transference relationship. When the clinician addresses the transference, he/she achieves several goals (Arlow 1987).

1. Generalization

The clinician is able to demonstrate to the patient how he/she distorts the current relationship (with the clinician) as a result of issues connected to his/her life. In this way, the patient gradually learns how he/she misperceives stimuli arising from other people, and how misinterpreting what is happening makes the patient prone to respond inappropriately.

For example, when a child with oppositional symptoms hears "No," he/she feels humiliation and thus retaliates. This, of course, will be repeated in the psychotherapy when the clinician inevitably says "No" about something. Over time, the clinician can first point out and discuss with the child his/her responses when the clinician says "No" to something. At a certain point, the clinician can gently ask something like, "How do you respond when (mom, dad, teacher, grandma, etc.) say 'No' to you?" This is an example where the clinician can use the knowledge obtained from the parents and try to make connections between what is happening in the sessions and what is happening in the child's real life.

> **The clinician can demonstrate the child's distortions in the current relationship with the clinician.**

2. Therapeutic realism

By addressing the nature of the interaction between child and clinician, as well as, implicitly or explicitly, its connection to other relationships, the treatment becomes experience-near and real for the patient and clinician. The clinician does not have to resort to reports from the family, does not have to conjecture about conflicts that are either unconscious or impossible for the patient to articulate. Addressing the nature of the interaction between both of them allows the patient and clinician to address the disturbing situation that is occurring in the present, even though its roots belong to the past or to other relationships.

> **By addressing what actually occurs between clinician and patient, the treatment becomes experience-near and real for the patient and clinician.**

For example, where the child responds dramatically to the clinician's "No," the clinician must first examine the interaction between the two of them. Only then can the clinician try to make a connection to the child's real life. The discussion between clinician and child about an interaction in which they both participate makes the issue real for the child in the present. Common protective devices that children utilize are denial and projection (Cramer 2006). These protective devices are easily activated when the child is in a stressful state because they are the most familiar to the child. As described by Otto et al. (2013), during stress, an individual's executive function is impaired, conscious deliberative choice cannot occur, and the person responds with habitual automatic processes. This maladaptive response to stress is particularly prevalent when the child has working memory impairment (e.g., deficits in the capacity to hold information in mind and manipulate it over short periods of time).

One can easily see that such a discussion with a child who utilizes intense denial and/or projection can lead to either the clinician communicating that he/she does not believe the child or the opposite, that the clinician "believes" the child and that the parent was unfair. Either resolution can lead to an impasse in the treatment because the clinician usually cannot set him/herself up as the judge of what really happened. By utilizing the interaction between clinician and child, the clinician does not have to rely on a third-person account and can also address the child's protective devices that the child will inevitably utilize in the sessions.

> **By utilizing the transference, the clinician avoids second-hand information. The clinician does not have to say, "I heard from your parents that . . ."**
> **Treatment thus focuses on what is happening right now.**

3. An evolving process

It is important to remember that addressing the interaction between clinician and child occurs over time and cannot be a "one-shot" deal. The nature of the work is that of a process that evolves throughout the duration of the treatment. The clinician must continuously assess how to respond to the dynamic interplay that occurs within the patient and between the patient and him/herself.

> **Psychotherapeutic treatment is a process.**

4. Displacement of externalizing behaviors to the clinician

Finally, and most importantly, when the relationship between the child and clinician intensifies, the conflictual issues between the child and his/her family can become fully displaced onto the figure of the clinician. This displacement often causes the disruptive symptoms to diminish at home and school. In that way, the symptomatic disruptive behavior can be worked through between clinician and patient.

> **Conflicted issues are displaced onto the clinician, allowing them to be worked through.**

D. Complications that may arise

1. Confusion in the parents

Children often say to the clinician: "My problems at home are fixed. You are my only problem; if I left here then everything will be OK." This can present several problems.

Parents can easily be swayed by the child's arguments and may request premature termination of the treatment. Thus, the clinician will need parental support for continuation of the treatment and will have to review with the parents the nature of the relationship between the clinician and the child. This should include discussion of the repetition (and the *__importance__* of this repetition) of the problems with the clinician.

> **Parents need to be made aware of the repeated nature of the psychotherapeutic process.**

Parents may also be disturbed by the child's responses to the clinician coming in or out of the sessions. In private moments, the clinician can discuss with the parents the difference between a therapy session and an interaction at school or at home. The emphasis in a therapeutic encounter is not on simply exhibiting socially acceptable behavior. Rather, the treatment will not succeed *without* the child demonstrating disruptive behavior.

2. Suboptimal behavioral diminishment in the real-world environment

Difficulties may occur when there is a continuation from the session to the real world of the "socially inappropriate" behavior. This is a situation where the clinician has to work with child and parents, trying to understand why the disruption continues: Is the therapy overstimulating the child? Is the clinician addressing the child's protective mechanisms too vigorously and too rapidly in a child whose protective mechanisms need to be reinforced instead of explored? Are the parents promoting or not controlling the disruptive symptoms? Are the parents trying to "imitate" the clinician, being "therapeutic" rather than parental with the child by setting rules?

An ideal situation occurs when a parent says: "I don't understand. I heard her screaming at you and soon as we walked out of the office, she was fine."

Parents need to be helped to understand the difference between expectations of the child in the therapy session and at home.
  Pitfalls to watch out for if disruption continues:

1 Is the therapy overstimulating the child?
2 Is the clinician addressing protective devices too vigorously and too rapidly in a child whose protective devices need to be shored up instead of explored?
3 Are the parents promoting or not controlling the disruptive symptoms?
4 Are the parents trying to "imitate" the clinician and not being parental with the child?

Ideal situation RFP-C:

Parent says:
  "I don't understand. I heard her screaming at you but as soon as we walked out of the office, she was fine."

E. Countertransference

The psychotherapeutic treatment of aggressive children is difficult because of the child's potential real threats to the clinician and his/her possessions. Counterreactions are inevitably evoked in the clinician. As with any other person, the clinician's experience of the patient is colored by residues from his/her own past (countertransference). That is why a clinician has to understand him/herself as much as possible. This is crucial since the clinician needs to discern, as much as possible, the degree to which his/her reactions to the child are derived from his/her own past, and how much is provoked by the patient.

1. Introduction to countertransference in children with disruptive behaviors

Children with regulation problems such as children with Oppositional Defiant Disorder (ODD) or Disruptive Mood Dysregulation Disorder (DMDD) can become aware of their effects on their clinicians. In order to protect themselves from the painful emotions of powerlessness, shame, and distress, they may attempt to cope with those feelings by exhibiting an attitude of superiority or attempting to control the clinician. They attack the clinician; they follow the motto: "A good offense is the best defense." The provocations of the clinician and the attacks on the clinician are often a repetition of the behaviors that occur at home and/or at school. In the sessions, the child may respond with disruptive attacking behavior to the clinician's absences, to the presence of other children in the waiting room, or to the clinician's attempts to discuss uncomfortable subjects. In order not to feel the shame of missing the clinician, the child will attack instead. These situations are often reenactments of significant precipitants of the disruptive symptoms in the child's life.

2. Clinical example of problematic enactment of countertransference

A problematic countertransference was illustrated in Chapter 1 and Chapter 9. We learn from this therapeutic impasse that counterreactions by the clinician are a ubiquitous problem when working with disruptive children. Children with ODD and DMDD often evoke common countertransference issues. The treatment of these difficult children would be enormously helped for clinicians to be aware of their inevitable countertransference responses. Group supervision in a safe environment can be very useful to help the clinician appreciate the universality of this phenomenon and learn ways to master his/her own emotional reactions. The clinician's self-understanding can allow him/her to be more secure in limit setting and maintaining a positive regard for the child in the face of relentless provocations.

> **The challenge:**
> **How to address the child's emotional sphere.**

3. Means of addressing common countertransference issues

a. Self-understanding

The greater the knowledge the clinician has about him/herself, the more effective the clinician can be. Self-understanding will also help the clinician balance implementation of a variety of techniques, such as limit-setting, direction, and, even, at times, physical control to prevent damage to him/herself, the child, or his/her possessions; all of these may be necessary during the treatment.

b. Limit setting

In a psychotherapeutic setting, clinicians inevitably make comments such as: "We cannot continue with such wildness" or "I am going to protect you and me from being hurt" or "I will discuss this with your mother so she can sit outside so you don't run away." Limit setting is often necessary with children with dysregulation problems, and, at times, a clinician's angry reactions are unavoidable. However, many have had the clinical experience that such interventions, whether more neutral limit-setting or angry response, never have more than transient effects, regardless of the nature of the comment or degree of firmness or anger by the clinician.

c. Positive regard

Since psychotherapeutic work with such children is often challenging, it is important for the clinician to have some genuine positive feeling towards the child and feel hope that he/she can help the child in order to be able to weather the storms that will inevitably occur in the sessions. However, positive regard for the child is never a sufficient therapeutic ingredient because, inevitably, the child will test the clinician in an effort to provoke punishment or rejection from the clinician as he/she does at home. It is important for the clinician to observe the attempts to hurt and punish the clinician as well as the attempts to provoke the clinician to retaliate.

F. Clinical example 1: Sherlock Holmes and the vacation

A key session with eight-year-old Billy occurred shortly before a vacation. In contrast to the previous session when the clinician felt provoked to the point of getting angry, in this session, the clinician was able to respond to the child's provocation in a firm, nonangry manner.

1. Accepting and discussing aggression in the child's language

The clinician told the boy that the boy already knew that the goal was to investigate the motives for his behavior and that his behavior indicated that there were problems with his feelings that he could not talk about. The boy responded, "I only act crazy here." The clinician said that they would have to try to figure this out together. The boy responded: "You act like you're Sherlock Holmes."

The clinician agreed that the two of them *were* like detectives trying to figure out why he did destructive things in here. The boy tried to engage the clinician in a physical fight. The clinician said that he was trying to provoke a fight with him and hurt him, and he knew that the session could not continue that way. By incorporating the child's language, the accusation was released of its aggression and used in a therapeutically constructive way.

2. Addressing a break in the treatment

The boy said, "I want you to call my mother and say to her, 'Mrs. Brown, I've spoken to you before, but I can't treat your son anymore.'" The clinician responded, "Now I see; you've been fighting with me much more since we talked about how we have to have a break after next week. You feel so angry about that, so you fight with me and want to hurt me and my things; but you are also trying to provoke me to throw you out before the time we have to stop for the break so you can be in control."

Very dramatically, Billy calmed down and matter-of-factly asked how the clinician would be getting home that evening. The boy said that he would be going to a play in which his friends were performing and that, like the clinician, he would take a bus. He spent the next session doing origami. This is an example of a dramatic emotional response to the clinician's intervention (understanding the defensive nature of the child's fighting). By fighting, the child masked the sad or other negative emotions about the separation. When the clinician communicated this understanding, the child became calm and communicated his positive attachment to the clinician. Explicit verbal insight, as adults experience this, was not necessary to appreciate that the child understood the nature of his defensive actions.

3. Summary and a discussion of insight

Through the process of the clinician addressing the myriad ways the child and clinician interact, the child will gradually become more in touch with his/her feelings that he/she tried desperately to keep out of his/her awareness. In dysregulated children, it is important that the clinician explore with the child: (1) the problem with his/her aggressive outbursts in the sessions, (2) their cause, (3) their consequences, and (4) the feelings that provoke them. Eventually children will be able to directly discuss the impact of the other children in the waiting room, their feelings about the clinician's or their own absences from the sessions, and perhaps the connection between the feelings with the clinician and the sources of those feelings in their relationships with their primary family.

It is crucial to bear in mind, that for children, unlike with adults, insight into their problems has to do with being in touch with their feelings, motivations, and behaviors, without necessarily reasoning or verbalizing the causes the way adults do (Sandler et al. 1980; Joyce & Stoker 2000). The most effective way to help the child to be in closer contact with his/her feelings, behavior, and motivation is to demonstrate them live in the interaction with the clinician. Within the session and the therapeutic relationship, the child can begin to experience the unwanted affects consciously, without needing to rigidly employ the maladaptive protective devices, such as aggression, which impeded his/her development as a result of the disruptive symptoms.

G. Clinical example 2: refraining from making transference prematurely explicit

While playing a game, eight-year-old John, who was adopted at birth, knocked over the clinician's phone twice. The clinician reminded him that in the previous session he told the clinician that he was angry with him. He denied his anger but went on: "That's not being angry, but I hate, hate you, and despise you." This was a boy who was severely disruptive at school and had resisted coming to see the clinician. The disruptive symptoms were focused in the sessions; however, although he repeatedly said that he did not want to see the clinician, he clearly enjoyed himself as he yelled at the clinician, messed up his office, and would not let the clinician talk.

So here, even though he communicated annoyance and anger, he was also expressing an attachment with the clinician. Simultaneously, he was protecting himself against potential loss by not acknowledging the attachment. The important technical point was that the positive attachment was not addressed because clearly there was some danger in openly acknowledging the close connection to the clinician. Instead, the clinician focused the intervention on acknowledging that there were feelings (which the clinician did not specify at this point, yet) that were hard to think about and this made the child fight with the clinician.

As the clinician reviewed some of the themes of the sessions with the parents, he learned that recently John had been thinking about his adoption and worried that he would lose his adoptive parents. The parents, of course, tried to reassure him; however, this did not calm John. Concurrent with these discussions, the behavior problems began in school, often triggered by an angry remark by the teacher.

None of this material appeared directly in the sessions with John. Instead, his complaints about the clinician continued. The clinician's comments were refocused, saying to John that he complained so much about the clinician because he wanted make sure that nothing good happened between the two of them. This line of interpretation, focusing on the boy's active avoidance of acknowledging closeness with the clinician, continued for several sessions with John ignoring the comment. After a few sessions, when the clinician made the same comment, the boy stopped and said he had something to do. He went out to the waiting room and got his school bag, saying that he had to complete an assignment for school. He came back with his notebook and told the clinician that he had to complete writing his life story for school. He would not let the clinician see what he was writing, saying that it was private.

This response to the clinician's intervention (that John was avoiding closeness) led the clinician to conjecture that the private data referred to the adoption.

However, the clinician very carefully did not express this conjecture to the patient. In other words, the clinician did not attempt to "read the boy's mind."

> **Even when it seems obvious, a clinician should avoid "mind reading."**

In the next session, the clinician focused on John's defensive avoidance of revealing private thoughts by reminding him that the last time he needed to keep his story private. John threw a toy at the clinician's head. The clinician said that when he has difficult feelings he gets very angry and starts to fight. John calmed down. A few sessions later, John did discuss with the clinician the autobiography for school and read what he had written. In the assignment, he spontaneously mentioned that he was adopted but that it did not matter to him. The clinician did not comment but listened respectfully.

In this example, the clinician very deliberately did not ask the boy to reveal what he did not want to reveal. Instead, the clinician focused on the boy's need to keep a distance from the clinician and needed to keep private thoughts to himself. In his mind, the clinician conjectured that the boy had to defend himself against the complex feelings about the adoption and his fear that he might be abandoned again.

H. Summary and conclusions

Transference and countertransference are important in RFP-C. This chapter has aimed to explain these processes. In each session of Step 2, these issues must be attended to. As with the preceding chapter, the following adherence scale should be completed following each session within Step 2.

In Chapter 12 we will discuss the transition from Step 2 to Step 3 and termination.

Bibliography

Andersen, S.M. & Chen, S., 2002. The relational self: an interpersonal social-cognitive theory. *Psychological review*, 109(4), pp. 619–45.

Arlow, J.A., 1987. The dynamics of interpretation. *The Psychoanalytic Quarterly*, 56, pp. 68–87.

Cramer, P., 2006. *Protecting the self: defense mechanisms in action*, New York, NY: Guilford Press.

Gerber, A.J. & Peterson, B.S., 2006. Measuring transference phenomena with fMRI. *Journal of the American Psychoanalytic Association*, 54(4), pp. 1319–25.

Høglend, P. (2014). Exploration of the patient-therapist relationship in psychotherapy. *The American Journal of Psychiatry*, 171(10), pp. 1056–66

Høglend, P. et al., 2011. Effects of transference work in the context of therapeutic alliance and quality of object relations. *Journal of Consulting and Clinical Psychology*, 79(5), pp. 697–706.

Høglend, P. et al., 2008. Transference interpretations in dynamic psychotherapy: do they really yield sustained effects? *The American Journal of Psychiatry*, 165(6), pp. 763–71.

Joyce, A. & Stoker, J., 2000. Insight and the nature of therapeutic action in the psychoanalysis of 4- and 5-year-old children. *The International Journal of Psycho-Analysis*, 81 (Pt 6), pp. 1139–54.

Otto, A.R. et al., 2013. The curse of planning: dissecting multiple reinforcement-learning systems by taxing the central executive. *Psychological Science*, 24(5), pp. 751–61.

Rosenfeld, A.A. & Terr, L.C., 1994. Resolved: the therapist – patient relationship is the crucial factor to change in child psychotherapy. *Journal of the American Academy of Child & Adolescent Psychiatry*, 33(7), pp. 1047–53; discussion 1053–1056.

Sandler, J., Kennedy, H., & Tyson, R., 1980. *The technique of child psychoanalysis: discussions with Anna Freud Cambridge*, Cambridge, MA: Harvard University Press.

Chapter 11

Step 2: ongoing parent contact
Check-ins and meetings

OUTLINE

A. Specific goals of ongoing check-ins and meetings
   1. Provide treatment update
      a. Emphasize the child's strengths
      b. Offer information about gains the child is making in treatment
      c. Reintroduce Malan triangle with specific information about the child's feelings, anxieties, and how the child regulates unpleasant emotions
   2. Check in with parents to address current concerns
      a. Emphasize parent and family strengths
      b. Utilize empathic listening to continue building a strong therapeutic alliance
      c. Employ reflective functioning capacities as in-vivo tool for building parental mentalizing skills, which will, in turn, help the child increase regulatory capacities
         a. Clinical example: babysitter and the Brute
   3. Offer further education on defenses and mind-mindedness
      a. Explain process of scaffolding
      b. Activate parents' reflective functioning in order to begin building a mentalizing system around the child
      c. Offer further resources to help parents learn about how everyone regulates unpleasant emotions in a variety of ways and how to help the child understand his/her own behavior
   4. Responding to parental concerns about their own functioning
   5. Provide education about upcoming termination
      a. Outline common experiences of children and families at the end of treatment

A. Specific goals of ongoing check-ins and meetings

Ongoing parent check-ins and meetings are a useful way to continue to build an alliance with parents and the child and to enhance family functioning. These contacts with parents are essential and should take multiple forms, varying in length and frequency. Brief, weekly check-ins with parents are highly recommended in this treatment. Most clinicians will meet with parents for ten minutes at the end of each child session and these brief contacts are referred to as "check-ins" throughout the manual. Children may be included in the check-ins, at the discretion of the clinician. Although the brief check-ins will require additional time, the rewards of ongoing contact with parents are many. Parents feel valued as they are included in the treatment process and this further contributes to the inherent empathic stance of the clinician. The child has the opportunity to share his/her gains with the parents in the presence of the clinician. Additional clinical data may be obtained from regular interaction with the parents and from observation of the child with his parents.

In addition to these regular, brief interactions, clinicians may choose to have two or three meetings with parents during the course of treatment in addition to the initial meeting/s and the second meeting (for a total of up to six full-length parent meetings). These longer (typically 45-minute) contacts with parents are referred to as "parent meetings" throughout the manual. The purpose of check-ins and meetings is to educate and support parents in order to foster a supportive environment for the child.

Parent check-ins and meetings are *not* to be a place for the provision of individual or family therapy. Instead, the check-ins and meetings are designed to enable a longitudinal discussion of reflective parenting and/or education about how their child regulates unpleasant emotions. This helps the parents to develop a secure, internalized sense of the clinician, which may help them bear their child's disruptive behaviors and the family problems in the intersession intervals. Much as the clinician attempts to strengthen a sense of object constancy (Burgner & Edgcumbe 1972) in the child, the similar techniques which are helpful to the child, including a warm regard, balanced reactions, and reflective functioning in lieu of impulsive action, are applicable to the parents. The content focus should remain on the problems of the child and his/her means of developing greater self-regulatory control; the process of listening, receiving, processing, and returning once-negative affects in a less corrosive form is the active agent of change in the parents, which is of perhaps of greatest help to the parents and, indirectly, to the child as the parents internalize this function and employ it in their interactions with their child.

The parent check-ins and meetings may indeed elicit statements from parents about their own reactions (either, to painful affects or to their child). The specific process for responding therapeutically to these self-statements will be addressed later in this chapter. The topics covered in this chapter should not be addressed within a single parent check-in or meeting; rather, they are intended to be discussed over the course of several parent contacts with dosing adjusted in accordance with the parents' individual needs and abilities. The content of weekly check-ins or longer, less frequent parent meetings is not distinct. The specific goals outlined in this chapter apply to both the check-ins and the more extensive parent meetings.

1. Provide treatment update

Parents are often eager to know how treatment is progressing, and offering feedback and updates can help quell feelings of anxiety about what is taking place in the consulting room. After several sessions with the child, the clinician will have a better understanding of the child's typical responses to painful affects and how the child's capacity to regulate them manifests itself behaviorally. Providing parents with a brief and updated conceptualization of the child's difficulties can help validate what they may already know about their child. It may also offer some parents a new way of thinking about their child's difficulties that will allow them to have greater empathy and to intervene more effectively with their child.

> **Being transparent about what is taking place in RFP-C can help parents feel more empowered to create a more supportive environment for their child.**

a. Emphasize the child's strengths

RFP-C is a strength-based approach to working with children. This style of psychotherapy understands the child as doing the best that he/she can, given the emotional and cognitive resources he/she currently has available. Clinicians should reiterate to parents that children with externalizing behaviors do not have sufficient internal strength (or implicit emotion regulation capacities) to tolerate the pain and anxiety of disturbing emotional states. This framing of the child's difficulties helps set the tone for the meeting as one of empathy and concern for the child. Although the concept of emotion regulation is associated with affective neuroscience, it is important that the clinician recognize the problem with becoming less empathic when biological causalities are stressed (Lebowitz and Ahn 2014). Clinicians are encouraged to provide parents with multiple positive statements about the child. For example, the clinician might say: "She is really able to let us know when she feels overwhelmed," or "He is taking some big risks in talking about his feelings a bit more directly," or "She has a great sense of humor that helps her cope with things that trouble her." These positive statements are somewhat more elaborate than those provided to parents in earlier meetings. They begin to make connections between underlying feeling states and what behaviors are actually observable in the child. This is the beginning of building parental understanding of the child's regulation capacities. These comments can also help invite parents into a discussion of their perception of their child. Parents may want to share how they view the child's adaptive and maladaptive reactions and should be encouraged to agree or disagree with the clinician's assessment. All parent meetings should be a collaborative process in which the clinician and parents are working together to better understand the child.

> **Parents need to learn that children with externalizing behaviors do not have sufficient internal strength to tolerate the pain and anxiety of disturbing emotional states.**

b. Offer information about gains the child is making in treatment

It is important that clinicians offer parents feedback about what the child is experiencing, learning, articulating, and acting out (through play, etc.) in treatment. This will help alleviate parental anxiety about how the therapy is progressing and will provide a foundation for parents in terms of how to respond empathically and effectively to their child's distress. Clinicians may want to provide specific descriptions of topics and emotions that the child appears to avoid and offer explanation as to why the child feels, on some level, that these *must* be avoided. Early on in the treatment, when clinicians are simply noticing the avoidant strategies of the child, an example of how this happens in the consulting room should be shared with the parents. This can provide a model for parents as they begin to think about how to engage with their child in new ways.

As treatment progresses, the clinician can share with parents other types of interventions that have allowed the child to express him/herself more freely. The clinician should also continue to highlight the child's strengths. This can include describing topics and feelings that the child appears to be more comfortable expressing or simply identifying the ways in which disruptive behavior sometimes allows the child to protect him/herself. In later parent meetings, the clinician can share with parents concrete indicators of improvement in the child. This table, first presented in Chapter 9, may help clinicians identify and frame specific gains for the parents that have been achieved thus far.

Indicators of improvement in the child

1. Greater comfort in sharing uncomfortable topics.
2. Revealing problematic events from his/her life.
3. More direct expression of feelings about the clinician.
4. Decreased aggression at home and at school.
5. Parents have greater comfort with child.
6. Reports of greater socially appropriate interactions at home and at school.
7. More direct discussion of aggression at home and at school.
8. Verbal attacks towards clinician instead of physical attacks.
9. Playacting aggression towards clinician rather than direct attacks.
10. Verbalization by the child that interactions are pretend.
11. Ability to play games by the rules and allow the clinician a chance of making points or even at times winning.
12. Greater use of humor in the sessions instead of direct verbal attacks.
13. More direct elaboration of fantasy material.

c. Reintroduce Malan triangle with specific information about the child's feelings, anxieties, and how the child regulates unpleasant emotions

Parents should now be familiar with Malan's Triangle of Conflict based on earlier meetings with the clinician. Malan's Triangle should be reintroduced to parents in each ongoing meeting; for some families, introducing a visual cue may be helpful (see Appendix A). In these later meetings with parents, the Triangle of Conflict can be employed to conceptualize the child's particular difficulties (WHAT feeling is being avoided, HOW the feeling is avoided, and WHY does that feeling need to be avoided). The clinician may want to share with parents a scene from the therapy that highlights the child's maladaptation and increasing adaptation to negative emotional stimuli. **(Note: Before sharing with the parents specific, detailed examples from the therapy, the clinician should obtain verbal permission from the child by discussing with him/her what can or cannot be shared with the parents.)**

For example, a child who becomes increasingly disruptive towards the end of a session is likely experiencing difficulty with feelings of loss associated with saying good-bye or a sense of being overwhelmed by an upcoming transition. In this case, the feared feeling of loss or a sense of uncertainty is being avoided and cannot be directly discussed by the child. This automatically leads to an experience of anxiety that is also difficult for the child to articulate. The manifestation of these two automatic processes is disruptive behavior, perhaps in the form of taking out numerous toys with no intention of using them, yelling, or attacking a doll or action figure within the play. Within the RFP-C paradigm, the clinician will have commented on the behavior in a nonjudgmental way with an emphasis on trying to understand why a particular feeling is being avoided.

At this time, parents should be invited to think about a recent interaction in the home in which the child's disruptive behavior was evident. The clinician may say something like: "This is one example from the work we've been doing in therapy but I am sure this is something that comes up at home many times a day. Can we think together about one of those incidents?" This process will allow parents to begin to think more effectively about their child's emotional regulation and its impact on the child's behavior. Some parents may want to relay an incident reported by a teacher or school counselor, but they should be encouraged to also describe an interaction that they observed and participated in themselves. Parents should be encouraged to describe incidents from their own perspectives: Either that they both witnessed or ones that only one witnessed and reported to the other. It is important for the clinician to stress that different people have a variety of perspectives and that by discussing them they can understand their similarities and differences. As parents report the incident, the clinician can gently guide them through a process of thinking about the child's behavior in a new way.

2. Check in with parents to address current concerns

In each parent meeting, parents should be given ample opportunity to express their concerns. These may include concerns about the treatment model, ongoing behavior problems at school or in the home, or about the clinician him/herself. Concerns should always be respected and addressed with special care taken to understand and empathize with the difficulty parents may be experiencing. Reassurance, comfort, structure, and kindness should be portrayed to the family in ensuring all questions have been answered to their satisfaction. If parents raise concerns in a brief check-in and there is not sufficient time to fully address them, this would be an opportune time to suggest a full-length parent meeting.

a. Emphasize parent and family strengths

Anecdotes shared by the parents during meetings with the clinician, stories relayed by the child in the RFP-C sessions, and the clinician's own observations form the basis of positive feedback that can be shared with the parents. That the family is seeking treatment at all is indicative of an inherent strength, and this should be acknowledged. It may be helpful to specifically identify the hopes and wishes the parents have for their family as strengths. For example, "It is clear how much you want to be able to do more activities together as a family," or "It's great to see how proud you are of your daughter's accomplishments in her after school program." There may be strengths within the couple (when there are two primary caregivers) that can be highlighted. For example, "The warmth and affection you show each other and your son is really special." These types of statements, if shared in the right context and in a genuine and authentic tone, can help relieve some parental anxieties and increase parental self-efficacy.

b. Utilize empathic listening to continue building a strong therapeutic alliance

As with all parent and child meetings in RFP-C, the clinician is advised to maintain a nonjudgmental stance and a warm, collaborative attitude. Many parents will express feelings of frustration, of simply not liking their child at times, and fear that things will never change. It is important that parents feel that the clinician can hear these concerns without becoming overwhelmed. Empathy is one aspect of the therapeutic relationship that makes it distinct from other types of relationships. Although parents have other people in their lives that they speak to regularly about their child, the level of vulnerability they show with the clinician may be greater than in their day-to-day interactions with others (Greenberg et al. 2001). Families come to therapy because they have a problem they have been unable to solve and often are unable to share with another person. Clinicians are the keepers of many, many secrets. But, how do clients know they can trust the clinician? Kohut (1984, page 82) defined empathy as "the capacity to think and feel oneself into the inner life of another person." This definition is useful to keep in mind in RFP-C as it combines the nonjudgmental stance that is required of the clinician with a mentalizing capacity that the parents and child are beginning to develop.

> Kohut (1975) also described empathy as "a fundamental mode of human relatedness, the recognition of the self in the other; it is the accepting, confirming and understanding human echo" (pages 704–5).

c. Employ reflective functioning capacities as in-vivo tool for building parental mentalizing skills, which will, in turn, help the child increase regulatory capacities

RFP-C is designed to increase children's abilities to think constructively about their own thoughts, feelings, wishes, motivations, and actions. In order for this process to flourish once treatment concludes, the child will need an environment that allows and even encourages this type of thinking. The task of the child, to engage in meta-cognition and meta-emotion processing, is complicated. The fact that *affect* is the central component that is being processed, understood, and discussed raises the stakes. Although the clinician may be quite skilled and able to tolerate a complex range of intense, sometimes overpowering, emotions, this may be a new skillset for parents.

This process, whereby feelings, thoughts, desires, and beliefs, are actively processed – rather than simply acted out – is often referred to as *mentalization* or *reflective functioning* (Slade 2005). Mentalization involves being able to think about one's own mind and the mind of another in a nondefensive way. Ideally, a parent will develop great abilities to hold, regulate, and fully experience their own emotions and those of their child. This use of mentalization and reflective functioning on the part of parents is termed *parental reflective functioning* or *reflective parenting*. It is not enough for the clinician and parents to simply empathize with the child's emotional and cognitive world; they must also work together to help the child effectively regulate emotional states and thoughts that trouble them.

In order to help parents begin to develop these skills, the clinician can utilize ongoing parent meetings to model reflective functioning in real time. By engaging parents in a mentalizing exercise about their child, the clinician can obtain a great deal of information about the parents' ability to provide a reflective parenting environment. By encouraging parents to focus on one of their own experiences with their child's disruptive behavior, the clinician is also obtaining data about the parent's cognitive and affective experience. What were they aware of feeling when the incident occurred (conscious affective experience)? Were they aware of any kind of anxiety in response to these feelings (signal anxiety)? How did they respond to the child's distress (possible defense against unconscious affective experience)? What feeling might have been present at the time, but was unable to be processed or attended to (hidden feeling/impulse)? Some parents may respond well to completing a Triangle of Conflict handout based on their own experience, whereas others may be resistant. The clinician should follow the parent's lead and engage in the discussion in a way that the parents can tolerate.

The clinician, in some cases, may employ a further step, though care must be taken to avoid delving too much into individual or family treatment with the parents. The clinician may notice the unfolding of an automatic, defensive response to affect within the session, which can be used to discuss how emotional regulation works both in adults and children.

The clinician's reflective stance with the child is manifested when the clinician observes a pattern of behavior and wonders about its significance with the child. "I notice that every time we are about to stop the session you throw toys. Maybe it's hard to tell me in words how you feel?" In such a situation, the clinician does not communicate certainty and does not communicate that the child should act more appropriately. Instead, the clinician wonders about the meaning of the behavior with the child. When talking with parents, the clinician takes the same stance: A self-reflective, curious stance. The clinician, in essence, models this kind of self-reflection when the clinician discusses problematic situations at home with the parents. For some parents, the introduction of this kind of reflective parenting may help them shift from being certain about their child's intentions to being curious about what motivated a particular behavior or response. By being curious about the child's motivation, the clinician implicitly helps the parents to be curious. A sign of progress occurs when the parents are able to say to themselves, "I wonder why he did that? I'm not sure how he's was feeling at the time." This state of mind creates more space and invites the parents and clinician to think about the child's actual experience.

I. CLINICAL EXAMPLE: BABYSITTER AND THE BRUTE

Luke's parents reported to the clinician that many things had improved at home since Luke had been in treatment; however, one problem persisted. When the parents would return home and the babysitter would leave, Luke was rough, bordering on aggressive. He would slam things around, push his sister, intentionally bump into his parents or the family dog and sometimes would break things. Luke's parents were able to connect his distress with the babysitter's departure and their return, but were at a loss as to what to do to improve the situation.

Luke's parents participated in weekly check-ins and had already participated in several parent meetings; as a result, Luke's parents knew enough to wonder about the feelings behind such seemingly angry behavior. They remained unsure of how to approach Luke about the disruptive behavior. Together, the clinician and the parents were able to brainstorm about possible feelings Luke may have been experiencing that he needed to avoid – sadness, loss, guilt, fear, confusion, etc. The clinician also reminded the parents that Luke had demonstrated similar behaviors towards the end of each therapy session during the first few weeks of treatment.

They revisited how the clinician had helped Luke anticipate the ending of the session, the impending transition from consulting room to being back with his parents, and how Luke had questioned: "Why do I have to stop doing something when I'm having fun? If we're playing here and then I have to leave, I'm missing out on everything!" Luke also shared how it reminded him of when the family had moved from another state and he had to leave behind his friends and teachers. The clinician said, "I think I am starting to understand. When you are faced with separating from people you care about, your 'tough guy' side comes out. You show everyone how strong and feisty you are – maybe because that is easier than sharing that you feel sad or that you are missing someone."

Luke's parents were then able to take these concepts home and help Luke become less of a "brute" during these difficult transitions. They also collaborated with the babysitter to help Luke anticipate the transition and engage in play that would help him express both his sadness and his anger about having to separate. Some months later, the parents contacted the clinician to report that Luke had shown them how drawing out the situation could help him process his feelings; they were impressed at how he was able to translate what he had experienced in therapy into an effective strategy at home.

3. Offer further education on defenses and mind-mindedness

a. Explain process of scaffolding

Once parents begin to learn about the skills they can develop and offer to their children, it can be helpful to discuss how *scaffolding* works in a developmental context. Although parents may not be familiar with the term, it is likely that they have been providing scaffolding around their child's physical, cognitive, and emotional development for many years. Common examples may include how they taught their children to speak, tie their own shoes, and dress themselves. The development of emotional regulation capacities mirrors these developmental tasks in terms of the role parents play in creating a supportive structure around their child's needs and emotional expression.

b. Activate parents' reflective functioning in order to begin building a mentalizing system around the child

Parents may begin to develop a two-way understanding of how emotional regulation works. The ability to link outer behavior with the inner workings of the mind is a reciprocal process. In order for children to develop regulatory abilities for intense or unacceptable emotions, the child's primary caregivers must also grow in their ability to tolerate unpleasant affect. *The clinician's collaborative attitude and self-reflective stance promotes the parents' growth.*

One child, who was raised from birth to age seven by her grandmother (before being transferred to an aunt's care), was not allowed to attend the grandmother's funeral because the child's aunt felt it would be "too upsetting." The aunt also chose not to attend the funeral, stating that she would, "Grieve in my own time."

The aunt's avoidance of feelings of loss and sadness were transmitted to the child and, not surprisingly, the child began to exhibit disruptive and aggressive behaviors in the face of nearly any ending – leaving for school in the morning, the end of the school day, saying good-bye to the babysitter, and when it was time to go to bed at night, all provoked uncontrollable rages for which the child had no words to explain. Both the aunt and her niece were coping with loss as best they could, given the resources available to them at the time. After several weeks of treatment, the clinician was able to broach the difficult subject of the loss of this family matriarch with the aunt, and this helped foster a new level of openness about feelings in the family. Over time, the child also began to draw and play around themes of death, abandonment, and fear of being left alone rather than yelling or throwing things at the clinician.

c. *Offer further resources to help parents learn about how everyone regulates unpleasant emotions in a variety of ways and how to help the child understand his/her own behavior*

Education about how children avoid disturbing thoughts and feelings can empower parents to understand the child's difficulties in terms of an adaptive response to stress. The following basic points about self-regulation should be communicated to parents:

1. Maladaptive behavior is often an automatic attempt to find a way to deal with stress, anxiety, and emotional discomfort.
2. The way in which children cope with distressing feelings is a largely automatic process; they are unlikely to even noticing they're doing it.
3. Everyone has ways to regulate difficult thoughts and feelings – some more adaptive than others. They are being used constantly in order to try to navigate life's challenges.
4. Problems arise when an individual has more maladaptive than adaptive ways of regulating affect, when these coping mechanisms are employed rigidly or without regard for the uniqueness of each situation, or without regard to the rights of others.

Once parents can understand self-regulation as a normal response to life's challenges, the clinician can begin to focus on how the child's ability to self-regulate is currently impeded by the child's current maladaptive regulatory style. Some parents may be eager to utilize the new skills and information they are learning. It is important to caution parents and remind them that the child's behavior (though often maladaptive) exists for a reason. Just as an infant turns his face away from the mother in order to have a break from "connecting," children also let us know when they need a break from being understood. Clinicians can highlight how important it is to be sensitive to the child's signal that some feelings may be too painful to talk about right away. The clinician can share how he/she avoided a topic when it was obvious that it was too intense for the child to continue to discuss. Parents may want to discuss with the clinician how to, gently and gradually, help the child become aware of and discuss those feelings willingly. Finally, it is important to reiterate to parents that children express their emotions in ways different from adults. These expressions may be nonverbal, through the use of metaphors or stories, demonstrated in play, or in the use of jokes. As these are all generally healthy ways to express emotion, children should be encouraged to utilize them and parents should be instructed to attend to these types of communications. In fact, being in touch with a child's feelings without having to verbalize the experience or cause of the feelings may be a more empathic and effective way of connecting with the child (Sandler et al. 1975).

4. Responding to parental concerns about their own functioning

For some parents, having a child in therapy can alleviate some of the burden of self-blame and judgment from other professionals about their child's behavior. It may be that the child is seen as the identified patient, that is to say, the one within whom all the problems reside. This parental response presents its own problems and can be addressed by identifying ways in which parent and child feed off of each other in difficult interactions. For other parents, the experience of RFP-C may raise new questions for them about their own functioning. Meetings with parents may illuminate ways in which their reactions to the child may at time exacerbate the problem. Or parents may begin to notice how their own histories, personality structure, and/or emotional regulation capacities influence their child. The purpose of ongoing parent meetings is not to provide individual psychotherapy for parents; however, parents who express a desire to look inward or to increase their own mind-mindedness should be encouraged to pursue outside resources. Many parents will benefit from a referral to individual psychotherapy or couples therapy, depending on the nature of the difficulties they face. The clinician may offer to speak with the parent's individual clinician in order to share a bit about RFP-C and the work that has been done thus far.

> **Having been helped to recognize and recapture the feelings which she herself had as a child and to find that they are accepted tolerantly and understandingly, a mother will become increasingly sympathetic and tolerant towards the same things in her child (Bowlby 1940, page 176).**

5. Provide education about upcoming termination

a. Outline common experiences of children and families at the end of treatment

Discussion of termination should be initiated with parents at least five sessions prior to the end of treatment. The clinician should explore with the parents how their child typically handles endings and separations and use this conversation as an opportunity to build additional, reflective parenting skills. Children with propensities to emotional dysregulation tend to have a difficult time with transitions, including separations and frustrations. Both the clinician and the parents can provide scaffolding around the child's experience by helping the child to be curious about what he/she might be feeling or thinking about the end of treatment. Parents may express relief or distress about the upcoming end of treatment. They should be encouraged to share these reactions with the clinician rather than with their child. Ample space and freedom should be afforded to the child to feel his/her own feelings about the separation.

The clinician should discuss with the primary caregivers areas in which the child has experienced significant growth and change as this can help foster healthy posttermination development. Parents should be prepared for normal and expected reactions to termination, which may involve a slight regression, or resurgence of symptoms, as termination approaches.

References

Bowlby, J., 1940. The influence of early environment in the development of neurosis and neurotic character. *International Journal of Psycho-Analysis*, 21, pp. 154–78.

Burgner, M. & Edgcumbe, R., 1972. Some problems in the conceptualization of early object relationships – Part II: the concept of object constancy. *Psychoanalytic Study of the Child*, 27, pp. 315–33.

Greenberg, L. S., Watson, J. C., Elliot, R., & Bohart, A. C., 2001. Empathy. *Psychotherapy: Theory, Research, Practice, Training*, 38(4), pp. 380–4.

Kohut, H., 1975. The psychoanalyst in the community of scholars. *Annual of Psychoanalysis,* 3, pp. 341–70.

Kohut, H., 1984. *How does analysis cure?* Chicago, IL: University of Chicago Press.

Lebowitz, M. S. & Ahn, W. K., 2014. Effects of biological explanations for mental disorders on clinicians' empathy. *Proceedings of the National Academy of Sciences of the United States of America*, 111(50), pp. 17786–90.

Sandler, J., Kennedy, H., & Tyson, R. L. 1975. Discussions on transference – The treatment situation and technique in child psychoanalysis. *Psychoanalytic Study of the Child*, 30, pp. 409–41.

Slade, A., 2005. Parental reflective functioning: an introduction. *Attachment & Human Development*, 7(3), pp. 269–81. doi: 10.1080/14616730500245906.

Chapter 12

Step 3: sessions 12–16
Termination

OUTLINE

A. Introduction to the termination process
B. Specific goals of the termination step: step 3
   1. First reminder of the approaching termination: session 12
      a. Discussion of past gains
      b. Delivery of the reminder
      c. Common patient reactions and responses
   2. Working through termination: sessions 13–15
   3. The final good-bye: session 16
      a. Restatement of the final good-bye
      b. Common patient responses
C. Clinical examples
   1. Clinical example 1: nonverbal communications
   2. Clinical example 2: use of metaphors
   3. Clinical example 3: use of drawing
   4. Clinical example 4: the avoidance of talking
D. Summary and final remarks

A. Introduction to the termination process

A psychotherapeutic relationship is an unusual relationship. On the one hand, it is a relationship like no other. Two people are in a room together with one of the participants free to make choices, talk, interact, remain silent, speak what is unspeakable in any other social situation, criticize, admire the other person in the room, and, with children, play and interact with few limitations.

This first person, the protagonist who drives the action between the two, is obviously the patient. The other person, the clinician, follows where he/she is led. Unlike the patient, the clinician does not direct but follows along and needs to act in the most impossible way – trying to understand and help the patient without inappropriately gratifying the patient while, at the same time, comfortably accepting that in this relationship the gratifications, which he/she expects from a normal everyday relationship, will not be forthcoming. The transformative power of the therapeutic relationship is ultimately derived from the unequal relationship between patient and clinician. The patient is able to express him- or herself in the most direct way possible and the clinician allows him- or herself to be the recipient of the patient's myriad complex feelings. At the same time, the clinician attempts to address the patient's struggles with his/her emotions as effectively as possible. This entire framework enables the patient, perhaps to understand, but certainly to master his/her complex feelings. In the language of a young child, the goal of psychotherapy is to allow the patient to be the boss of his/her feelings instead of allowing the feelings to be the boss.

This unique arrangement between clinician and patient allows the clinician to organize and articulate for the child how the clinician understands the child, particularly the child's difficulties managing painful emotions. Essentially, clinicians communicate to patients (implicitly or explicitly) that, in this room, they are safe to explore their conflicts and to express their thoughts and feelings without retribution.

Yet, this is a relationship that usually cannot go on forever.

Despite psychotherapy being such an intimate encounter, it inevitably does have to end, whether it is a planned, short-term endeavor as described in this manual or a longer endeavor. There is, however, an inherent paradox in this intimate relationship when there is a built-in termination point. The clinician, implicitly or explicitly, promises close attachment to the patient while at the same time explicitly stating that it can only exist for a designated amount of time. The ending of the relationship can, thus, be a particularly painful situation for the child.

> **Paradox:**
> **Short-term psychotherapy is an intimate encounter with a built-in ending.**

Despite this inherent paradox,[1] this manual for a short-term approach is a valuable instrument in order to make this treatment available to a larger number of children. Clinical experience has shown that a significant amount of symptomatic improvement can occur in children with difficulties regulating their emotions during a period of a few months.

> **Value of short-term, Regulation-Focused Psychotherapy for Children:**
> **A significant amount of symptomatic improvement can occur in just a few months.**

There is much more written and thus much more known about when and how to begin a child in psychotherapy than there is about when and how to end it (for example, Anna Freud 1957; Fabricius & Green 1995). In addition, the problem of premature termination from child psychotherapy is a significant problem (Kazdin 1997) and can be as high as 60% (Midgley & Kennedy 2011). In fact, time-limited therapy has been shown to be one of the strategies to avoid premature termination (Ogrodniczuk et al. 2005). Regardless of how psychotherapy concludes, whether by mutual agreement or interrupted prematurely, usually by parents, there are a variety of ways in which the ending is experienced.

Some parents and children do not think or talk about the ending of the treatment, acting as if it will never end. In those situations the ending, despite discussion at the beginning, feels like a surprise when the clinician comments on the nearing of the termination date. Some parents understandably may miss sessions for their children, following such an announcement.

The various responses to termination indicate the importance of helping children (and parents, see Novick & Novick 2002) master termination since dealing with endings and separations will be an ongoing challenge throughout life. Separation from the clinician may trigger memories of old disappointments, anger, and rage at people who disappointed them earlier in their lives. Some parents openly express anxiety that they will be left without the support of the clinician. Parents manifest similar defenses or regulating mechanisms as they try to cope with the loss of the clinician as a supportive adult who helps their child.

B. Specific goals of the termination step: step 3

When children have difficulties regulating their painful emotions, these difficulties usually reemerge as the ending of the treatment approaches. It is very important that every instance of psychotherapy include a period of time for the patient and clinician to work through the process of separation and take leave of one another. This is called the termination phase. The goal of the termination phase is to help the child master the painful emotions associated with separation in the most effective way possible.

> **Goal of termination phase:**
> **Help child master the painful emotions associated with separation.**

In a treatment of 16 or so sessions, as in this manual, a period of five sessions need to be devoted to dealing with the termination of the treatment. During this period, ongoing therapeutic work continues in the mode of Step 2 of this manual, but proceeds with a focus on the approaching separation.

During this period, many of the issues addressed during the bulk of the therapy will be repeated and reviewed. The major focus of the clinician will continue to be the exploration of the child's attempts to avoid painful emotions, such as by denial or aggression within the relationship with the clinician. Most importantly, since children with propensities to emotional dysregulation have such difficult times with transitions, including separations and frustrations, the termination of the therapy will give the clinician an opportunity to address with the child his/her difficulty directly addressing reactions to leaving the clinician. By acknowledging this difficulty, the clinician can help the child modify his/her tendency to become dysregulated and, instead, more effectively manage the inevitable separations that will occur in the future.

> **During the termination phase, the clinician addresses the child's difficulty directly, addressing his/her reactions to leaving the clinician.**

1. First reminder of the approaching termination: session 12

Many children express the wish to leave treatment as soon as they experience symptomatic improvement or if the clinician broaches on uncomfortable topics. At those times, one usually conceptualizes the wish for a premature closure as a device utilized by the child to protect him/her from painful emotions and wish to get away from the clinician. Other children do not consciously think about termination. With those children, the clinician could begin to note the impending ending date in session 12.

a. Discussion of past gains

During this discussion, the clinician can review the course of the child's treatment to date, what they have worked on, and what the child feels they need to further accomplish. Most children will not reveal anything in particular, and in response, the clinician should leave it at that.

b. Delivery of the reminder

When addressing the treatment, the clinician has an opportunity to discuss the impending separation, including explicitly naming the potential feelings the child may have about the end of the treatment, including sadness, loss, or anger.

c. Common patient reactions and responses

Many children will not express any reaction to the clinician's discussion of termination. Some will be glad to leave; others will say they should leave now or that they should not leave. Some children may begrudgingly say: "I guess this has helped me, maybe I'll miss it a little." Others may miss the next session. And, still others may play out their feelings.

Seven-year-old Judy avoided the clinician's comment about the forthcoming termination. After a few minutes of not knowing what to do, the little girl started to play with the Barbies in the office. She created a wedding scene where Ken was going to marry Barbie. She set up a very complex scene with guests, furniture, a priest, the parents of Barbie, and the parents of Ken. She started to sing "Here Comes the Bride" as all of the guests were waiting expectantly. Suddenly one character (a friend of Ken's) rushed into the scene and yelled, "Ken has left! He does not want to get married!" Barbie started to cry.

The clinician empathized with Barbie, saying how bad Barbie feels that Ken left her. "It is very tough to be left." It is important to note that the clinician did *not*:

1 Tell Barbie that she did not have to cry.
2 Translate the play directly to the child's life, but instead made a generalized statement of how hard it was to be left.
3 Immediately ask why Ken left.

The clinician rightly assumed that this play and its themes would continue in subsequent sessions (which it did and the girl said that Ken did not like her). At a later point, the clinician, outside the play, could discuss that the reason for termination was not that the clinician did not like her.

When a child plays out a separation or an abandonment theme, the clinician does not directly symbolically interpret the play to mean that the child is expressing feelings about the termination of the treatment.

2. Working through termination: sessions 13–15

Throughout the manual, we have tried to make it clear that children do not necessarily verbalize their understandings about themselves as adults do. Instead, they communicate their understanding in a more implicit manner and can have insights into their feelings without reasoning about them or verbalizing the cause of the feelings. In fact, children often can tolerate only indirect recognition of the emotions that they have attempted to mask. This indirect recognition may be viewed by observing the child's physical demeanor as well as his/her play and activity. In essence, through this indirect expression children gain implicit insights into their current conflicted situations and can develop new ways to meet the conflicts. Through play, children can work through their conflicts over experiencing painful emotions via this age-appropriate substitute for direct verbalization. In fact, being in touch with one's feelings without necessarily reasoning about and verbalizing the cause of the feelings may be nearer to a child's experience than to an adult's (Sandler et al. 1975; Joyce & Stoker 2000).

> **Children can be in touch with their feelings without directly verbalizing them.**

There are a variety of ways children implicitly communicate their understanding of their protective devices and their readiness to tolerate separation from the clinician:

1 Nonverbal communication with the clinician such as a change in eye-contact, smile, or other facial communication,
2 Use of metaphors and stories by both clinician and child,
3 Communication through play and activity and not by talking,
4 Use of jokes.

> **Ways children implicitly communicate their understanding of their feelings:**
> 1 **Nonverbal communications.**
> 2 **Use of metaphors.**
> 3 **Though play and activity.**
> 4 **Jokes.**

3. The final good-bye: session 16

a. Restatement of the final good-bye

Some children will note the fact that this is their last session. Some will be happy, some sad, and some neutral. If the child does not mention the fact, the clinician should comment on that early in the session, without any specific commentary, waiting to hear the child's associations.

b. Common patient responses

When listening to children's responses to the last session, one has to listen with a "third ear." In other words, the clinician should not just listen to the manifest expressions of happiness or sadness but to the child's spontaneous associations and spontaneous play and activities. One child, who always played catch with the clinician, "accidentally" broke a light bulb. The child jokingly said that he will never break a lamp again. Staying in a joking mode, the clinician said, "It is hard to tell me in words how you feel about our ending. Using your words is something we have talked a lot about. Maybe you are worried now that we won't be meeting."

The little girl, who played with Barbie, played out that Ken came back and told her that he was sorry but he could not marry her. He had to go to another country. Barbie was very sad but accepted it without crying. Towards the end of the session and after the play had finished, when the child was speaking outside of play, the clinician said to the little girl that he knew how much she would miss playing with him. The little girl agreed.

Another child denied vociferously that he would miss the sessions. Suddenly he said that he would have to change next Monday's session, because he had an extra baseball practice. The clinician responded that he saw how hard it was to remember that today was the last session and say good-bye.

C. Clinical examples

The following clinical examples are offered as a means of showing the variety of ways that children engage with the clinician as their therapeutic contact ends. The first clinical example demonstrates the use of metaphor and visual contact with the clinician as an indicator of the child's implicit understanding and modification of his avoidance of painful emotions. The second example shows a child's expression of understanding with the use of metaphor. In the third clinical example, the child's understanding emerges through drawing. The final example shows a child who is "not so into talking."

1. Clinical example 1: nonverbal communications

Two sessions before they were scheduled to terminate, eight-year-old Alexander was reluctant to join the clinician in the room. He entered with a forlorn look. He asked the clinician whether he had brought him a present. When he realized that the clinician had not, he angrily threw all of the pillows off a couch, yelled at the clinician and declared in a loud voice, while coming up to the clinician's face, that they were not going to do anything today because the clinician did not bring him the video game that he had demanded.

The clinician said that he understood how angry and upset Alexander was because in a week they would be having their last session. Alexander responded, "I don't care, I just wanted the game." Alexander walked out of the playroom and stayed out for ten minutes. The clinician knew the child was safe because his mother always waited for him. The clinician did look out to the waiting room when Alexander left. Upon his return to the playroom, he reiterated the list of things that he wanted the clinician to bring him. The clinician suggested that since there was confusion today, they should write a list of what they would do during the last session. Because the clinician did not explicitly say that he would not be bringing a present, Alexander assumed that he would. It is important to note that the clinician did not confront Alexander but rather used the more neutral word, "confusion."

Alexander seemed content with the idea of the clinician writing a list. The clinician wrote a very detailed account of the things Alexander suggested that they do during their last meeting. Alexander followed very closely how the clinician wrote everything down. While writing, the clinician looked at Alexander and said: "You know we have been meeting for quite some time, we know each other pretty well and. . ." Alexander interrupted the clinician in mid-sentence, dramatically looked at the clinician, and said furiously, "Shut up!" The clinician responded: "Yes, it is difficult to talk about our ending our sessions."

With this comment, the clinician implicitly communicated, "It feels better to yell at me than to talk about feeling sad about our termination." In essence, with this comment, the clinician addressed Alexander's anger as a protective device to prevent addressing negative emotions in the transference about the termination, such as sadness. Anger as a protective device had been a common theme throughout the therapy.

After the clinician finished writing the list of activities for the last session, Alexander suggested that they play a board game ("Guess Who"), which Alexander used to play in the sessions but which they had not played in a while. Alexander played without cheating, using the right logic of asking questions about the figures in order to try to guess the figure that the clinician had hidden. During the second game instead of asking the usual questions about the figure, the clinician asked: "Does your person look sad?" "No," Alexander said quickly. Alexander proceeded to ask the same question of the clinician's figure. The clinician answered, "No, he doesn't look sad but I think he is sad inside." This time Alexander did not respond but simply looked at the clinician and smiled. They continued to play until the end of the session and the clinician commended him for playing very well. With that question, the clinician communicated with a metaphor. Instead of saying that Alexander was sad inside even though he did not show it, the clinician transposed those feelings to his character from the "Guess Who" game. One can safely infer that Alexander's smile implicitly communicated that he knew the reference of the clinician's comment and felt helped by it.

The last session went without incident as they played as planned. The clinician mentioned a couple of times that there were difficult feelings to talk about since it was their last session and Alexander would miss playing games with the clinician. Alexander just listened to the clinician without denying and without interrupting. It is important to note that a child need not verbalize such painful feelings. However, the stark contrast between the defensiveness of the next-to-last session and the relative calmness of the last session illustrates that Alexander had greater tolerance for the experience of the unpleasant emotion associated with the separation from the clinician.

2. Clinical example 2: use of metaphors

A very bright, nine-year-old boy, Sam, responded effectively to RFP-C as his dramatic reactions to frustration came to the fore of his psychotherapeutic work with the clinician. The effectiveness of the psychotherapeutic work is indicated by his positive responses (such as stopping a tantrum while the clinician communicated her understanding).

During one session, towards the end of the psychotherapy, after they had discussed the date of the last session, Sam made an error on a picture he was drawing. He became frustrated and angry, but did not scream as he would have in the past. The clinician said to him that his reaction to the mistake was similar to what Sam had reported about school. Sam said, "Do you mean like when I do work and I think it is right and then my teacher comes over and says it is wrong?" Sam had angrily told the clinician many times in the past that he would do work in school and the teacher would mark him wrong even though he had the right answer. As he described the situation now, he was less dysregulated than in the past.

Sam repeated that he wants to do well in school. The clinician responded that Sam had told her in the past that he felt a great deal of pressure to behave well and how proud he was when he had a good day. In response, Sam mentioned another child he saw leaving the clinician's playroom before his session. Sam told the clinician that he wanted a pair of sneakers just like that boy was wearing. The clinician reminded him how he used to scream at her when he saw other children leaving the playroom. She said, "Sam, maybe you are concerned about not being here in a couple of weeks and that I will be playing with the other boy and not with you."

Sam did not respond directly to the clinician's comments. But he said to her that she was trying to figure things out about him just like he was learning about "approximation" in math class. The clinician responded that it was not easy to talk about their ending soon. The boy ignored the statement and continued playing, but without any disruption.

This child clearly demonstrated greater frustration tolerance. Sam's connection of the therapeutic work with the concept of "approximation" indicated that he had an implicit understanding of the link between his behavioral symptoms and his response to the unpleasant emotions triggered by the presence of a rival. Furthermore, allowing the clinician to bring up the termination, without disruption, was a further sign of greater mastery of his unpleasant emotions.

3. Clinical example 3: use of drawing

A seven-year-old boy, Eli, participated in RFP-C because of a chronic irritable mood and severe aggressive outbursts when he was easily frustrated. During his last session with a woman clinician, Eli was not overtly aggressive, but instead expressed his intense feelings via his drawings, demonstrating greater mastery over his aggression.

He drew a very complicated picture. He drew himself stabbing a woman. Then, he drew many different people hurting that same person. The clinician said, "Everyone is angry with her. Why?" He continued drawing many attacks and included a blotch of red which he said was blood dripping from her head. He made a slip calling the person who was being attacked as "you" instead of calling the person "she" as he had been doing all along.

Without any reference to the picture, the clinician said that Eli was upset and angry that they were ending their therapy. Eli denied this, saying, "That's not true." But unlike other sessions when he would drown out the clinician, or close his ears, he listened to the clinician and looked at her and did not fight.

At some point, he stopped drawing and mentioned some schoolwork that he had to do. The clinician said that she heard how well he was doing. Eli then did a group of arithmetic problems, showing the clinician how he could do complicated subtraction.

It was very significant that at this point, at termination, Eli expressed in tremendous detail his very aggressive feelings that dominated the very beginning of the treatment. The difference, however, was that the aggressive feelings were expressed in fantasy through drawing and words in contrast to the early profoundly disorganized anger he expressed with physical threats towards the clinician. These aggressive ideas receded to the background (though were always there) and came out in full force with the impending termination.

4. Clinical example 4: the avoidance of talking

Throughout the treatment, Patrick, a ten-year-old boy who had difficulty with separations, filled sessions by playing games of Connect Four, Chess, Checkers, and Monopoly. He remained focused on strategy and frequently used his significant intelligence to teach the clinician better techniques. Patrick used games to solidify his relationship with the clinician as well as a way to avoid talking about problems. Addressing this avoidance of talking about problems was not useful. When the clinician tried to ask questions or chat about events he had learned during the initial meetings, Patrick became anxious and uncomfortable. He said many times, "I'm not so into talking." The oppositional symptoms and aggression that were prevalent in school did not occur in the sessions. When the clinician noted his avoidance, he would grin and acknowledge that he just did not want to talk. He only wanted to chat about the games and activities they played.

Patrick did talk about his dislike for his school, perceiving it as overly strict. He denied any issues in school despite his mother showing the clinician disciplinary reports from the teacher.

The day after the clinician reminded Patrick that their therapy was to be concluded, the clinician learned from the mother that Patrick got into trouble because, as Patrick said, he "accidentally" threw his bag at another student. At the next session, the clinician used this sequence to address with Patrick how hard it was for him to use words when he gets upset, like the therapy ending. These comments were made several times, with Patrick denying them but listening to the clinician's words.

D. Summary and final remarks

In many dysregulated children, a course of Regulation-Focused Psychotherapy will result in symptomatic improvement as a result of the development of an increased tolerance of painful emotions. One can conjecture that the therapeutic process facilitates the development of an awareness that painful emotions do not have to be so vigorously warded off. From a neural perspective, the implicit emotion regulation has developed the capacity to process difficult emotional threats. The sustained limbic and brainstem hyperarousal witnessed in children with underdeveloped implicit emotion regulation systems resolves, and thus the child is less prone to the enactment of fight/flight stance. The stress of termination, especially in children who have separation problems, provides an opportunity to help the child master more effectively the painful emotions that accompany "good-byes."

The child reaches an implicit awareness within the relationship to the clinician that can then be expanded, again implicitly to his/her life situations in home and at school. In other words, painful emotions can be mastered more effectively and the child's use of aggression as his/her main coping device is diminished.

> **As a result of Regulation-Focused Psychotherapy, the child can master painful emotions more effectively and has less need for the use of aggression as his/her main coping device.**

Note

[1] To our knowledge, there is only one critique of the concept of brief therapy: Migone, Paolo (2014). What does "brief" mean? A theoretical critique of the concept of brief therapy from a psychoanalytic viewpoint. *Journal of the American Psychoanalytic Association*, 62(4), pp. 631–56.

Bibliography

Fabricius, J. & Green, V., 1995. Termination in child analysis: a child-led process? *Psychoanalytic Study of the Child*, 50, pp. 205–25.

Freud, A., 1957. Termination of child analysis. In *The Writings of Anna Freud, VII*. New York, NY: International Universities Press, pp. 3–21.

Joyce, A. & Stoker, J., 2000. Insight and the nature of therapeutic action in the psychoanalysis of 4- and 5-year-old children. *The International Journal of Psycho-Analysis*, 81(Pt 6), pp. 1139–54.

Kazdin, A.E., 1997. Practitioner review: psychosocial treatments for conduct disorder in children. *Journal of Child Psychology and Psychiatry, and Allied Disciplines*, 38(2), pp. 161–78.

Midgley, N. & Kennedy, E., 2011. Psychodynamic psychotherapy for children and adolescents: a critical review of the evidence base. *Journal of Child Psychotherapy*, (September 2012), pp. 232–60.

Novick, K. & Novick, J., 2002. Parent work in analysis: children, adolescents, and adults. Part four: termination and post-termination phases. *Journal of Infant, Child & Adolescent Psychotherapy*, 2, pp. 43–55.

Ogrodniczuk, J.S., Joyce, A.S., & Piper, W.E., 2005. Strategies for reducing patient-initiated premature termination of psychotherapy. *Harvard Review of Psychiatry*, 13(2), pp. 57–70.

Sandler, J., Kennedy, H., & Tyson, R., 1975. Discussions on transference – the treatment situation and technique in child psychoanalysis. *Psychoanalytic Study of the Child*, 30, pp. 409–41.

Chapter 13

Conclusion

With Regulation-Focused Psychotherapy for Externalizing Behaviors (RFP-C), the focus of the treatment is not to promote cognitive (intellectual) change in the child (classical insight) ("Oh, now I understand"), but to promote implicit awareness that:

1. The emotional state that is feared or is seen as overwhelming by the child is not as overwhelming as he/she thinks it is and that it will not destroy him/her.
2. There are better ways to manage those emotions than to fight.
3. The clinician will not be hurt by those feelings, and then the child will feel that those feelings will not destroy him/her.
4. The clinician, by understanding that the behavior has meaning, is always implicitly communicating that to the child and communicating that the child is not bad.

With many dysregulated children participating in a course of RFP-C, success will result in symptomatic improvement as a result of the development of an increased tolerance of painful emotions. The therapeutic process facilitates development of an awareness that painful emotions do not have to be so vigorously warded off. The child reaches this implicit awareness within the relationship with the clinician that can then be expanded to his/her life situations in home and at school.

In other words, painful emotions can be mastered more effectively and the child's use of aggression as his/her main coping device is diminished. As a result of Regulation-Focused Psychotherapy, the child can master painful emotions more effectively and has less need for the use of maladaptive protective devices such as fighting.

The child reaches this implicit awareness within the relationship with the clinician that can then be expanded to his/her life situations in home and at school. In other words, painful emotions can be mastered more effectively and the child's use of aggression as his/her main coping device is diminished.

> As a result of Regulation-Focused Psychotherapy, the child can master painful emotions more effectively and has less need for the use of aggression as his/her main coping device.

Appendix A

Regulation-Focused Psychotherapy for Children with Externalizing Behaviors

A new, short-term psychotherapy approach to working with children who suffer from irritability, oppositional defiance, and disruptiveness.

- The goal of RFP-C is not to promote cognitive (intellectual) change in the child (classical insight) ("Oh, now I understand") but to promote implicit awareness that:
  - The emotional state that is feared or is seen as overwhelming by the child is not as overwhelming as he/she thinks it is and that it will not destroy him/her.
  - There are better ways to manage those emotions than to be disruptive.
  - That the clinician will not be hurt by those feelings and then the child will feel that those feelings will not destroy him/her.
- The clinician is always implicitly communicating to the child that behavior has meaning, and that the child is not bad through conceptualizing Malan's Triangle:
  - Which of the child's emotions are avoided.
  - How the emotion is being avoided.
  - Trying to understand why that emotion is being avoided in a maladaptive way.
- Treatment includes three phases:
  - Phase 1: Introductory meeting/s with the parents, two initial sessions with the child, and a feedback meeting with the parents.
  - Phase 2: Twice weekly individual sessions with the child and regular check-ins with the parents, as well as a full-length meeting with parents midway through the treatment.
  - Phase 3: Termination phase of therapy with a focus on preparing for separation and reviewing progress.

- In many children with disruptive behaviors, a course of RFP-C can:
  - Achieve improvement in problematic symptoms and mature developmentally as a result of increased ability to tolerate and understand painful emotions by addressing the crucial underlying emotions.
  - Decrease the child's use of aggression as the main coping device by allowing painful emotions to be mastered more effectively.
  - Help to systematically address avoidance mechanisms, talking to the child about how his/her disruptive behavior helps him/her avoid painful emotions.
  - Facilitate development of an awareness that painful emotions do not have to be so vigorously avoided, within the relationship with the clinician, which can then be expanded to life situations at home and at school.
- Integrates psychodynamic techniques with behavioral interventions such as limiting dangerous behavior in the therapy room.
- Utilizes play – children's primary means of communicating difficult thoughts and emotions – and allows the child to lead play and discussion in order to help identify the meaning of symptoms and disruptive behavior.
- A systematic, individual psychotherapy that is an alternative or complement to PMT, CBT, and psychotropic medication, which shifts focus away from simply helping parents manage their children's misbehaviors.
- The clinician helps parents to understand the idea that all behavior has meaning and learn to reflect on both his/her own as well as the child's distressing feelings.
- The clinician and the parents work together to help the child learn to regulate his/her own emotions.

Appendix B

Chapter 6
Adherence scale for initial interview/s with parents

A. Goals of the encounter

    _____ 1. Establishing an alliance with parents
    _____ 2. Approaching in a nonjudgmental manner
    _____ 3. Presenting a warm, collaborative attitude
    _____ 4. Empathizing with parents' feelings about the child's difficulties
    _____ 5. Empathizing with parents' feelings about seeking consultation for their child
    _____ 6. Communicating that behavior has meaning

Total Score _____ of 6 Total

B. Parents' views of child's problems

    _____ 1. The parents' ideas of the child's symptoms: "Why now?"
    _____ 2. Discussing and developing areas of difficulties
    _____ 3. The parents' conception of the child's ideas about the problem
    _____ 4. Review triggers and conflicts, which provoke child's symptoms
    5. The nature of the child's interaction with other people

        _____ a. Inventory of relationships
        _____ b. The "best friend" question

    6. The nature of the child's development

        a. Eliciting a developmental history

            _____ i. Language and motor milestones
            _____ ii. Social and emotional history

        _____ b. Discussion of developmental progress and/or concerns

    _____ 7. Review of clinical psychiatric examination
    _____ 8. Review of symptom inventories
    _____ 9. Emphasizing family and child strengths

Total Score _____ of 12 Total

C. Summary at the end of the initial meeting/s with parents

    _____ 1. Recapitulating the meaning of behavior within the model of Malan's Triangle of Conflict (provide parents with a copy of Appendix A)

    _____ 2. Scheduling two child sessions and a second meeting with parents

    3. Helping the parents to approach the child about the treatment

        _____ a. Discussing with parents the nature of their prior discussions with the child about the problems

        _____ b. Anticipating children's questions and how to respond

        _____ c. Talking about how to address clinician

Total Score _____ of 5 Total

Total Score for Parent Meeting 1: _____ of 23

Chapter 7
Adherence scale for initial interviews with child

A. First contact with the child

    1. Initial moments of meeting

        _____ a. Creation of collaborative atmosphere

        _____ b. Spontaneous interaction between clinician and child

        _____ c. Addressing any issues related to separation with parent

    2. The play environment

        _____ a. Suitable toys and activities

        _____ b. Does clinician allow child to lead the play/activity?

        _____ c. If child does not spontaneously play, does clinician give choices?

        _____ d. Does clinician minimize giving directions to child?

    3. First question

        _____ a. Does clinician address with the child what he/she knows about visit?

        _____ b. Does clinician review with the child the parents' concerns in appropriate language?

        _____ c. Does clinician note to child difficulty in discussing a particular subject?

        _____ d. Does clinician communicate an attitude of trying to understand?

Total Score _____ of 11 Total

B. Unstructured techniques
- _____ 1. Does clinician identify patterns of play and activities, repetitions, and play disruptions?
- _____ 2. Are limits utilized?
- _____ 3. Does clinician need to set rules of the space?
- _____ 4. Are moments of transference-like phenomena identified?
- _____ 5. Does clinician note other defensive maneuvers (note which)?
- _____ 6. Are issues related to leaving session identified?

Total Score _____ of 6 Total

C. Structured techniques
- _____ 1. Are structured techniques utilized? (Identify specific techniques) (This is not counted to total adherence score, because it is optional.)

D. Global Goals
- _____ 1. Approaching in a nonjudgmental manner
- _____ 2. Establishing an alliance with child
- _____ 3. Presenting a warm, collaborative attitude
- _____ 4. Empathizing with child's feelings about the child's difficulties
- _____ 5. Empathizing with child's feelings about coming to consultation

Total Score _____ of 6 Total

Total Score for Initial Child Meeting 1: _____ of 23

Chapters 8 and 11
Adherence scale for feedback meetings with parents

Goals of the encounters

_____ 1. Present a warm, collaborative attitude

2. Communicate issues about child to parents in a nonjudgmental manner
    - _____ a. Discussion of clinician's impressions of the meetings with the child (noting with parents that information was reviewed with the child)
    - _____ b. Emphasize the child's strengths
    - _____ c. Avoid judgmental statements, including good/bad descriptors

3. Continue to promote alliance with parents
    - _____ a. Recognize and address parental experiences and concerns

_____ b. Empathize with parents' feelings about their child
_____ c. Empathize with parents' feelings about the discussion of the child's problems

4. Review of child's issues

_____ a. Use of Malan's Triangle with specific information about the child's feelings and anxieties and how the child regulates unpleasant emotions
_____ b. Clinician reflects out loud about child's symptoms, conveying that there is meaning to his/her behavior
_____ c. Clinician asks parents to reflect on their conception of the child's behavior

_____ 5. Addressing parental concerns
_____ 6. Ongoing review of treatment plan and timeline

Total Score for Ongoing Parent Meeting 1: _____ of 12

Chapters 9, 10, 12
Adherence scale for ongoing sessions with child

A. **Global goals**

_____ 1. Approaching in a nonjudgmental manner
_____ 2. Establishing an alliance with child
_____ 3. Presenting a warm, collaborative attitude
_____ 4. Empathizing with child's feelings about the child's difficulties
_____ 5. Empathizing with child's feelings about coming to consultation

Total Score _____ of 6 Total

B. **Addressing child's avoidance of painful states (emotions and activities)**

1. **Precautions**

_____ a. Remains experience-near
_____ b. Avoids unnecessary, simple reassurance
_____ c. Avoids any moralistic stance
_____ d. Uses a variety of supportive interventions when indicated
_____ e. Encourages development of new play activities without interference
_____ f. Discusses play actions within the play
_____ g. Avoids direct interpretation of symbolic meaning of play
_____ h. Uses information from play to address conflicted issues outside of play
_____ i. Recognizes the importance of addressing interruptions of treatment

Total Score _____ of 9 Total

2. **Expressive interventions**

   ____ a. Remains experience-near
   ____ b. Sets, observes, and addresses response to limits to the play
   ____ c. Identifies patterns of play and activities, repetitions, and play disruptions
   ____ d. Interprets avoidance
   ____ e. Other defensive maneuvers are noted (note which)
   ____ f. Issues related to leaving session are identified

   Total Score ____ of 6 Total

3. ____ **Demonstrates an effective balance between supportive and expressive interventions**

   Total Score ____ of 1 Total

C. **Assessment of clinician–patient relationship in the treatment (transference)**[1]

   ____ 1. Focuses on interactions within the therapeutic relationship
   ____ 2. Allows for displacement of disruptive behaviors to the clinician, without interference
   ____ 3. Makes comments generalizing behaviors with clinician to real-world situations

   Total Score ____ of 3 Total

D. **Complications that may arise**

   ____ 1. Clinician contains countertransference responses appropriately
   ____ 2. Clinician uses limit setting when appropriate
   ____ 3. Clinicians maintains a general positive regard throughout the session

   Total Score ____ of 3 Total

E. **Interventions during termination step**

   1. **First reminder of the approaching termination: Session 12**

      ____ a. Discusses past gains
      ____ b. Delivers the reminder of time length
      ____ c. Receives and effectively processes the child's reactions and responses

      Total Score ____ of 3 Total

   2. **Working through termination: Sessions 13–15**

      ____ a. Hears parental anxieties and provides empathic listening
      ____ b. Responds to parental protective measures

      Total Score ____ of 2 Total

3. **The final good-bye: Session 16**

   _____ a. Restates treatment goals and gives a final good-bye
   _____ b. Effectively addresses child's responses

   Total Score _____ of 2 Total

Note

1   Compare this scale to Ulberg, R., Amlo, S., & Høglend, P., 2014. Manual for transference work scale; a micro-analytical tool for therapy process analyses. *BMC Psychiatry* 14, p. 291 (http://www.biomedcentral.com/1471–244X/14/291)1).

   1) The therapist addressed transactions in the patient therapist relationship (address transaction).
   2) The therapist encouraged exploration of thoughts and feelings about the therapy and the therapist's style and behavior (thoughts and feelings about therapy).
   3) The therapist encouraged patients to discuss how they believed the therapist might feel or think about them (beliefs about therapist).
   4) The therapist included him-/herself explicitly in interpretive linking of dynamic elements (conflicts), direct manifestations of transference, and allusions to the transference (linking therapist to dynamic).
   5) The therapist interpreted repetitive interpersonal patterns (including genetic interpretations) and linked these patterns to transactions between the patient and the therapist (repetitive interpersonal pattern).

   (Reprinted with permission from the journal)

Appendix C
Rating scales

1. Modified target symptom rating scale (TSRS)[1]

Family Conflict	None	Mild	Moderate	Severe
Peer Relationships	Good	Mild Problem	Moderate	Severe
Depression	No signs	Mild	Moderate	Severe/debilitating
Anxiety	None	Mild	Moderate	Pervasive
Psychosomatic	None	Mild	Moderate	Severe
Suicidality	None	Mild	Moderate	Serious
Self-destructive/ Dangerous Behaviors	None	Mild	Moderate	Severe
Aggression	None	Mild	Moderate	Severe
Substance Abuse	None	Mild	Moderate	Severe
Psychotic Symptoms	None	Mild	Moderate	Severe
Runaway/ Out of control/ Legal Problems	None	Mild	Moderate	Severe
Impulsivity	None	Mild	Moderate	Severe

Affective reactivity index (ARI – P)

Name of participant _____ Age:____

For each item, please mark the box for Not True, Somewhat True, or Certainly True.

In the *last six months* and compared to others of the same age, how well does each of the following statements describe the behavior/feelings of your child? Please try to answer all questions.

	Not True	Somewhat True	Certainly True
Is easily annoyed by others			
Often loses his/her temper			
Stays angry for a long time			
Is angry most of the time			
Gets angry frequently			
Loses temper easily			
Overall, *irritability* causes him/her problems.			

Thank you very much for your help.
© *2012* Stringaris, A. (King's College London), Goodman, R. (King's College London), Ferdinando, S. (King's College London), Razdan, V. (National Institutes of Health), Muhrer, E. (National Institutes of Health), Leibenluft, E. (National Institutes of Health), Brotman, M.A. (National Institutes of Health).

This material can be reproduced without permission by clinicians for use with their own patients. Any other use, including electronic use, requires the prior written permission of the authors.

Affective reactivity index (ARI – S)

Name of participant _____ Age:_____

For each item, please mark the box for Not True, Somewhat True, or Certainly True.

In the *last six months* and compared to others of the same age, how well does each of the following statements describe your behavior/feelings? Please try to answer all questions.

	Not True	Somewhat True	Certainly True
I am easily annoyed by others			
I often lose my temper			
I stay angry for a long time			
I am angry most of the time			
I get angry frequently			
I lose my temper easily			
Overall, my *irritability* causes me problems			

Thank you very much for your help.
© *2012* Stringaris, A. (King's College London), Goodman, R. (King's College London), Ferdinando, S. (King's College London), Razdan, V. (National Institutes of Health), Muhrer, E. (National Institutes of Health), Leibenluft, E. (National Institutes of Health), Brotman, M.A. (National Institutes of Health).

This material can be reproduced without permission by clinicians for use with their own patients. Any other use, including electronic use, requires the prior written permission of the authors.

Oppositional defiant disorder rating scale (ODD-RS)

(0 = *not at all*, 1 = *just a little*, 2 = *pretty much*, 3 = *very much*)

1.	Often loses temper	0	1	2	3
2.	Often argues with adults	0	1	2	3
3.	Often actively defies or refuses to comply with adults' requests or rules	0	1	2	3
4.	Often deliberately annoys people	0	1	2	3
5.	Often blames others for his/her mistakes or misbehavior	0	1	2	3
6.	Is often touchy or easily annoyed by others	0	1	2	3
7.	Is often angry and resentful	0	1	2	3
8.	Is often spiteful or vindictive	0	1	2	3

From: Hommersen, P., Murray, C., Ohan, J. L., & Johnson, 2006. *Journal of Emotional Behavioral Disorders*, 14(2), pp. 118–25.

Note

[1] Original scale published in Barber, C.C. et al., 2002. The Target Symptom Rating: a brief clinical measure of acute psychiatric symptoms in children and adolescents. *Journal of Clinical Child and Adolescent Psychology!: The Official Journal for the Society of Clinical Child and Adolescent Psychology, American Psychological Association, Division 53*, 31(2), pp. 181–92.

Index

Abrams, Samuel 71–2
adaptive states 59
addressing defenses 165–6
affect 37–8, 69, 175
aggression 10, 16, 17; clinical example "Luke" 201–2; severe clinical example "Pete" 173–4
American Academy of Child and Adolescent Psychiatry 93
American Psychological Association 93
amygdalo-cortical connections 82
Andersen, Susan 35
anger/irritability symptoms (AIS) 20, 47
antipsychotic medications 13
antisocial personality disorder (ASPD) 17
anxiety: emotion regulation 85; over externalizing behavior 45; parental anxieties in first meeting 105; punishment anxiety manifestations 139
attacks on clinician 167
Attention Deficit/Hyperactivity Disorder (ADHD) 12, 94
avoidance mechanisms 25, 54, 98; of talking clinical example "Patrick" 215–16

Benveniste, Daniel 65
biosignatures 4
Bornstein, Berta 69, 70–1, 95
break in treatment 190–1
Brenner, Charles 53–4

callous-unemotional (CU) traits 94
childhood bipolar disorder 18
Children with Conduct Disorders: A Psychotherapy Manual (Kernberg, Chazan) 20–1
child's cognitive, language and motor development 112–13

child therapy: allowing parents into 138; approaching about treatment 116–17; "Betty" clinical example 165–71, 175–6; "Brenda" clinical example 134–5; clinical examples 164–5; communication in displacement 138; comparisons between children 142–3; conclusion 143, 177–8; discontinuity of play 141; discussing real-life problems 170–1; disruptive behavior limits 141–2; first question 122–3; giving direction during 139–40; goals 143–4, 162–3; "Henry" clinical example 137; history of prior discussions with 117; initial meeting 121–2; initiation of 160–1; interaction with others 112; interactions surrounding leaving or staying 141; obsessive play 140–1; outline 120–1, 158–9; "Pete" clinical example 173–4; play environment 124; precautions 163–4; punishment anxiety manifestations 139; rationale and goals for 137; regulation-focused approach 174–5; repetitive themes 140; scoring points 171; specific goals 159–60; "Stacy" clinical example 137–43; "Stephanie" clinical example 172–3; structured techniques 131–3; summary 133–4; supportive interventions 175–7; transference moments 142; unstructured techniques 125–31; *see also* parent meeting; play activities/therapy; psychodynamic psychotherapy; Regulation-Focused Psychotherapy for Children with Externalizing Behaviors; termination process
clinical psychiatric examination 113–14
clinician-parent relationship 104–5

Index

clinician-patient relationship: "Billy" clinical example 189–91; complications with 186–7; countertransference concept 187–9; introduction 180–1; "John" clinical example 191–2; overview 179; transference concept 181–3
Cognitive Behavioral Therapy (CBT) 59, 93
common childhood experiences 149–50
communication in displacement 138; reticence clinical example "Brenda" 134–5
Comprehensive Assessment of Defense Style (CADS) 64
computer activities in play therapy 124
Conduct Disorder (CD) 94
coping mechanisms/skills 23, 58–9
Coping Power program 11
countertransference: by clinician 7–8, 46; clinician/patient relationship 187–9; enactment clinical example "Stephanie" 172–3; means to address 188–9; in psychodynamic psychotherapy 50
Cramer, Phebe 63, 65

Default Mode Network (DMN) 38
defense mechanisms (DM): in child therapy 130–1; clinician addressing 67–9; defined 4–5, 63; the ego 38–9; emotional regulation 74–5; evaluation of 63–5; internal conflict over 53–5; interpretation of 70–4; in psychodynamic psychotherapy 53–5, 58–62
deficient emotional self regulation (DESR) 18
denial mechanisms (DM) 4, 54, 60–1
developmental perspective 34
Diagnostic and Statistical Manual of Mental Disorders (DSM) 63, 80
direct verbalization 73
discontinuity of play 141
displacement of affect 69
disruptions in play therapy 127–8
Disruptive Disorders (DD) 15
Disruptive Mood Dysregulation Disorder (DMDD) 94, 114, 188
divergence in handling external problems 155–6
divergence in parent perspectives 106–7
dorsal anterior cingulate cortex (dACC) 81, 84

dorsolateral PFC (dPFC) 81
drawing in child therapy 131–2; clinical example "Eli" 214–15
drive derivatives 36
dynamic model of understanding 150–6

education on termination 205
education providers, role of 107–8
the ego 35, 38–9, 61–2
electroencephalography 84
emotion regulation (ER): defense mechanism and 74–5; defined 4; impaired 7, 15; implicit ER 35, 72, 96–7; maladaptive emotion regulation 23, 46–8; neurocognitive concept of 94; neurophysiology and development 81–2
emotions, defined 37–8
empathic listening 104–5, 199
experience-distant intervention 47, 73
experience-near intervention: basic perspective 47, 72–3; clinician/patient relationship 180–1; importance of 168; overview 96
Exposure with Response Prevention (ERP) 95
expressive interventions 48–9, 176–7
externalizing behaviors: countertransference 7–8; defense mechanism 4–5, 54–5, 62; development of 44–6; displacement of 185–6; dynamic approach to 25–6; emotion regulation 4; lack of treatments 12–17; nature of 3–4, 14–16; therapeutic failure 6–7; treatment challenges 69; varieties of 9–11; *see also* oppositional defiant disorder

family/child strengths 108–9
family strengths, emphasis of 199
Federal Drug Administration (FDA) 14
Fonagy, Peter 21–2
Freud, Anna 21, 60–1, 70–1
Freud, Sigmund 35–6, 38–9, 49, 59–60
frontal lobe of the brain 38

generalization discussions 151–2, 184
genetic determinants 165
Gray, Paul 70, 73
Great Smoky Mountain Study 18
Gross, James 37–8, 59, 81, 99
group delinquent reaction of childhood 17

headstrong dimension (argues, annoys, blames, and defies) 18
"headstrong" symptom cluster 81
Hierarchy of Verbal Interventions 21
hurtful dimension (vindictive) 18
hyperkinetic reaction of childhood 17

id 35, 36–7, 43
implicit emotion regulation (ER) 35, 72, 96–7
improvement indicators 197
impulsive behaviors 84
Individualized Educational Plan (IEP) 114
Individual Parent Management Training 93
Individuals with Disabilities Education Act (IDEA) 114
influence of the past on the present 35
insight 15, 24, 100, 181, 190, 210, 218, 221; implicit 181, 190, 210; implicit awareness 218
internal conflict and defenses 53–5
internalizing behaviors 14–16, 61
Internet in play therapy 124
interruptions in child therapy 167–8
irritable dimension (touchy, angry, temper) 18
"irritable" symptom cluster 81

judgmental statements 148

Katan, Anny 39
Kennedy, Hansi 21
Kernberg, Paulina 20–1, 95
Klein, Melanie 70–1
Kline, Paul 69

MacArthur Story Stem Battery (MSSB) 65
Major Depressive Disorder (MDD) 20, 80
maladaptive aggression 10, 165
maladaptive emotion regulation 23, 46–8
maladaptive implicit emotional regulatory mechanisms 46–8
maladaptive states 59
Malan's Triangle of conflict 115–16, 153, 198
marital discord 146
maturational cognitive (ego) 42
McCullough, Leigh 37, 95, 98
mentalization 40, 200
Mentalization-Informed Child Psychoanalytic Psychotherapy (MBT-C) 21–3

metaphor use clinical example "Billy" 189–91; clinical example "Sam" 214
Moran, George 21
multigenerational families 107
mutative factor and transference 181, 183–6

National Institute of Health Blueprint for Neuroscience Research Workshop 82
Negative Valence Systems 94
negativism clinical example "Henry" 137
noncompliant symptoms (NS) 20
nonjudgmental attitude of the RFP-C clinician 106
nontraditional parent families 107
non-verbal communication clinical example "Alexander" 212–14

Obsessive Compulsive Disorder (OCD) 94
obsessive play 140–1
Oedipal period 41
ongoing parent contract: check-in goals 194–5; education on termination 205; further education offers 202–4; "Luke" clinical example 201–2; outline 194; response to parental concerns 204; treatment updates 195–8
oppositional defiant disorder (ODD) 4–7; behavioral approaches to 79–80; countertransference in 188; dimensions in 19–20; emotional components in 18–20; emotion regulation deficit concept 83–4; historical context 17–18; meeting criteria for 114–15; prevalence of 9–10, 12; systematic dynamic approach 94
orbitofrontal cortex (OFC) 81

parental anxieties in first meeting 105
parental conception of child's idea of problem 110–11
parental idea of child's symptoms 109–10
parental protective measures 105–6
parental strengths, emphasis of 199
parent management training (PMT) 10–11, 13, 20, 79, 94, 95
parent meeting, introductory: chief complaint, by parent 105–8; clinician-parent relationship 104–5; conclusions 115–17; global goals of 118–19; goals of 104–17; organizing parental concerns 108–15; outline 103–4

Index   235

parent meeting, second: addressing concerns 156–7; dynamic model of understanding 150–6; individualized treatment plans 157; "Josh" clinical example 154–5; outline 145; recognition of common concerns 146–8; revising treatment timeline 157; "Stacy" clinical example 152, 153–4; stress-diathesis model of understanding 148–50
patient resistance 68
patterns in play therapy 125–6
performance goals in play therapy 128
Perry, J. Christopher 66
personal responsibility 15
play activities/therapy: patterns in 125–6; performance goals in 128; with referents 166–7, 169; toys in 124; unstructured initiation of 160–1
positive regard 189
postponement of affect 69
prefrontal cortex (PFC) 84–5
problematic emotionality 12
progression of tasks in child therapy sessions 161–2
projection as defense mechanism 4
psychoanalytic perspectives: the ego 35, 38–9; id 35, 36–7; overview 34–5; superego 35, 39–42
psychodynamic psychotherapy: defense mechanisms 53–5, 58–62; expressive interventions 48–9; internal conflict and defenses 53–5; listening to children from 43–8; maladaptive implicit emotional regulatory mechanisms 46–8; nature of 48–52; overview 42–3; relevance building 85; supportive interventions 51–3; transference 49–51
psychological agency 42
psychotropic medication 94
punishment anxiety manifestations 139
pupilometry 84

reaction formations 40, 168
recognition of common concerns 146–8
reflective functioning capacities 200–1
Regulation-Focused Psychotherapy for Children with Externalizing Behaviors (RFP-C) 23–6, 46; alliances formed during 118; biological underpinnings 86; central features 98–9, 181; central tenet of 69; child therapy sessions and 162; defense mechanisms 64; goals 100; impact of 218; impulsive behaviors 84; introduction 79–80; major focus 180, 218–19; Malan's Triangle of conflict 115–16; procedure 99–100; review of 174–5; roots of 95–6; short-term approach to 97, 207; as strength-based approach 196
relationship 7, 36, 43, 48–52, 104, 109, 112, 115, 118, 133, 143, 156, 161, 170, 179–92, 199, 206–9, 218, 222, 227
Research Domain Criteria (RDoC) project: benefits and promise 85–6; from categorical to dimensional 80–1; common childhood experiences 149; constructs and levels of analysis 83–5; emotion regulation 81–2; introduction 4, 79–80; systematic approach 94–5
respectful demeanor in child therapy sessions 160
response to parental concerns 204
rules of space in child therapy 129–30

Sandler, Joseph 21, 61–2
self-esteem 5, 21, 62, 110
self-understanding 188–9
sensory gating 148–9
severe inhibitions in children 45
severe mood dysregulation (SMD) 18
short-term psychotherapy 207
sleep/wake disturbances 83
strength-based approach 196
stress-diathesis model of understanding 148–50
suboptimal behavioral diminishment 186–7
superego 35, 39–42
supportive interventions 51–3, 175–7
suppression, defined 64–5
symptom inventories 114–15
Systems for Social Processes 94

Target, Mary 21–2
Target Complaint (TC) 67
Target Symptom Rating Scale (TSRS) 115
temperamental variations 148–9
temper dysregulation disorder with dysphoria (TDD) 18
temper tantrums 10, 46, 97, 173
termination process: "Alexander" clinical example 212–14; education on 205; "Eli" clinical example 214–15; final

goodbye 211–12; introduction to 206–8; outline 206; "Patrick" clinical example 215–16; reminder of 209–10; "Sam" clinical example 214; specific goals of 208–12; summary 216; working through termination 210–11
theoretical organization in child therapy 128–9
therapeutic failure 6–7
therapeutic realism 184–5
three-wishes question in child therapy 132–3
Tourette's Disorder (TD) 94
toys in play therapy 124
transference: avoiding premature interpretation clinical example "John" 191–2; in child therapy 142; clinician/patient relationship 181–3; defined 35, 182; mutative factor and 181, 183–6; in psychodynamic psychotherapy 49–51

Treatment of Maladaptive Aggression in Youth (T-MAY) guidelines 16
treatment process clinical example "Betty" 165–71, 175–6
treatment updates 195–8
Triangle of Conflict 95, 98
Tyson, Phyllis and Robert 21

unconscious defense mechanisms 35
unconscious mental activity 34
uncorroborated readings/conclusions 125–6
unsocialized aggressive reaction of childhood 17
unstructured initiation of play in child therapy sessions 160–1

Vaillant, George 58
ventral anterior cingulate cortex (vACC) 81
ventromedial PFC (vmPFC) 81
verbalizations in child therapy 134–6